SALOMON GESSNER

ANGLICA GERMANICA SERIES 2
Editors: LEONARD FORSTER, S. S. PRAWER *and* A. T. HATTO

Other books in the series

D. Prohaska: Raimund and Vienna: A Critical Study of Raimund's plays in their Viennese Setting

D. G. Mowatt: Friderich von Hûsen: Introduction, Text, Commentary and Glossary

C. Lofmark: Rennewart in Wolfram's 'Willehalm': A Study of Wolfram von Eschenbach and his Sources

A. Stephens: Rainer Maria Rilke's 'Gedichte an die Nacht'

M. Garland: Hebbel's Prose Tragedies: An Investigation of the Aesthetic Aspects of Hebbel's Dramatic Language

H. W. Cohn: Else Lasker-Schüler: The Broken World

J. M. Ellis: Narration in the German Novelle: Theory and Interpretation

Maurice B. Benn: The Drama of Revolt: A Critical Study of Georg Büchner

SALOMON GESSNER

HIS CREATIVE ACHIEVEMENT
AND INFLUENCE

JOHN HIBBERD

Lecturer in German, University of Bristol

CAMBRIDGE UNIVERSITY PRESS

CAMBRIDGE

LONDON · NEW YORK · MELBOURNE

Published by the Syndics of the Cambridge University Press
The Pitt Building, Trumpington Street, Cambridge CB2 1RP
Bentley House, 200 Euston Road, London NW1 2DB
32 East 57th Street, New York, NY 10022, USA
296 Beaconsfield Parade, Middle Park, Melbourne 3206, Australia

First published 1976

Printed in Great Britain
by W & J Mackay Limited, Chatham

Library of Congress Cataloguing in Publication Data
Hibberd, John.
Salomon Gessner: his creative achievement
and influence.
(Anglica Germanica: Series 2)
Bibliography: p. 171
Includes index.
1. Gessner, Salomon, 1730–1788 – Criticism
and interpretation. I. Series.
PT1886.Z84   831'.6   [B]   76-7139
ISBN 0-521-21234-0

CONTENTS

v

ILLUSTRATIONS

The half-page vignettes at the head of chapters are from the fol-
lowing sources: Introduction – *Contes moraux et nouvelles idylles
de D... [Diderot] et Salomon Gessner* (1773); Chapter 1 – Gessner's
Schriften (1762); 2 – *Contes moraux et nouvelles...*; 3 – Gessner's
Schriften (1762); 4 – Gessner's *Oeuvres* (1777); 5 – Gessner's
Oeuvres (1777); 6 – *Contes moraux et nouvelles...*; 7 – Gessner's
Oeuvres (1777); Conclusion – Gessner's *Oeuvres* (1777).

[With one exception, these and plates 3–8 above are reproduced
from *Geist und Schönheit im Zürich des 18. Jahrhunderts*, published
by Orell Füssli Verlag, Zurich, in 1968; the vignette at the head of
Chapter 1 is reproduced from Salomon Gessner, *Sämtliche Schriften*, Band II, published by Orell Füssli Verlag, Zurich, in 1972.]

ACKNOWLEDGEMENTS

I wish to thank my friends and colleagues in Bristol, Zurich and Munich who helped and encouraged me in my work on Gessner, and the editors of *Anglica Germanica* who kindly suggested improvements to my text. My indebtedness to other scholars is great, and perhaps inadequately reflected in the notes and bibliography to this volume. Any errors and shortcomings that remain are my own.

Much of my research on Gessner and related topics was facilitated by grants from the Alexander von Humboldt-Stiftung (Bad Godesberg) and Pro Helvetia (Zurich). Through a generous subvention Pro Helvetia also made possible the publication of this book in its present form. For their support I am especially grateful.

Bristol, 1976   JOHN HIBBERD

INTRODUCTION

Salomon Gessner was the first imaginative writer in German to achieve international renown. His works – two collections of idylls and a biblical epic – enjoyed a phenomenal success, a fame and popularity such as was later equalled only by Goethe's *Werther* and Heine's *Buch der Lieder*. They were translated into many languages, read and re-read with enthusiasm at courts and in humbler middle-class homes from Portugal to St Petersburg. In the mid eighteenth century, when German was generally regarded as a barbaric tongue, he caused the nations of Europe to recognise it capable of subtle and powerful poetic expression, and his most fervent and influential admirers were found in Paris, the traditional stronghold of refinement and good taste. To a Europe increasingly conscious of the evils of civilisation he became a symbol of natural virtue, reminding his readers that innocence might still exist in the countryside. Largely through his influence his native Switzerland came to be seen as a haven of rural happiness and true morality. His descriptions of natural beauty encouraged many to reverence nature and to make pilgrimages to the scenic delights of his country. His house was a temple visited by worshippers of nature and simplicity, and an object of curiosity to every traveller conversant with the literary scene. He became a legend in his own time. Many of the thoughts and sentiments now associated with the name of Rousseau became familiar to the reading public of Europe through Gessner's works; they seemed all the more convincing and appealing because expressed by a man who was believed to be utterly genuine and untainted by civilisation and formal education. The simplicity of his writings appealed directly to the taste of the age; they were taken as proof that great poetry, rivalling that of the Ancients, could be written in modern Europe.

Yet all these remarkable facts are now largely forgotten and today Gessner is scarcely read. Even his name is not widely known, though he may be encountered as a fictional figure, the jovial host in the story *Der Landvogt von Greifensee* by his now more famous fellow townsman, Gottfried Keller. Were it not for Swiss academics eager to proclaim his importance, for a couple of French scholars exploring the main trends of Pre-Romanticism, and attempts to rescue the best of German Rococo literature from total neglect, Gessner might well have disappeared, even as a figure mentioned in passing, from histories of literature and taste. The very bases of his appeal in his own time have become, to a large extent, apparent grounds for critical condemnation. The sentiments he expressed now all too often strike readers as maudlin sentimentality. What once seemed touching simplicity has been rejected as foolishness. His style, the epitome of all that was natural to his own generation, has been condemned many times as utterly artificial. Most of his works belong to the pastoral tradition, itself felt to be artificial and dead, inaccessible to modern taste. He became one of the many German writers to be obscured by the long shadows cast back into literary history by the phenomenon of Goethe and by that revolution in taste called Romanticism.

All the qualities of Gessner's work, so manifest to his contemporaries, have not, however, become faults with the passing of time. Many may be appreciated still, more particularly by a reader willing to come to terms with eighteenth-century taste. Changes in fashion do not, in any case, diminish his historical importance. The study of Gessner reveals various facets of an age that is often, when called the Age of Reason, reduced to only one of its aspects. Rational optimism, Pre-Romantic sensibility, Rococo playfulness, and the beginnings of Neo-Classicism are each reflected in his writings. They are mirrored, too, in his etchings and paintings, for Gessner was also a talented artist (indeed a businessman, local administrator and patriot as well). Familiarity with his work leads to a greater understanding of the cultural unity of the eighteenth century. Seen as a representative of his time, Gessner is a fascinating figure. He made an undoubtedly great contribution to the development of the German idyll and his works were imitated in several languages. But his real significance is much wider, it lies in several factors that, whilst they have for the most part been recognised in isolation, have in combination eluded recent generations trained to concentrate on narrowly defined disciplines.

To evaluate Gessner as writer and artist, to explain his short-lived success, and to measure his historical importance we must cross frontiers of language and scholarly discipline. He must be seen as a product of a German-speaking environment and of Zurich as a cultural centre, but also in the wider context of Western Europe. For his significance is European. He belongs to Switzerland, to German literature, and to Western culture – as a man sensitive to the beauties of nature and of language, who, despite the limited scope of his genius, gave artistic form to the sensibility of his age.

This, the first book about Gessner in any language other than German, has been written in the conviction that his work is worthy of detailed study and deserves greater international recognition, both in its own right and as a key to the taste of Europe in the era of Rousseau, Goethe and William Blake.

1 · TOWARDS A SYNTHESIS

In 1775 Gessner was visited in his summer home outside Zurich by an aristocratic French lady and admirer of his works, herself a writer, Mme de Genlis. She imagined that the famous poet who sang the Arcadian pastoral scene must live in an ideal realm, far removed from the shortcomings of everyday reality. Her expectations met with disappointment:

Gessner m'a invitée à l'aller voir dans sa maison de campagne; j'avois une extreme curiosité de connoître celle qu'il a épousée par amour, et qui l'a rendu poète; je me la représentois sous les traits d'une bergère charmante, entourée de bocages et de fleurs, que l'on n'y buvoit que du lait, et que, suivant l'expression allemande, *on y marchoit sur des roses*. J'arrive chez lui, je traverse un petit jardin, uniquement rempli de carottes et de choux, ce qui commence a déranger un peu mes idées d'églogues et d'idylles, qui furent tout à fait bouleversées, en entrant dans le salon, par une fumée de tabac qui formoit un véritable nuage, au travers duquel j'aperçevois Gessner, fumant sa pipe et buvant de la bière, à côté d'une bonne femme en casaquin, avec un grand bonnet à carcasse, et tricotant; c'étoit madame Gessner.[1]

The vision of Gessner's wife as a shepherdess and of the cottage surrounded by flowers may have been conjured up after the event for literary effect, but in essence the account rings true. Gessner was not the man that most of his contemporary readers imagined him to be, nor was the Switzerland in which he lived an Arcadia, as many people thought. (Nor, indeed, did Gessner's wife inspire his depiction of shepherdesses – he wrote most of his idylls before meeting her.)

His life was in a sense idyllic. It was not without excitement, and the formative years of his youth especially included travel and contacts with interesting personalities. He was, indeed, never cut off from the latest literary and intellectual developments. Yet the mature Gessner showed little desire to seek novelty, and his most outstanding characteristic was serenity of mind. The relative stability of Switzerland and of his personal situation undoubtedly helped to determine the way he thought and wrote. But he was able, whatever the reality around him, to create his own world of peace and contentment, not only for himself, but for other people too. Mme de Genlis soon realised that a kind of idyll was possible amid the unpoetic carrots and cabbages, tobacco-smoke and beer of a middle-class Swiss home. Gessner's imagination coloured his appreciation of life, just as it created the vision of harmony found in his writings; and it was fed by the poetry, art and ideas with which he came into contact. Thus it was above all his experience of poetry, rather than the political, social or economic realities around him, that formed the basis of his creative writing. As a citizen of Zurich he was relatively free from worries about economic hardship and political unrest. Yet he was, as we shall see, concerned about the sufferings of the poor, and his idyllic visions, despite their connections with rural Switzerland, were in essence a foil to reality. They contained a reminder that Utopia was a dream, a theoretical goal rather than an established fact.

Many of the poets from whom he learnt are scarcely remembered now, but he read them with a thrill of discovery, his personal excitement increased by the knowledge that they were breaking new ground and striving towards an excellence that, it was thought, had not been achieved in German literature before. He was a modest individual who did not engage in the theoretical and polemical activities associated with the prominent literary figures of his time; though anxious to win recognition from the authors and critics he admired, at first he can hardly have dreamt that his own writings would conquer Europe. His early literary experiments, indeed, attracted little more than the polite enthusiasm of his friends. Nevertheless, in them we can now trace the seeds of his more successful work and a struggle towards an idiom that would please divergent tastes.

But the young Gessner's main concern was to escape the cares of mundane existence and to seek harmless enjoyment. To the staid citizens of Zurich he may have seemed a frivolous youth, but he was in no way a rebel, and by his early twenties he was coming to terms with the puritanical spirit of his home town. Like most authors of his time, he never regarded writing as more than a spare-time occupation, yet the breakthrough in his literary development came when he discovered how to combine moral seriousness with his love for lighthearted amusement.

Salomon Gessner was born on 1 April 1730 into a well-established middle-class family. His father owned and ran a printing and publishing business and a bookshop, and was a member of the 'Grosser Rat' of Zurich, the assembly of citizens with rights of self-government. Conrad Gessner, the 'German Pliny', a celebrated polymath of the sixteenth century, and Johannes Gessner, distinguished botanist and friend of the eighteenth-century poet and natural scientist Albrecht von Haller, were distant members of the same family. But Salomon showed no signs of becoming a learned man like them and his school-teachers thought him a hopeless pupil. His young friends appreciated him as a merry companion not averse to buffoonery. At an early age he began to write imitations of *Robinson Crusoe* that were later burnt, but of which it is reported that the hero was fond of pipe tobacco and that raging seas and storms figured prominently.[2] Like most early German imitations of Defoe,[3] Gessner's stories probably concentrated on adventure and did not necessarily indicate a leaning towards idyllic subject-matter. In the classroom he liked – surreptitiously – to make wax figures of men and animals, a pointer to his later interest in the visual arts. The academic curriculum did not capture his imagination, nor learning by rote suit his temperament.

6

Since he made little progress at school, Gessner was sent at the age of fifteen to a private tutor, a parson in a village between Zurich and Schaffhausen, with whom he lived for about two years. By the end of this time in Berg am Irchel he could read Latin and French, though his command of standard German (as opposed to Swiss German) was still shaky. Later in life he learned some Italian, but never English or Greek, although he was able to read most of the classics in translation. He had plenty of time to enjoy the pleasant vine-clad hills overlooking the Rhine. The parson's daughter engaged his emotions. But the verses he now wrote were inspired by the poetry he read rather than by nature or love. The sixteen-year-old boy begged his father to allow him to keep a copy of Brockes, and some of Gessner's earliest verses, clumsy alexandrines written at this time, show the influence of that poet in both content and style.[4]

Barthold Hinrich Brockes' large collection of poems, *Irdisches Vergnügen in Gott* (1721–48), immensely popular in Germany in the mid eighteenth century, introduced Gessner to a type of poetry that had a decisive influence on his own writings. Brockes' descriptive and reflective poems marked a new stage in man's attitude to nature and were, despite their rather dryly rational style, one of the first signs of Pre-Romantic feeling in Europe. He never tired of stating that the world was created beautiful, good and useful to man, as a reminder of the benevolence of God and of the possibility of happiness on earth. Gessner was at once delighted and impressed by Brockes' descriptive power and was by no means out of sympathy with his message.

Brockes' poetry appealed to Gessner's feeling for nature, already developing in these years, but he was equally entranced by the lighthearted muse of Friedrich von Hagedorn and J. W. L. Gleim, who also became models for his early inauspicious attempts in verse. They introduced delicacy, charm and wit to modern German lyric poetry, Rococo characteristics that contrasted with the serious and rather prosaic tones of Brockes, the poet of the early Enlightenment. Gessner was soon acquainted with much German Anacreontic and Rococo poetry, and absorbed its mood of joy. In the 1740s it was new and dominated poetic production in Germany, but long afterwards it continued to provide him with inspiration.

He wrote much in Berg am Irchel, verses with and without rhyme, pieces of mixed verse and prose, fables, stories, satires and Anacreontic songs, though few examples of this immature work were preserved. Probably at this time too he read Ovid's *Metamorphoses*, a book that he always loved and which nurtured his penchant for demigods and magic transformations. But it was not until a few years later that classical poetry made a decisive impact on him.

In 1748 Gessner returned to Zurich to enter his father's business. He was inclined to conviviality rather than hard work, but his contacts with other young men of the town widened his intellectual and cultural horizon, and he now began to spend much time drawing. Very soon, however, he was sent to Berlin to learn more about the book trade. He remained in the bookshop there for only a short time, for he refused to submit to the discipline and the menial tasks imposed on him. His father discontinued his allowance, but a reconciliation was soon forthcoming when Gessner announced that he was seriously studying to be a landscape painter. Through another visitor to Berlin from Zurich, J. G. Schulthess, he was introduced to the 'Montagsklub', a circle of artists, poets and intellectuals which, only a few years later, the young Lessing was to frequent. Gessner approached the court painter Hempel, who was astonished: Gessner knew nothing of technique, his paints were mixed wrongly and would not dry, yet his artistic efforts showed considerable promise. But his mentality was that of a dilettante. He continued to regard himself as a budding poet, but had little time for poetics, and made no contact with J. G. Sulzer, a follower and friend of Bodmer, the literary doyen of Zurich; already a respected academic, Sulzer later became a leading writer on aesthetics.

It was in Berlin, however, that Gessner met the critic and poet Karl Wilhelm Ramler, whom he was to count as a friend for the rest of his life. Ramler, a perfectionist in matters of prosody, was entrusted with the task of polishing the verses of several leading poets of the time, including Gleim and the Prussian officer Ewald von Kleist. He was critical of Gessner's work and, according to one report,[5] advised him to give up his struggle with metre and adopt poetic prose. If this is correct, his advice was a turning-point in Gessner's career as a writer. But it seems that Gessner did not stop writing verse immediately, though he certainly respected Ramler's judgements and was later encouraged by his example to polish and perfect his own poetic language.

In 1750 Gessner returned to Zurich. He did not hurry back, for his journey lasted four months. He visited Hempel in Magdeburg, and saw Gleim in Halberstadt, Gärtner, Zachariä and Ebert in Braunschweig – all poets of the Rococo movement reacting against the seriousness of Enlightenment rationalism. The highlight of his trip was six weeks spent in Hamburg, where he was delighted to be welcomed by Hagedorn. They spent many hours together, talking and drinking or taking boat trips. Gessner probably then went by ship from Hamburg to Amsterdam to look at Dutch paintings. Nearer home, in Strasbourg, he met quite by chance an acquaintance from Berlin, an actor called Dancourt who was playing Harlequin when Gessner in his enthusiasm advanced on to the stage, giving the actor extra opportunity for improvised comedy.

Gessner was still impetuous and not minded to take work in his father's business too seriously. But he knew that he had much to learn as an artist or poet. He knew that a command of correct German (in so far as there was standard practice) was important if he were to meet the classical poetic demands of correctness and clarity that determined Ramler's perfectionism and Hagedorn's poetic style. He knew, too, that he had to work hard to polish his verses if they were to come anywhere near the standards set by Ramler and Gleim.

The Zurich to which Gessner returned in 1750 was a town of about ten thousand inhabitants. A further sixteen thousand lived in the rural parts of Canton Zurich. Power lay in the hands of some two thousand burgesses, and the political system, though thought to be constitutionally superior to that of the absolute states of France and Germany, was extremely conservative. Zurich was an oligarchy, ruled by a few families successful in industry or commerce. An English visitor in 1784 observed that no new citizen had been admitted for a century and a half,[6] and only citizens could set up in business, enter the church, become officers in the army or hold senior administrative posts. The town flourished, largely due to its stake in the silk and cloth trades. The guilds were strong and manners simple, even antiquated. The prosperous citizens went about their affairs in wigs and frock coats; but the peasants of the canton, who provided a pool of cheap labour for the textile industry, were poor and without political rights. The Reformed Church, on the whole a reactionary body, had enormous power. Religious and secular authorities together kept, at least in theory, a tight watch over the morals of the populace (even their dress), and wielded a strict censorship of all publications. They were suspicious of foreign, especially French, influences, which were felt to threaten morality and religion. Nevertheless by Swiss, indeed by European standards, Zurich was relatively liberal in spirit, and it had the lion's share of the cultural achievements of German-speaking Switzerland. It was an important publishing centre. Even before Lavater, Pestalozzi and Füssli were known, Ewald von Kleist judged that Zurich far outshone Berlin as a centre for men of genius. But one man there stood supreme – Bodmer, intellectual and man of letters whose ambition was to change the course of German literature. He and his followers concerned themselves with moves towards liberalisation in the spirit of the Enlightenment. Whilst proud of Swiss traditions, they were open to foreign ideas. There was, in fact, considerable traffic in French culture, and English thought and literature were championed by Bodmer and his associates. He was able to attract to the town two of the most promising young German poets, Klopstock and Wieland; both fulfilled their promise, though not exactly as Bodmer had hoped. Johann Jacob Bodmer and his friend and collaborator Breitinger were the outstanding literary theorists and critics of the period, and together they had made Zurich the most important literary centre in the German-speaking world. Their ideas promised to release poetry from the restrictions of earlier theory, and Bodmer's famous quarrel with Gottsched in Leipzig, the leading literary theorist of the early Enlightenment, had attracted the attention of all those interested in poetry. It focussed on the merits of Milton's *Paradise Lost*, which Bodmer praised and translated into German, but which to Gottsched represented the excesses of the Baroque age that he had endeavoured to eradicate from German letters. Bodmer defended the poetic imagination. The first cantos of Klopstock's *Messias* which appeared in 1748, with their sublime expressions of religious sentiment, marked for him a most welcome innovation in German poetry, and when Gessner came back to Zurich he found that Bodmer was playing host and mentor to Klopstock and had little thought for anything else but his already famous protégé.

The unworldliness of Klopstock's work evidently did not appeal to Gessner, who made no attempt to meet him. When, in 1752, Bodmer's next great protégé, Wieland, arrived in Zurich, Gessner was again not keen to make his acquaintance. Yet Gessner's friends formed the Bodmer circle, and no aspiring poet could afford to ignore him or his opinions. Furthermore, Gessner had business reasons for being on good terms with this prolific author and arbiter of taste: in 1753 he was anxious to repair a breach of relations between Bodmer and his father's firm. He moved progressively closer to Bodmer, and the poetry of 'Empfindsamkeit', as represented by this man and his circle, was the next decisive influence on his creative work. Gradually he came to accept that poetry should be more than graceful, witty and amusing, that it should portray virtue and appeal to moral sentiment.

But Gessner did not embrace 'Empfindsamkeit' immediately, nor did he rush to curry favour with Bodmer. Rather he made friends with the poet Ewald von Kleist, who in his capacity as Prussian officer came to Zurich in 1752 on a recruiting drive that met with some local opposition. He kept Gessner informed of literary currents and opinions in North Germany, and encouraged him to write. His own most famous work, *Der Frühling,* was published in a new edition by the Gessner firm in 1754, with a title page engraved by Gessner himself. The poem belonged to the type of nature poetry familiar to Gessner through Brockes, though in its emotional response to nature it was close to the tone of Klopstock. In combining these two aspects, this minor masterpiece pointed the way to Gessner's future poetic development.

Gessner's other companions in Zurich could appreciate both Anacreontic and sentimental poetry. They too were sons of prosperous citizens, keen to enjoy themselves before embarking on responsible and demanding careers. For all were soon to assume offices and dignities. Many were ordained ministers in the Reformed Church. Several were later known as authors: J. G. Schulthess and J. J. Steinbrüchel who translated from English and Greek, and J. G. Hirzel, who became a European celebrity when he wrote a book about the virtues and practicalities of a farming life. Klopstock, in his famous ode 'Der Zürchersee', recorded the gaiety of these young people. Gessner was not present on the boat trip described there, but there were many other expeditions into the countryside, where they would drink and dance and sing. Gessner described one such party:

ich wolte beyde Hirzeln, Kellern und den Füssli zu unserm Stein am Bach führen, wir verirten [uns] an dem Bach, und statt zum Stein zu kommen, stunden wir plötzlich bey einem Wasserfall, er stürzte recht hoch durch grünen Moss herunter und rauschte so lieblich: bis hierher ruft ich und nicht weiter, hier lasst uns wohnen, wir lagerten uns da ins Grüne, und assen und tranken, da im Kühlen, dann stund Keller in unsre Mitte und blies auf seiner Flöte das *est mihi propositum*...und wir danzten im Cirkel um ihn her und sangen...wir waren recht unvergleichlich froh.[7]

Bodmer was rather indulgent in his attitude to these young men, although he required considerable discipline from his most promising protégés. In 1750 Gessner and his friends had founded a society, the 'Dienstags-Compagnie'. Its meetings were devoted mainly to merriment, though more serious moments were given to criticism of the members' own writings, and to the reading and discussion of literature in general. Bodmer, Breitinger, Klopstock and Wieland were present on occasions. In conjunction with Bodmer some of the members produced the periodical *Crito*. In winter or in inclement weather they met in a member's house, but they preferred to let their hearts expand in the countryside. They relished several aspects of contemporary poetry, including the cult of friendship, as sung by the poets of 'Empfindsamkeit', and the pleasures of wine favoured by the Anacreontics. Gessner and his friends welcomed any poem that expressed joy in life and contrasted with the sobriety and self-interest of everyday reality.

Wieland was then known as a writer of rather unworldly, religious and reflective poetry. In 1752 Gessner expressed derision of him and all his kind who had, as he put it, no warm blood in their veins.[8] Soon, however, he discovered that Wieland was quite capable of enjoying life. By 1753 he noted, with some surprise, that both Bodmer and Wieland seemed well disposed towards him, and it was not long before he struck up a close and lasting friendship with the poet who was, a few years later, to become the great representative of German Rococo literature. At this stage, however, an association with him meant a rapprochement with Bodmer.

In 1752 Gessner considered publishing some Anacreontic verses. But he received no encouragement from Bodmer, who disapproved of such frivolities, and Gessner, unsure of himself, promised him to write no more in this vein.[9] At the same time he sought the opinion of others, but with similar results. Whereas Bodmer objected to the content of the verses, Gleim was critical of their form, agreeing with Ramler that Gessner had not mastered the art of prosody.[10] Accordingly, Gessner did not appear in print as a verse poet until some years later. If verses by him appeared anonymously in Zurich periodicals in the early 1750s, as seems likely, such pieces cannot be distinguished from those by other aspiring Anacreontic poets.[11]

The earliest poem that he acknowledged as his own, by later including it (with minor alterations) in his *Gedichte* of 1762, was the 'Lied eines Schweizers an sein bewaffnetes Mädchen', six rhymeless stanzas, each of four lines, that first appeared anonymously in *Crito* in 1751. It is based on an episode from the history of Zurich. In 1298 the town was besieged, and in order to give the foe a false impression of the defenders' strength, women in armour were placed alongside the men on the walls. In Gessner's poem a young man sees his girl in armour, regrets that this attire conceals some of her charms, but delights to observe that delicate feet and knees are exposed to view. The poem shows some witty invention in the final 'pointe', where the girl is compared with the angel guarding paradise, but it is otherwise scarcely worthy of critical attention.

In the *Gedichte* of 1762 and in his idylls of 1772 Gessner published four other verse poems. They were probably written shortly before their publication, but they could equally well date from the early 1750s. Both 'Die Schiffahrt' (1772) and 'An den Amor' (1772) are weak Anacreontic pieces. Compared with the songs of Gleim or any of the better Anacreontics, they lack the smooth rhythm and polished expression that was the chief attainment of this school. 'Morgenlied' (1762) is another lightweight poem: the poet at dawn thinks of his beloved and asks a zephyr to carry her a message. 'An den Wasserfall' (1762) describes a pleasant spot by a waterfall, now in winter bleak and cold, but imagined as it was in summer and will be in spring. Much is conventional, but this is the only verse poem in which Gessner reveals his eye for moving patterns of light and for details in nature. The details are part of an exclamation; within the development of German nature lyrics this represents a step beyond the objectivity of Brockes towards the more subjective manner of Goethe:

> Da wo sonst deine klare Quelle
>   Auf Schaum und Moos sich stäubend stürzt;
> Da blinkt von Eis itzt eine Säule
>   Vom hohlen Felsen hoch herab.
>
> Wie öd', wie nackt sind die Gesträuche,
>   Wo sonst im dunkeln Laubgewölb'
> Die Zephyr mit den Blüten spielten,
>   Und mit dem sanftbewegten Laub,
>
> Dass schnellverschwundne Sonnenstrahlen
>   Auf Wellen, Schaum und weichem Moos,
> Wie Lichter durch den Schatten blitzten;
>   Wie öd', wie nackt hängt ihr herab![12]

There are Anacreontic elements here, but the poem is less stilted than Gessner's other verses, and suggests that he might have done better to have broken completely with the Anacreontic mood and to concentrate on nature lyrics. But of his few published verses, most are lighthearted pieces. His pastoral drama *Evander und Alcimna* (1762) includes some poor rhymeless verse, intended to express innocent love in a lyrical but very formal style.

It was Ewald von Kleist who encouraged Gessner to publish *Die Nacht*. His earliest extant attempt at poetic prose, it appeared anonymously in December 1752, but with the date 1753. Despite its title, this work is not connected with the influential *Night Thoughts* of Edward Young and the beginnings of graveyard Romanticism. It sings of night in the countryside in a largely conventional Rococo manner, but with touches of realistic detail. Perhaps because he was free of the limitations of a verse form that he could not master, Gessner here expresses an emotional response to nature with some force:

Welch Entzücken! Welch sanftes Taumel fliesst durch mein wallendes Herz! (F, 3)

...dort eilt der rieselnde Bach, ich hör, ich höre sein Rauschen; er stürzt sich an moosichte Steine und eilet schäumend ins Thal und küsst mit hüpfenden Wellen die Blumen des Ufers. (F, 4)

The natural scenery is, however, little more than a background for an erotic encounter and youthful revelries with wine and song, and an excuse to introduce classical deities. In a satirical digression the poet compares the songs of unnamed poets with the croaking of frogs. In 1762 he added a frivolous piece of invented mythology on the creation of the glow-worm. *Die Nacht* lacks unity of theme, but it shows that by 1753 Gessner had already developed a distinctive style of poetic prose, characterised by euphony, simplicity and expressiveness. This style is quite similar to that of the idylls, a few of which, written in the I-form, probably date from 1752 or 1753: 'Der Wunsch', which like *Die Nacht* concerns friendship and the joys of drink; 'Der Frühling', mentioned by Gessner in 1752,[13] which sings of spring much as *Die Nacht* sings of night; and 'Der feste Vorsatz'.

15

Gessner was no doubt encouraged by his German friends' comments on *Die Nacht* as reported to him by Kleist:

Gleim empfiehlt sich Ihnen aufs Beste. Ihre 'Nacht' hält er für ein Meisterstück, nicht nur der Erfindung und Gedanken wegen, sondern auch des Wohlklangs wegen, und alle Leute von Geschmack, die ich gesprochen, Cramer, Sucro, Giseke u.s.w. urtheilen wir er. Trösten Sie Sich also über das Urtheil der armen Theologen in Zürich und machen Sie nur mehr dergleichen, wenn Sie für ein Genie und witzigen Kopf gehalten sein wollen![14]

Despite its stylistic achievement, the piece undoubtedly did not recommend itself to the 'poor theologian' Bodmer. It lacked moral seriousness. The word 'heilig' was used indiscriminately in a secular context or to refer to classical gods. Furthermore, one passage was suspiciously like a parody of a section from Bodmer's *Syndflut*.[15] This passage was later shortened and became obscure, but in the original version it is clear that spirits of men as yet unborn but destined to be friends in life flit like butterflies from one delight of the Rococo world to another:

...und Seelen der künftgen Trinker...spielen, und sind jetzt schon Brüder. Auch wir waren schon Brüder ihr Freunde, da wir noch Atomen waren, da lachten wir schon im holen Reb-Blatt, und schlüpften über den perlenden Becher, oder schlummerten auf Rosen, die junge Mädchen auf den Busen pflanzten.[16]

Perhaps Gessner did not intend to parody, but made a clumsy attempt to imitate part of the fifth canto of *Der Syndflut* where the theme of eternal friendship is presented in an almost Rococo manner:

Die Seelen der Bryder
Wurden von ihrem Feinde, der Flut, aus den Leibern gejaget;
Alsdann sahen sie auf, wo die dienstbaren Zephyre lauschten,
Die da kamen, sie auf balsamische Flygel zu nehmen,
Dass sie zu aufgeschwollenen Trauben sie trygen; sie wollten
Wieder da spielen, und wie sie schon ehmals Bryder gewesen,
Als sie noch Atome waren, wer glaubts nicht den taumelnden Kelchglas?
Wieder so werden, und auf dem Weinstoke lachen, sie wollten
Yber dem perlenden Becher her hypfen, und wieder auf Rosen
Schlummern, die junge Mädchen auf ihrem Busen sich pflanzten.

The language and the motifs of *Die Nacht* are sometimes reminiscent of Klopstock and Bodmer, yet its subject-matter is somewhat frivolous. No wonder, then, that Bodmer felt that Gessner was mocking him and his illustrious disciple.[17]

Gessner's next work, the pastoral novel *Daphnis* (1754), found Bodmer's approval, at least after it had been re-written to include sentimental and morally satisfying episodes. There appears to be no similar work in previous German literature, and he considered he was breaking new ground.[18] An inexperienced and unknown writer, he would doubtless not have ventured into this field had he not been inspired by a classical model, the pastoral novel *Daphnis and Chloe* by the Byzantine writer Longus, which he knew in the French translation by Amyot.

Daphnis tells of the love of the shepherd Daphnis for Phillis from their first encounter until their wedding, a period of less than six months. Divided into three books, corresponding to the cantos of a short verse epic, it consists of a number of rather loosely connected scenes or situations. The characters express their emotions in lyrical speeches, sometimes reminiscent of pastoral drama and close in technique to Gessner's idylls. One of the many self-sufficient, and essentially static sections is the opening description: shepherds gather to honour the river-nymphs, adorn their images, in a cave on an island in the river, with flowers, and sing songs, the texts of which are given. Another is the harvest scene, again with songs, when Daphnis, suffering from the pangs of love, helps with the seasonal work. Stories and songs are introduced throughout at the slightest excuse. When the lovers shelter in a cave, they meet an unknown shepherd and entertain him with a song; in return he sings about the nymph of the grotto. The presence of a certain Damon at the wedding serves to introduce a story of how he met Amor and, as a result of this, a girl.

Longus's narrative is more extended, has more characters, and a more involved plot. He begins with the birth of the two lovers and ends with their wedding. They are foundlings, discovered in similar circumstances by two sets of shepherd foster-parents, and their lives follow parallel courses. Both are abducted by pirates and foreign raiders. This symmetry of structure is imitated by

Gessner only in so far as the introductions of Daphnis to Phillis's mother, and of Phillis to Daphnis's father, form parallel climaxes in his story. He omits the adventures with pirates and soldiers and the threat of war. Longus's attitude to the pastoral world is somewhat ambiguous: his landscape is the idyllic scene of happy love, but there is also mention of hardships and of less pleasant aspects of country life and the swains are occasionally referred to as coarse rustics. It is implied that the lovers' nobility of character is connected with their noble birth, and when their real identity is discovered, they look forward to a life of greater ease. They appreciate more sophisticated food than they enjoyed as shepherds, and Chloe is said to look more beautiful in fine clothes. Their princely parents are honest and upright, although some men at court are foolish and wicked. In Gessner's story town and court are unambiguously places of wickedness and unhappiness, from which the virtuous man must flee. Noble birth and possessions mean nothing to his shepherds, who rejoice in a contented spirit. Longus equates innocence with ignorance. He describes nascent love with some tender sympathy, but also with irony and more than a hint of lascivious enjoyment. His lovers do not understand their own feelings. Quite by chance they discover the thrill of kissing and embracing. When a grasshopper alights on Chloe's bosom, Daphnis discovers the delights of this anatomical feature. An experienced woman gives him a practical lesson on how to satisfy his amorous desires. Gessner's Daphnis knows from the beginning that he is in love, and knows how he will express his love when he meets Phillis again. Both his lovers have a definite sense of propriety and modesty, even if this does not coincide with the conventions of eighteenth-century society.

Besides the basic story, Gessner took a few details from Longus: notably the grotto of the nymphs and the lovers' meeting with a strange shepherd. Longus's wine-harvest becomes a corn-harvest to fit in with the reduced time scale. Other features of Gessner's work, the songs telling of legends and metamorphoses, the singing contests and the Greek deities are part of the pastoral tradition and not peculiar to *Daphnis and Chloe*.

The adventures that separate the lovers in the Greek novel break the peace of the idyllic world. Gessner reduced the dramatic impact by replacing these with Daphnis's accident on the river. He probably originally intended to dispense with the rival lover altogether, only finally to reinstate him in order to increase the dramatic interest; for, according to Gessner's biographer Hottinger, his friend Hirzel persuaded him to include more drama and a moral tendency.[19] The latter was added mainly through the figure of the old man Aristus who has fled from the wicked town of Croton; he comments on the beauties of nature and the virtues of country life in a fine, if overlong, passage of hymnic prose, stylistically the highlight of the novel. Though Longus sets the scene within a few miles of Mitylene on Lesbos at the outset, Gessner does not mention the town of Croton until the second book. This would seem to confirm that the story of Aristus was added as an afterthought.

The moment of danger as Daphnis is swept away by the river is passed over quickly. Gessner concentrates on the scene in the fisherman's hut after the rescue, and on their joy at being able to aid Daphnis in his distress. The turbulent floods endanger the peace of the pastoral world. Not only is Philetas dispossessed by floods, but Daphnis's father also recalls boats swept away and men drowned in the river. There is no suggestion that the victims deserve their misfortune, rather calamity serves to introduce scenes of virtuous compassion. The story of Philetas is exploited to give a number of sentimental situations. First Daphnis hears the unhappy tale, and wishes he could help, anticipating the joys of charity and the blessing of the gods that would result from a good deed. Then, when Philetas has been given the cottage, he overflows with gratitude, and Daphnis with joy. Philetas's son is introduced to add poignancy. His father weeps to see his ignorance of misfortune, and the child's reactions accompany the effusions of the adults:

Inzwischen dass sie so sprachen, hatte das unschuldige Kind die kleinen Arme um des Daphnis Knie gewunden und lächelte zu ihm herauf, als ob es ihm Dank zulächelte... [Daphnis] hob indes das Kind auf seinen Arm und küsst' es, indem

19

es lächelnd mit der kleinen Hand in seinen Locken und auf seinem glatten Kinne spielte. (F, 47)

The realistic details connected with the harvesters and the fisher-men are negligible. The fishermen use flares to lure their catch at night, and the walls of their hut are hung with nets. The meal they give to Daphnis is, of course, fish, but the emphasis is on their pride and joy in the exercise of hospitality, and the repast con-tinues with traditionally idyllic fare, bread, fruit and fruit-juices. In the harvest scene Gessner gives a pleasing visual impression of rows of men moving in unison, the sun flashing on their sickles. In the same sentence he moves on from the work to rest after work. The labour itself seems little more than an appetiser for food, drink and song:

> In langen Reihen gingen sie teils hinter den Ähren her und mähten sie vor sich weg mit der blickenden Sickel; teils banden sie die Garben zusammen, und wenn der Mittag kam und der Abend, dann sammelten sie sich unter dem Schatten naher Bäume, sich durch Speisen und den kühlenden Trunk zu erfrischen, und sangen Erntelieder der Ceres, indes der weite Krug herumging. (F, 17)

The stylisation is even more apparent when the men, divided into reapers and binders, sit facing each other and sing in two choruses. Little attention is paid to the reality of work in the fields.

Nor is there much realistic description of nature in the novel, indeed the scenery plays only a minor role. Trees and flowers are sometimes named, but more often, as in Aristus's glowing speech on the countryside and country life, the overall impression of the peaceful landscape, 'die ganze schöne Natur' with its variety of sights and sounds, is more important than exact detail:

> er bestieg einen nahe gelegenen Hügel und sah da eine ausgebreitete Gegend im Morgenlicht, buschreiche Hügel, ferne blaue Berge, weit ebene Felder und Wiesen voll fruchttragender Bäume und zerstreute Wälder von geraden Tannen und schlan-ken Eichen und Fichten. Fernher rauschte der Fluss zwischen Feldern und Hügeln und Hainen und Felsenwänden mit majestätischem Getöse; nahe Bäche lispelten durch das Gras, oder rauschten in kleinen Fällen sanft in das Getöse, und ein Heer von schwärmenden Vögeln sang froh auf betauten Ästen oder hoch in glanzvoller Luft einen mannigfaltigen Gesang, untermischet von den Flöten der Hirten und dem Gesange der Mädchen, die gesellschaftlich auf fernen und nahen Hügeln oder ebenen Wiesen die Herden weideten. Erstaunt mit unstetem Blick irrte der Greis, bald in weiter Entfernung, bald in Kräutern und Blumen, die duftend vor seinen Füssen lachten, voll von frohem Entzücken schwoll ihm die Brust. (F, 34f)

In the whole novel only one image strikes the reader as an observed, picturesque detail; that of fruit-trees whose branches are supported by props (F, 45).

The characters are idealised figures, vehicles for the portrayal of generalised emotions and virtues. The hero and heroine have two functions, as lovers and as loving and dutiful children. The father and mother are loving parents, Aristus a lover of nature and virtue. Through all the characters, with the exception of the rival lover Lamon, Gessner reveals the connection between virtue and happiness. They overflow with moral goodness, and are extremely tender in their emotions, given to unselfish deeds and compassion, full of piety towards the gods and of loving regard for the family. A guest at the wedding, Damon, has many abilities more realistically allocated to several different persons in Haller's *Die Alpen*:[20] knowledge of astrology and of the properties of herbs, prowess in singing, and skill as a wood-carver, musician and poet.

The long speeches of the characters are accompanied by exaggerated and stylised gestures. When Daphnis learns of Phillis's supposed unfaithfulness, he almost swoons:

er stund betäubt da, seine Knie bebten, Angstschweiss floss von den Gliedern; er wäre gesunken, wenn Lamon nicht unterstützend ihn an das Ufer geführt hätte.

(F, 37)

As soon as he is alone, he throws himself on the ground in misery and despair. The language of sentiment is sometimes heightened to pathos. Gessner evidently tried to emulate the high epic style in parts of the novel. Phrases reminiscent of Baroque rhetoric occur in Aristus's speeches, and some expressions have biblical associations. The verb 'hub an', with its epic connotations, introduces unprepossessing prosaic utterances. When Daphnis is swept away in his boat, his fear is described by means of an extended simile:

Wie das zarte Lamm zittert, wenn es von der Löwin mit starken Zähnen den Jungen zugetragen wird, die hungrig aus der Höhle ihr entgegen brüllen: so zitterte Daphnis...(F, 31)

Not all attempts at sublime poetry are as inept as this. The language varies from polished lyrical prose of considerable distinction to passages written with less care.

A few passages in *Daphnis* are impressive, but it lacks overall integration. A short episode is skilfully handled, and a tableau vividly presented, but the reader's interest is not sustained over the length of the novel. The characters do not seem to be capable of any development; as in many novels of the time, their ideal qualities, present from the beginning, are revealed in varying circumstances. The background of nature remains vague and colourless, despite the expressions of love of nature. Yet in one sense *Daphnis* was unique: there would appear to be no other pastoral novel in German Rococo literature.

The censors in Zurich were not impressed by the mixture of Christian and pagan elements, and *Daphnis* was allowed to be printed only on the condition that the author's name and the place of publication were suppressed. Kleist recommended it to Gleim, who began to correspond with Gessner, and in his first letter praised the naiveté and style of the novel:

Was für Natur, welche Naivetät, wie viel angemessene Schönheit im Ausdruck! Aber ich kann Ihnen diessmal nicht sagen, wie sehr alles an dem kleinen Schäfer-romane gefällt...[21]

Yet *Daphnis* passed virtually unnoticed by the wider public until some years later, when it was the object of a cult in certain circles, particularly in France during the period of Gessner's greatest fame. Nevertheless, it at once found the approval of Bodmer, who informed a friend that a young man in Zurich had written a pastoral prose work, full of 'Natur, Unschuld und Genie'; it would surely make the Germans think highly of Zurich's poetic potential.[22] With *Daphnis* Gessner had allied himself to the poets of 'Empfindsamkeit'. He had retained the lightness of touch of Rococo literature, but abandoned its amorality. The novel made its appeal to the readers' sensibility through the depiction of morally satisfying episodes. He had advanced a little further in his search for a style and a subject-matter most suited to his gifts and his mentality, and recognition by Bodmer doubtless gave him greater confidence.

Gessner took no public part in Bodmer's feud with Gottsched, though he did try to find a publisher for Bodmer's polemics.

Privately, in 1755, he wrote scathingly of Gottsched and his followers, who seemed associated with all that was old-fashioned, inimical to poetic freedom, and foolish in the extreme; and in the same year he persuaded Gleim to declare against Gottsched.[23]

But he did not agree with the attacks made by Bodmer and Wieland on the Anacreontic poet Johann Peter Uz. He assured Gleim, who defended Uz, that he was not associated with all that Bodmer did. Yet he had imbibed enough of the spirit of Zurich to disapprove of Uz's disregard of conventional morality. He wrote to Gleim that he did not rush to take sides in any dispute: he was 'kein streitbarer Held', but a conciliatory and peace-loving man:

Ich habe Herrn Utzens neue Ausgabe seiner lyrischen Gedichte gesehen. Sie wollen, dass man ihn verschone; für mich sag' ich's Ihnen zu, denn ich bin kein streitbarer Held. Ich ruhe mit Feder und Dintefass gern im Schatten des Friedens. Bodmer und Wieland sind beleidigt; ich zweifle aber, dass sie ausziehen werden ...Gewiss wird Utzens Ausspruch viele determiniren, die noch zweifelhaft waren, denn seine Lyrischen Gedichte werden die meisten mit Recht bewundert; sie haben oft den stürmisch fortreissenden Schwung, den poetischen Taumel; oft fliessen sie sanfter, wie kleine Wellen durch Blumen. Seine Bilderchen und Gemälde sind fein und ausgemalt, nicht zu karg, und nicht zu häufig. Kurz, die meisten sind Meisterstücke, und ich wünschte nur, dass seine Sittenlehre zuweilen wenige frei wäre.[24]

There is a touch of humour in this letter, as Gessner speaks of his own peaceful nature in a hexameter (a verse form associated with Klopstock and Bodmer) and ascribes Klopstockian qualities to Uz.

Some years later, in his letters of the 1760s, Gessner criticised Bodmer's vanity and lack of moderation. Yet by the mid-1750s he had espoused, at least with one half of his nature, the cause of moral and sentimental poetry, and he accompanied Bodmer and Breitinger on their regular strolls beside the river in Zurich, when they discussed eruditely and he, presumably, listened respectfully. In December 1755 he informed Ramler that Bodmer, Breitinger and others had encouraged him to publish his idylls. They were now in the press. Wieland had probably played a large part in bringing him closer to Bodmer. On hearing some of Gessner's idylls read in 1755, he recommended him to develop their moral content.[25] At about this time Gessner was writing a sequel to a narrative poem by Bodmer, probably with the author's encouragement.

In this piece Gessner broke completely with the Rococo manner; it is a sentimental, melodramatic tribute in poetic prose to the power of remorse and the innate goodness of man.

Bodmer's hexameter poem, published anonymously in 1756, told of Thomas Inkle, whose story had first been narrated in the *Spectator* (13 March 1711). Inkle, a Londoner, had sailed on a trading expedition to the West Indies in 1647. On the American coast his companions were attacked by Indians and only Inkle escaped alive. He was then helped by an Indian girl, and after some months together they arrived in Barbados, where he sold her into slavery, for a good price, because she was pregnant. Gellert had already retold the story in rhyming iambics.[26] The contrast between the inhumanity of the 'civilised' Englishman and the goodness of the 'savage' girl captured the imagination of men looking for signs of natural virtue in unsophisticated peoples. Both Gellert and Bodmer ended by damning the hero, but Bodmer added that he would have preferred the episode to end differently, and suggested an alternative conclusion:

> Also erzählt die Geschichte mein Author und schweigt und bedenkt nicht,
> Dass er uns traurig da stehn lässt, die Brust mit Abscheu erfüllet.
> Dürft' ich dazu was dichten, so dichtet' ich: Der Käufer
> Fürchtete Gott, er erbarmte sich über die arme Verstossene,
> Hält sie wie seine Tochter und gab sie nach etlichen Tagen
> Ihrem Vater und Volk und ihren Gespielinnen wieder;
> Diese fluchen, von ihrer Geschichte gekränket, dem Weissen,
> Der das schändlichste Herz in seinem Eingeweid führet.
> Aber sie fluchet ihm nicht, sie liebt ihn auch untreu und wünschet
> Ihm nur ein menschliches Herz und wünschet sich selbst ihm zur Sklavin.[27]

The poet of the optimistic age liked to think that virtue would triumph over moral depravity.

Gessner took up Bodmer's words in the introduction to his own *Inkel und Yariko, Zweyter Theil* (1756):

> ...stünde der Leser traurig da, die Brust mit Abscheu erfüllt, wenn man das gute Mädchen ungerettet liesse, so wär es nicht weniger erfüllt: liess man ihn von Inkeln weg, ohne Spuhren der Reu, ohn ein Merkmahl der Menschheit in ihm zu finden. So sehr kan die Güte kein Herze verlassen, dass nicht ein Rükfall der Tugend, kein Schauer der Reue, mächtig ihn fasse, dass nicht seine Fähigkeit gut zu seyn, durch das Unkraut der Leidenschaften in seinem Busen mächtig hinauf bebe. So erzehl ich denn Yarikos Rettung und Inkelns Reue.

Gessner's Inkel immediately regrets his deed. The slave-owner hears Yariko's history, and the commandant of the island condemns Inkel to five years' hard labour. He welcomes his punishment as due penance before God. Yariko is allowed to return to her homeland; she goes sadly, reluctant to leave him, and, learning of his remorse, returns a year later, with her baby, and secures his release. He does not desire freedom, but wishes to continue his penance, until he meets Yariko and both fall into each others' arms. Inkel's despair and remorse are shown as 'Angstschweiss' covers his features, he calls himself 'ein Schandflek der menschlichen Natur', and calls upon the birds to be silent and to flee, for his presence creates 'eine Wildniss, wo ein stinkendes Aas liegt'. As in *Daphnis,* a dramatic moment leads Gessner to use an extended simile taken from his imagination or some third-class poet:

hier bebt' er, wie einer bebt, der izt eine reizende Unschuld verlezen will, wenn ein brüllender Donner den Baum zersplittert, in dessen Schatten er die viehische That begann.

The short work seems lacking in inspiration: the potentially moving story is not exploited to the full, and the psychology is rudimentary. Direct speech is used throughout irrespective of any demands of probability: a third person reports at length the exact words used by Inkel to Yariko.

Inkel und Yariko was never published in Gessner's works during his lifetime, probably because it was incomplete without Bodmer's poem, the first part. It bears witness to Gessner's interest in tragic subjects involving pathos and his desire to present them in a sentimental and morally satisfying manner, with a happy conclusion. In this respect it was an exercise that pointed forward to *Der Tod Abels* of 1758, the biblical epic that, together with his idylls, made his reputation.

Gessner's verses, his *Die Nacht, Daphnis* and *Inkel und Yariko* reveal different moods and styles. By 1756 he had adopted the manner of 'Empfindsamkeit', but only in *Inkel und Yariko* had he abandoned altogether the style of German Rococo literature. To some of his contemporaries frivolous Rococo literature and moralising 'Empfindsamkeit' seemed poles apart, and historians often stress the contrast between them. But perhaps because of his conciliatory nature, Gessner was more aware of what they had in common. His readiness to absorb and reconcile was not a sign of indiscriminating eclecticism. For, despite all their differences, the poetic works that he admired and that influenced him all reflected a reverence for nature and natural man. Nature, indeed, rather than reason, was the central concept of the age. A belief in providential nature underlay the optimism of those who put their faith in reason and those who saw feeling as the chief motive force in human life. Nature's purpose was invariably held to be the same: the progress of man towards perfection, to virtue and happiness. In an age dominated by the Leibnizian theory of pre-established harmony and the best of all possible worlds, few people questioned this notion. All faults in society were believed to follow from man's rejection of the voice of nature. Natural religion, natural law and natural morality were generally accepted as ideals consistent with the realities of experience. This acceptance seemed to be justified by pragmatic evidence, for the travel literature of the time told of 'natural' societies in America, Africa and the East untouched by the evils of civilisation. The myth of the Golden Age, that appeared to be substantiated by such reports, fascinated writers, and took various guises in literature, including the depiction of patriarchal life in Bodmer's biblical epics; all in some way influenced the Arcadia that was the setting for most of Gessner's works.

Brockes had written of the happiness that could be gained from the contemplation of nature, the Anacreontics of the more frivolous joys of flirtation and the flowing bowl, Bodmer and Klopstock of the satisfactions of virtue and the exultation of the pious soul; Gessner's shepherds were to know all these experiences. Each poet he admired implied that one kind of experience was natural and basic to all men; he was to portray them all. In style, too, contemporary poets strove for a form of expression natural to their themes. Gessner appreciated the 'naturalness' of Brockes, the Anacreontics, Bodmer and even Klopstock. But above all he found that everyone agreed that the Ancients were unsurpassed.

Gessner himself, in a letter to Gleim in 1755, declared that more of the classics should be translated into German, since they were indispensable for the formation of good taste.[28] His intention in *Daphnis* was to capture the natural spirit of the Ancients. In 1754 he mentioned, again in a letter to Gleim,[29] his sources of inspiration for his pastoral novel: not only Longus, but also Theocritus, Virgil, Homer – and Anacreon. Evidently he felt that the German Anacreontics understood naturalness in poetry as well as anyone else; at least he flattered Gleim by saying that he was an obvious judge of 'Naivetät'.[30] Since Gessner looked to the Ancients with an eye accustomed to Brockes, Hagedorn and the Anacreontics, he was attracted to pastoral and idyllic works rather than the heroic epic or grand tragedy. His predisposition was not purely personal. Bodmer's epics were sentimental and idyllic rather than heroic. Sublime deeds and great heroes were not favoured by the middle-class taste that was beginning to dominate literary production. Domestic crisis, family love and examples of charity, recognised by Diderot as the proper subjects of modern drama, satisfied most desires for excitement in literature. What could appeal more to the citizen of Zurich, anxious to believe in the goodness of God and man, but not too enamoured of reality, than a vision of natural man, happy, virtuous and pious?

Such a vision was present in *Daphnis*, which also combined Rococo and sentimental elements in a pastoral framework. Perhaps, while writing it, Gessner realised that he was better equipped to produce shorter pieces of poetic prose and chose to write idylls for that reason. Others, Ramler or Bodmer, may have given him advice. Certainly Ramler advised him to concentrate on idylls and recommended Theocritus as a model; but this was in 1755, by which time most, if not all, of Gessner's first collection had been written. Ramler stated that Gessner was particularly suited to the genre, by virtue of his character, and because Switzerland offered examples of idyllic existence in reality. He may have left unexpressed a third reason: pastoral poetry was traditionally considered suitable for a young poet's first experiments.[31] But whatever moved Gessner to write idylls, and to choose Theocritus as his prime model, his decision was a fortunate one, for here he found the form most suited to his genius and one with which his name will always be associated, not as an experimenter, but as a master.

2 · A TASTE OF NATURE

It was a few years before Gessner's idylls became a sensation. His first collection (1756) was favourably received in Zurich and Germany, and a second edition appeared in 1758. In 1757 a reviewer in the Zurich periodical *Freymüthige Nachrichten,* evidently expressing Bodmer's opinion, declared that Gessner had more than fulfilled the promise shown in *Daphnis,* and could be said to have excelled the Ancients. He pointed out the poetic properties of Gessner's prose, found great novelty in the situations and emotions he portrayed, and dismissed unfavourable comments, emanating probably from the Gottsched school, as signs of envy and prejudice. Yet this reviewer implied that these idylls were quite compatible with the theories of Fontenelle and comparable with the eclogues of that writer.[1] Gessner's work was not seen as revolutionary. Albrecht von Haller, writing in the *Göttinger Anzeigen* of 1756, found Gessner preferable to Theocritus, because more refined and more moral.[2] Wieland also noted with approval that Gessner's swains were more virtuous than those of Theocritus, but was not entirely happy with his use of Greek gods: he would have preferred shepherds with monotheistic beliefs.[3] Ewald von Kleist and Gleim were fervent admirers.

Encouraged by the reaction of his friends, Gessner began writing *Der Tod Abels* (1758) soon after the publication of his idylls. This biblical epic was again well received in Zurich, but initially made little impression elsewhere. A visit, with Wieland in 1758, to a touring theatrical company in Winterthur (Wieland's *Lady Johanna Gray* was performed) evidently aroused his interest in the theatre, and he subsequently wrote two short plays, published in 1762.

Meanwhile Gessner's works were introduced to a small circle in Paris, and the story of his fame was about to begin. A poor French translation of *Daphnis*, published in Rostock in 1756, had made no impression. But now Johann Caspar Füssli, painter, art historian, and member of the 'Dienstags-Compagnie', sent a copy of *Der Tod Abels* to an acquaintance in Paris, the engraver J. G. Wille. The work became known among a group of Germans, mostly artists, in the French capital. It passed into the hands of Michael Huber, a Bavarian who taught German to well-to-do Parisians and who did much to make German literature known in France. The short epic, with its relatively simple language, was suitable reading for students of German, and its poetic qualities recommended it as an introduction to German literature. One of Huber's pupils was Turgot, an important man in cultural as well as economic and political affairs, who a few years later became Louis XVI's Finance Minister. With Turgot's encouragement and assistance, Huber rendered *Der Tod Abels* into French, and began to translate the idylls, which then appeared in 1762, two years after *La Mort d'Abel*, as *Idylles et poèmes champêtres*. Turgot found a publisher and wrote introductions to the works. Diderot, who also knew Wille, played an important part in the spread of Gessner's fame. In 1759 and 1760 Lessing and Moses Mendelssohn, both writing in the *Literaturbriefe*, praised the style and content of Gessner's idylls. But now, in France, he was seen as an utterly new departure in literature and as the outstanding poet of nature. Reviews, articles and private letters all expressed, in glowing and excited terms, admiration for the simple poetry of his prose and the naturalness of his subject-matter. As soon as *La Mort d'Abel* appeared, a critic declared in the leading periodical, the *Journal des Sçavans*,[4] that it was 'un de ces ouvrages si rares, faits pour attirer l'attention de tous les Pays et de tous les siècles, et pour servir d'époque à la littérature universelle'. He found in Gessner 'tous les traits qui distinguent les génies consacrés à l'immortalité'; familiar with Gessner's idylls before they had appeared in translation, he announced that in their portrayal of virtue they represented a new and remarkable departure from tradition. Gessner became a best-seller in France. Edition after edition was printed, many of them luxury volumes with engravings by Gessner himself. It is doubtful whether any other poet has ever been re-issued in translation so often in so short a period.

The reception in Paris had its effect in Germany. Beginning in 1762, Gessner produced nine German editions of his collected writings over twenty-five years. This figure excludes individual works published separately, two smaller collections entitled *Gedichte*, and pirated editions.

Turgot, politician, physiocrat and linguist, was keenly interested in literary novelties and foreign poetry and a regular guest in the Parisian 'salons'. He was mainly responsible for the enthusiasm for Gessner in France and Europe, just as he started the craze for Ossian by his translation of Macpherson. In his introduction to the French translation of the idylls he wrote:

il me semble que M. Gessner a traité le genre de l'idylle d'une manière neuve, en évitant également, et la rusticité dans laquelle sont tombés quelques Anciens, et les lieux communs tant rebattus par leurs serviles imitateurs, et la fade galanterie que les Modernes y ont souvent substituée.[5]

Gessner himself declared that he did not look to the French for inspiration, but only to Theocritus and Virgil:

Freylich hab ich zu meinen Idyllen den Theokrit gelesen; ihn alein und den Virgil, bey diesen alein ist die Dichtarth in ihrer Volkomenheit; die verzärtelten Franzosen hab ich nicht gelesen, sie [sind] zu sehr von ihm abgewichen...[6]

We cannot be sure how widely Gessner read. He did not take his work in his father's business too seriously, and had time to read. Neither business, nor administration (in which he was later to become involved) were as time-consuming then as they are now. But he was no book-worm, and much of his time was given to convivial amusement, to writing, painting and drawing. Perhaps he relied on the opinions of others when he rejected French idylls as artificial. His dismissal of the French tradition and preference for the classics may be linked with the widespread reaction against the hegemony of French taste in Germany. In the context of idyllic poetry it promised a new departure.

Certainly he learnt little from German pastoral poetry. It is doubtful whether he read much, for no German writer had achieved great fame in this genre. Early eighteenth-century poets had used the pastoral scene either as a framework for occasional poetry or to describe the sentiments of lovers. One Rococo poet who had written pastorals, quite well known in Gessner's time, was Johann Christoph Rost. Gessner later referred to him as the epitome of lasciviousness in poetry until Wieland published his *Comische Erzählungen* in 1762.[7] Rost wrote to entertain; the style of his *Schäfererzählungen* (1742) is fluent, graceful and witty, comparable with the best of Wieland's Rococo verses. His shepherdesses pretend to be innocent, but are not; the poet plays with his reader, leaving enough to the imagination to avoid outright indecency. In contrast to Rost's erotic fantasies, C. F. Zernitz's pastorals are sermons. In a dryly rational tone and halting style, his *Versuch in Moralischen und Schäfer-Gedichten* of 1748 preaches of virtue and divine providence. Neither poet, the one lacking seriousness, the other imagination, was likely to appeal to Bodmer or his followers.

Gessner turned to the Ancients, and preferred Theocritus to

Virgil: 'Ich habe den Theokrit immer für das beste Muster in dieser Art Gedichte gehalten' (V, 17). This, too, was a break with tradition. For more than two hundred years it had been generally accepted that Virgil was a more skilled and more refined poet than Theocritus and his *Eclogues* had been recommended as the model for imitation. The preference for the more refined Virgil reflected the belief that the world of pastoral had nothing to do with realism. The tendency towards idealisation and stylisation in the idyll culminated in Fontenelle's *Discours sur la nature de l'églogue* of 1688, an essay that became the basis of most theories of pastoral in the early eighteenth century. Fontenelle argued, contributing to the 'Querelle des Anciens et des Modernes', that the Ancients could be surpassed, and made mocking attacks on Theocritus's supposed lack of taste. He maintained that the pastoral swain had nothing in common with real shepherds; pastoral poetry should depict the emotions of lovers; it was imitation of nature in so far as it selected from reality, painting the pleasant aspects of rural existence, but suppressing all that was less amenable to polite taste. Fontenelle's own pastoral poetry was even further removed from rural realities than his theory suggests. In England, Pope, in his *Discourse on Pastoral* of 1704, declared that this type of poetry portrayed an idealised existence; he, too, rejected the realism of Theocritus, and stressed the moral usefulness of pastoral as a reminder of virtue and innocence. The first notable German theorist of the eighteenth century, Gottsched, followed Fontenelle and Pope: the poet should not take real country folk as his subject, for his swains must be virtuous and happy.[8] The prejudice against realism in pastoral was so strong that Gottsched himself and his followers were accused of tastelessness and crudity in their idyllic works. For there was some divergence between theory and practice. In a satirical essay entitled *Vom Natürlichen in Schäfergedichten* (1746), J. A. Schlegel ironically castigated Fontenelle as a corrupter of taste and judged pastoral poems by the number of dung-heaps and swear-words they contained. In 1751 Schlegel gave his real opinions in an appendix to his translation of Batteux's *Traité des beaux arts*: he distinguished between realistic descriptive poetry whose subject was country life, and pastoral that described an imaginary world. Schlegel preferred Virgil to Theocritus and praised Gresset's French version of Virgil's eclogues that 'improved' the original. Gessner, in the foreword to his idylls, refers to Gresset's adaptation as an example of exaggerated and unnatural 'politeness'.

If this were the whole picture of the theory of pastoral before Gessner, his preference for Theocritus would have been extraordinarily provocative. But there were other voices. In England, Ambrose Philips published in 1709 pastorals set, not in an idealised Arcadia, but in the English countryside; his shepherds, ignorant of classical mythology, talked of native folklore. These poems were lauded in Addison's *Spectator*. In a series of articles in the *Guardian* of 1713 Theocritus was preferred to Virgil because he was thought to show more simplicity and virtue; Ambrose Philips was praised, Pope ignored, and local colour and realistic detail expressly called for. The English periodicals had great influence in Germany, and particularly in Zurich. Bodmer, in his *Neue Critische Briefe* of 1749, compared Theocritus, Virgil and Gresset, and concluded that Virgil did not match Theocritus in power and grace, and that Gresset had turned Virgil's shepherds into courtiers. He tentatively defended the 'crudities' of Theocritus by suggesting that they might be signs of true simplicity.[9] In the same year he contrasted Theocritus with the artificiality of German pastoral poetry.[10] He believed real shepherds on the whole too vulgar to be presented in pastoral, but allowed that some aspects of country life were suitable for poetic treatment. Ramler, too, as we have seen, was an admirer of Theocritus. But we may assume that Gessner was influenced mainly by opinions in Zurich, where there was evidently a lively interest in the idyll. For the Zurich periodical *Das Angenehme mit dem Nüzlichen* published in 1756 a translation from Theocritus, and in the previous year a rendering of Pope's pastorals into German alexandrines, a pastoral dialogue in undistinguished prose, and a further piece modelled on the Greek poet. This is a dialogue and singing contest, entitled 'Das Zweis [sic], ein Schäferstük, nach der würklichsten Natur'.[11] It contains rustic weather lore (one herdsman talks of cows raising their tails before a storm), references to popular superstition, unrefined imagery and peasant expressions of abuse and endearment. There are also humorous touches, emphasised by the contrast between colloquialism and formal verse structure.

Bodmer appreciated vivid imagery, but he did not call for realistic comedy in pastoral poetry. Realism could offend good taste. The innocent swain became incongruous among dung-heaps and cabbages – we recall Mme de Genlis's consternation on meeting Gessner. Alongside the shepherd of pastoral stood another stock literary figure, the rustic clown, and it was dangerous to confuse the two. Bodmer and Breitinger stressed the role of the poetic imagination, for them the world of poetry was a 'possible' world. Bodmer's own poetry, that of Klopstock and the early Wieland could hardly be described as realistic. Gessner's praise of Theocritus was therefore circumspect:

Ich hielt mich indess zu keinem von den Kunstrichtern, die entweder dem Theokrit alles zur Schönheit, oder alles zu Fehlern anrechnen. Er ist göttlich, aber er hat für Leute von andern, vielleicht bessern Sitten gesungen; ich kann den Käse und die Nüsse im Gedicht auch nicht zu oft ausstehen. Es ist kein Fehler, aber wir empfinden was dabey, das bey so ganz veränderten Sitten nicht ausbleibt.[12]

On the other hand he wrote critically of that hypersensitive taste that found crudity even in Virgil:

Zwar weiss ich wol, dass einige wenige Ausdrüke und Bilder im Theokrit, bey so sehr abgeänderten Sitten uns verächtlich worden sind...Ich meyne aber hier nicht dergleichen, die ein französischer Übersetzer [Gresset] in dem Virgil nicht ausstehen konnte; die ich meyne, hat Virgil, der Nachahmer des Theokrit, selbst schon weggelassen. (V, 18)

What Gessner appreciated in Theocritus was not realism as such, but closeness to nature:

Bey ihm findet man die Einfalt der Sitten und der Empfindungen am besten ausgedrükt, und das Ländliche und die schönste Einfalt der Natur; er ist mit dieser bis auf die kleinsten Umstände bekannt gewesen; wir sehen in seinen Idyllen mehr als Rosen und Lilien; seine Gemählde kommen nicht aus einer Einbildungs-Kraft, die nur die bekanntesten und auch dem Unachtsamen in die Augen fallenden Gegenstände häuft; sie haben die angenehme Einfalt der Natur, nach der sie allemal gezeichnet zu seyn scheinen. Seinen Hirten hat er den höchsten Grad der

Naivität gegeben...Sie sind weit von dem Epigrammatischen Witz entfernt, und von der schulgerechten Ordnung...(V, 17)

Gessner, the admirer of Brockes, found in his Greek model details in the description of nature that were not conventional formulae. There could be little problem of taste here, provided that the poet described what was beautiful or pleasant.

But what sort of man was natural man, and what was naiveté in shepherds? The answer seemed clear. Natural man was happy, virtuous and pious. He had been portrayed many times by eighteenth-century writers. The popularity of pastoral poetry in this age arose largely from the scope it gave for depicting man as happy and innocent. Natural man had appeared in other guises too. One was the 'noble savage' of travel literature. Natural man belonged to a society that was contrasted with European civilisation, and he had figured in several imitations of *Robinson Crusoe* and in utopian novels. Schnabel's successful novel *Die Insel Felsenburg* (1731–43) told of men shipwrecked on a South-Sea island who founded an ideal state without social or religious differences. Schnabel's characters live close to nature and reveal man's innate goodness and honesty. In Bodmer's biblical epics the patriarchs are basically happy because of their virtue and piety. They live in a virtual paradise, a variation on the Golden Age.

The Golden Age, or something like it, existed in Switzerland itself, if various writers of the age were to be believed. Ramler referred to this picture of Switzerland when advising Gessner to write idylls.[13] There could, therefore, be some connection between idylls and Swiss reality. Gessner wrote to Gleim in 1754 that he disagreed with those who would have pastoral poetry set in a purely imaginative land – those who

aus allzugrosser Gefälligkeit für ausschweifend zärtliche Leute, die Bilder und Gemälde aus dem wirklichen Landleben wegweisen, und die Schäferwelt nur zu einer poetischen machen wollen; denen eckelt, wenn ihnen in der Ekloge der Sinn an den Landmann und seine Geschäfte kommt. Das ist zu hart. In einem Lande, wo ein hochgräflicher Herr Graf, oder ein gnädiger Herr Baron den Landmann zum armen Sclaven macht, da mag letzterer kleiner und verächtlicher seyn, als bey uns, wo die Freiheit ihn zum besser denkenden braven Mann macht; und ich getraute mir, auf unsern Alpen Hirten zu finden, wie Theokrit in seiner

Zeit, denen man wenig nehmen und wenig leihen dürfte, um sie zur Ekloge zu bilden.[14]

Some followers of Gottsched had argued that idyllic poetry was impossible in the modern world, since the poet had no idyllic reality to portray. In a foreword to an edition of Gottsched's poems of 1736, Joachim Schwake addressed his reader thus:

Du weisst, dass ein Dichter die Natur zum Vorbild hat und nur deren Schönheiten nachzuahmen sucht. Wo zeigt aber itzt die Natur das alte Schäferleben?...Wie kann ein Dichter das wieder vorstellen was er nirgends mehr erblickt?[15]

The Swiss could not agree with this. For the national character, the Swiss constitution, the proximity to nature had, it was thought, preserved at least some men from the evils of civilisation. Gessner himself believed that the town of Zurich was relatively untouched by the worst aspects of civilisation; he wrote to an Italian correspondent:

Permettez-moi de vous détailler un peu notre Situation, et notre manière de vivre...Il n'y a pas de ville en Suisse où il y aye plus d'égalité entre la bourgeoisie et plus d'esprit de liberté. Nous sommes un peuple laborieux, et notre recource principale est le Commerce. Avec cela nous avons encor conservé une certaine Simplicité des moeurs, et le peu de Comunication que nous avons avec les étrangers, la médiocrité de nos fortunes et nos lois ont mis des bornes au luxe, qui est beaucoup plus avancé p. e. à Berne.[16]

The puritanical outlook, and the strong sense of civic duty encouraged by the Reformed Church, ensured that social differences were less marked here than elsewhere. There was no obvious contrast between the rich and an urban proletariat, and the paternal régime was accepted by most with cheerful acquiescence. Even more simple, of course, was the life of the Swiss countryfolk. One of Bodmer's friends, Laurenz Zellweger, was a doctor in the village of Trogen near Appenzell, and in that district the intellectuals of Zurich found much that reminded them of the Golden Age. In 1751 one of them wrote to a German about a visit to Trogen; he insisted that in many respects the Swiss countryman was eminently suitable for poetic representation:

Alles ist wahr, nach dem Buchstaben wahr, was Ihre Freunde Ihnen von diesem sonderbaren Volk in Prose und in Versen erzählt haben...Es ist Wahrheit, nicht

Poesie oder Roman, dass hier der Mensch sich noch nicht vor dem Menschen schämet, und zu ungeschickt ist, sein Herz zu verbergen...(V, 158f)

Patriotic sentiment had, indeed, long insisted that Swiss manners were simple and natural, particularly when compared with those in France. Johann Jakob Scheuchzer's *Naturgeschichten des Schweizerlandes* (1706) painted a picture, in an ostensibly scientific work, of a nation enjoying great freedom and equality; the mountain people, in particular, represented an ideal of simplicity, their huts were compared with those of the first men on earth, and the countryside with Canaan. In a similar vein, Muralt's well-known *Lettres sur les Anglais et les Français* of 1725 contrasted the natural simplicity of manners in Switzerland and England with the artificiality of French life. Haller's poem *Die Alpen* (1729) equally famous throughout Europe, also purported to give an objective picture of the Alps and their inhabitants, yet told of men sheltered from civilisation, pure in spirit and contented with their lot, kindly and charitable, of simple religious faith, and at one with nature.

Much literature of the time showed the innocence of country life as opposed to the depravity of the towns. Of course, men saw what they expected to see: sailors in the South Sea saw natural innocence, and the townsman saw virtue in the countryside. But in Switzerland examples of natural man were located with greater exactitude than elsewhere, and described in greater detail. The forest cantons of Schwyz and Uri provided amazing examples of pure democracy at work. Now that an aversion to the artificiality of court and town life was growing in Europe, it seemed that Switzerland was a happy hunting ground for anyone looking for naturalness. Gessner's friend Johann Caspar Hirzel, member of the 'Dienstags-Compagnie' and the official town doctor in Zurich, wrote of a farmer he knew. This man, Jacob Guier, known as Kleinjogg (he was the younger of two Jacobs in the same family), had through hard work and common-sense achieved a near miracle on two farms loaded with debts and ill-favoured by nature. Hirzel was concerned with the problem of agriculture, for he knew that unless farming methods were improved Zurich and Switzerland would become more and more dependent on imported foodstuffs. Traditionally, little corn was grown, and there was considerable resistance to the introduction of clover or to anything that was not time-honoured practice. Hirzel described methods of manuring and irrigation and of animal husbandry evolved by Kleinjogg. The bulk of Hirzel's book contains practical advice and hard facts. In an age interested in progress and in nature, and therefore in agricultural economics, his *Wirtschaft eines philosophischen Bauers* (1761) – *Le socrate rustique* in its French version – was widely read. Hirzel and Kleinjogg became famous throughout Europe, even in America. Hirzel maintained that a farmer followed the worthiest of occupations, since close to nature. Kleinjogg himself is said to have put many more educated and sophisticated men to shame by his common-sense. It was believed that his moral uprightness, his hard work and his belief in providence not only determined his success as a farmer, but also derived from his closeness to nature.

An Englishman in Switzerland a few years later noted 'the well-being of the peasantry... scarcely surpassed by any spot on the globe' in the district around Zurich, and wrote of Canton Appenzell:

Among the chief part of the inhabitants, the original simplicity of the pastoral life is still preserved; and I saw several venerable figures with long beards, that resembled the pictures of ancient patriarchs.[17]

But such pictures were very one-sided. In practice a few families ruled over the Swiss countryside, the farmers were often exploited by the richer townsfolk, they were poor and superstitious, and their manners matched the rigours of their existence. Oliver Goldsmith recorded in his poem *The Traveller*, based on a journey made in 1755, that the inhabitants of the Swiss Alps were contented with their lot, but lacked refinement. The small communities might appear like natural societies based on the family unit, but they also encouraged inbreeding and idiocy. Not surprisingly, Gessner was very cautious in selecting details from Swiss reality to include in his idylls – so cautious that there are few explicitly Swiss features in his shepherds, or, indeed, in the natural scenery. He set his idylls in a remote, timeless Arcadia; in that way, he thought, the naturalness he described would seem more credible:

Diese Dichtungs-Art bekömmt daher einen besonderen Vortheil, wenn man die Scenen in ein entferntes Weltalter sezt; sie erhalten dadurch einen höhern Grad der Wahrscheinlichkeit, weil sie für unsre Zeiten nicht passen, wo der Landmann mit saurer Arbeit unterthänig seinem Fürsten und den Städten den Überfluss liefern muss, und Unterdrükung und Armuth ihn ungesittet und schlau und niederträchtig gemacht haben. Ich will damit nicht läugnen, dass ein Dichter...nicht sonderbare Schönheiten ausspüren kann, wenn er die Denkungsart und die Sitten des Landmanns bemerket, aber er muss diese Züge mit seinem Geschmak wählen, und ihnen ihr Rauhes zu benehmen wissen...(V, 15f)

He declared that he painted a Golden Age that was not a myth but a fact of history: Homer and the stories of the Old Testament patriarchs could convince us of this (V, 15).

His idylls, indeed, helped to form and encourage the picture of Greece that was to have such a profound effect on European culture in the following decades. The myth of Greece as the land of beauty, goodness and happiness underwent considerable transformations during the late eighteenth and early nineteenth centuries, but the world of Gessner's idylls is still recognisable in the words of Goethe's Faust:

> Hier ist das Wohlbehagen erblich,
> Die Wange heitert wie der Mund,
> Ein jeder ist an seinem Platz unsterblich:
> Sie sind zufrieden und gesund.

Like Shaftesbury, and like Winckelmann, the father of Neo-Classicism (whose *Gedanken über die Nachahmung der griechischen Werke* appeared in 1755 while Gessner was preparing his first idylls for publication), Gessner dreamed of a beautiful Greece inhabited by almost perfect mortals. Winckelmann recognised in Gessner's vision of Arcadia something of that noble simplicity that he proclaimed the characteristic of Greek art; he read his idylls with enthusiasm whilst visiting the ruins of Paestum. The growth of interest in Greek art and the discoveries at Pompcii and Herculaneum encouraged Gessner in his own work and facilitated its reception throughout Europe. To a world somewhat disenchanted with the 'myths' of Christianity, the myth of Ancient Greece offered a secular alternative. Gessner himself, although a

firm believer in God and in Christian morality, was not enamoured
of orthodoxy as represented by the Reformed Church in Switzerland, and dreamt of a more natural form of religious behaviour.

The idyll seemed very suitable for portraying natural man. But
what was an idyll? It is probable that Gessner had some doubts
about the distinction between pastoral and bucolic poetry that was
a talking-point in contemporary theory. But there is no sign that
he was greatly worried about definitions. The idyll had not been
clearly defined. The Greek word was thought to mean a small
picture or description, and this meaning seemed convincing in an
age when all poetry was understood as imitation of reality, comparable to painting. Only in the nineteenth century was it discovered that idyll probably originally meant no more than a short
poem belonging to no defined genre.[18] A 'picture', moreover,
seemed adequate as a description of many of Theocritus's idylls,
particularly those that depict the pastoral scene. And it was these
that had been imitated by Virgil in his *Eclogues* or pastoral poems.
Since the Renaissance pastoral poetry had taken many forms, and
the idyll or eclogue was not distinguished clearly from this broad
tradition, so that the three terms became almost synonymous.
Gottsched headed a section of his *Critische Dichtkunst* of 1730 'Von
Idyllen, Eklogen oder Schäfergedichten'. Gessner's attempt to
renew the idyll by returning for inspiration to its original form as
given by Theocritus implied a rejection of much of the idyllic and
pastoral tradition. Linked with the idea that the idyll should be
set in the remote past, and that Theocritus's poems were more
natural than Virgil's, was the belief that man, and therefore poetry,
was more natural at earlier stages of civilisation. Pastoral poetry
was assumed by many to be one of the earliest, if not the earliest
form of poetry. Yet Theocritus belonged to an age that has been
called decadent, and his idylls have that mood of longing for lost
simplicity that was the lifeblood of all pastoral.

Theocritus gave Gessner his model: short, self-contained poems
depicting a scene and portraying basic human emotions, pieces
moving quickly between description and narrative, dialogue,
lyrical monologue and song. Several times Gessner uses as the

basis for an idyll another feature of pastoral poetry derived from Theocritus – the song-contest. Individual descriptions, of a cage for crickets made from rushes, of a basket, a drinking gourd, a lamp and a pitcher, are similarly based on the Greek poet. The simplicity of the ideas and emotions in Gessner's idylls owes much to Theocritus, as does the simplicity of the language. Gessner imitated Theocritus's similes, comparing song with running water or honey, human love and joy with the emotions of animals in spring, movements of delight with a fawn springing to its dam or a lamb skipping in the pasture. His practice of listing comparisons in a balanced sentence may also derive from the same source. Apostrophes to valleys, hills, trees and flowers are found in both poets.

But Gessner followed general practice, and not Theocritus, in confining his idylls to the pastoral setting; in 1777 he grouped together, under the title 'Vermischte Gedichte', several non-pastoral pieces originally called idylls in the 1756 collection. The pleasant spots in nature, shady nooks beside running water, with a flowery mead or a mossy bank in the spring or summer sunshine, described or evoked many times by Gessner, are variations on the 'locus amoenus', a literary topos that is traced back to Virgil rather than Theocritus. There are other signs of indebtedness to Virgil, notably in Gessner's story of a faun bound hand and foot and forced to sing. Gessner's idyllic world is an imaginative world, a 'possible' world in the sense of Bodmer's poetics, made up of elements taken mainly from literature and art. In externals it does not differ greatly from the traditional pastoral scene. His work was not so revolutionary that it could not be immediately accepted by contemporary readers. The characters are shepherds, goatherds or cowherds. One is found diverting a stream, others mention the care of fruit trees, vines and bee-hives, another is about to build a fence. But these activities are not described, and Gessner's idylls are of little interest to the agricultural historian. His shepherds have Greek names commonplace in pastoral – Daphnis and Damon, Phillis and Chloe. Their world is populated by the gods and demigods of Greek mythology.

This fictional world contrasted with reality. Yet to many of his readers, who hoped and expected to find aspects of ideal humanity present in areas remote from the main centres of civilisation, in the countryside untouched by the manners of courts or the heavy hand of tyranny, his idylls were not complete fabrications. They were poetic elaborations of something that was felt to be real, and could therefore evince a very real sense of longing.

Gessner did not, like many pastoral poets after Virgil, use the form to comment on contemporary events and personalities. Nor did he write elegiac idylls: the lover's complaint and mourning for the dead were favourite themes in pastoral, but where these occur in Gessner he handles them in such a way that they do not conflict with his vision of happy harmony. For, as Turgot claimed, Gessner was not a slavish imitator. He used forms and ideas taken from Theocritus and Virgil but adapted them and the idyll to his own taste, which was largely that of his age. He did not talk, as did Theocritus, of homosexuality, rutting animals and black magic, but of innocence and virtue and happiness. His idylls had aspects that appeared new, or at least corresponded to the taste of his time, and they were so successful, and Gessner was so pleased with his own formula, that he scarcely varied it when he wrote his second collection some sixteen years later. Indeed Gessner's idyllic vision remained essentially unchanged throughout his career as a writer, from about 1754 to 1771, and works that he published separately from the two collections of idylls may conveniently and appropriately be examined together with them.

Many features of his idylls are already present in *Daphnis*. There the townsman, Aristus, contrasts the virtues of the country with the vices of the town. He inveighs against the leaders to the city of Croton, who, unmindful of their duties, of the gods, virtue and justice, are guided by lust and self-interest. He expounds on the happiness of the shepherds:

Wie glücklich ist der Hirt, wie glücklich der Weise, der dem grossen Pöbel unbekannt, in lachenden Gefilden jede Wollust geniesst, die die bescheidene Natur fordert und giebt, und unbemerkt grössere Thaten thut, als der Eroberer und der angegaffte Fürst!...ihr Hirten! wie nahe seid ihr dem Glücke! Ihr, die ihr

unselig die Einfalt der Natur verliesset, ein mannigfaltigeres Glück zu suchen, ihr
Thoren!...ewig mühsam, ewig unzufrieden irret ihr da...(F, 35)

Since such a contrast between the country and the town, naturalness and artificiality, was both a common theme in eighteenth-
century literature and a part of the pastoral tradition, Gessner
could assume that his readers would understand it implicit in his
work. Yet he states the contrast explicitly, in the foreword to the
1756 collection, and in a few idylls.

In 'Menalkas und Aeschines, der Jäger' (V, 47) a huntsman from
the town, lost in the mountains, is rescued by the shepherd
Menalkas. In gratitude Aeschines offers to take him to the town,
where he will drink from cups of gold, eat from silver plates, hear
sophisticated music in marble palaces and see beautiful girls whose
skin has not been touched by sun or rain. But Menalkas is quite
satisfied with the bounties of nature, with well-water, fruits and
flowers, with thatched cottages, suntanned lasses, pastoral songs
and the music of the birds. He has no use for the gold he is
offered and asks rather for a gourd bottle engraved with Bacchus
and Loves. In an idyll from the 1772 collection, 'Daphne' (V, 113),
a rich townsman tries to seduce a country girl; in her innocence
she is slow to understand his intentions, and it is implied that his
immoral conduct is unheard of in the country.

The contrast between idyllic retreat and contemporary reality
is the theme of 'Der Wunsch' (V, 66f), the only idyll clearly set in
Gessner's own time. Untrammelled by an Arcadian disguise, and
before 'Erlebnisdichtung' was fashionable, Gessner speaks of his
longing for escape into nature. A rather rambling piece, 'Der
Wunsch' contains many echoes of conventional eighteenth-
century nature poetry, including a brief survey of rural life during
the four seasons. Love of nature is reflected in exclamation and
detailed description. Like Ewald von Kleist in *Der Frühling*, the
poet dreams of a country cottage, with a simple garden, an
orchard and a yard with poultry; he speaks of the joy of observing
and helping his gardener, of visiting neighbouring farmers, and of
walking in the moonlight. He wishes to escape from the claustro-
phobic town, from silly conventions and those he despises,

socialites and fops, gossips and carping critics of political leaders, gluttons and misers, immoral and irreligious men. Here there is a note of satire, but the poet quickly turns away from distressing reality to dream of happiness in nature. He does not wish to put all culture behind him: in winter he would study engravings of nature, write poems, and read classical authors and his favourite modern poets – Bodmer, Klopstock, Wieland, Kleist, Gleim. Nor would he turn his back on all other men, but would welcome convivial companions.

The contrast between town and country is largely a moral one, but 'Menalkas und Aeschines' includes another, aesthetic factor. The garden admired by the townsman is arranged in a regular, geometrical pattern and ornamented with statuary:

dort hat man auch Bäume und Blumen, dort hat sie die Kunst in gerade Gänge gepflanzet, und in schön geordnete Beeten gesammelt; dort hat man auch Quellen, Männer und Nymphen von Marmor giessen sie in grosse marmorne Beken. (V, 48)

The shepherd prefers the irregularity of the natural landscape:

Schöner ist der ungekünstelte schattichte Hain mit seinen gekrümmten Gängen...

The reader is expected to share this taste, which we find expressed again in 'Der Wunsch':

Denn, was entzüket mehr als die schöne Natur, wenn sie in harmonischer Unordnung ihre unendlich manigfaltigen Schönheiten verwindet? Zu kühner Mensch! was unterwindest du dich die Natur durch weither nachahmende Künste zu schmüken? Baue Labyrinte von grünen Wänden, und lass den gespizten Taxus in abgemessener Weite emporstehn, die Gänge seyen reiner Sand, dass kein Gesträuchgen den wandelnden Fusstritt verwirre; mir gefällt die ländliche Wiese und der verwilderte Hain, ihre Manigfaltigkeit und Verwirrung hat die Natur nach geheimern Regeln der Harmonie und der Schönheit geordnet, die unsere Seele voll sanften Entzükens empfindt. (V, 68f)

The landscapes of Gessner's idylls are determined by this principle of 'harmonische Unordnung'. They are not chaotic and confusing, although he occasionally mentions labyrinthine features formed by bushes or by meadow grasses seen from close quarters. The scenery is welcoming, it is like a garden or park. Indeed, Gessner scarcely distinguishes between gardens and countryside, the aspects that appeal to him in each are the same. He mentions one or two straight lines, for instance the trunks of fir trees, but he delights in irregular curving forms, a winding brook, twisting branches. His feeling for asymmetrical beauty and freedom of line was shared by many of his contemporaries. It foreshadows the popularity of the 'English garden' or park in Europe in the later eighteenth century. Like the great English landscape gardeners, Gessner owed something to the classical landscapes of Poussin and Claude, both in his literary output and, as we shall see, in his own work with the brush. In the later idylls he introduced classical temples with marble columns, but his idyllic landscape is pleasant rather than heroic or grand, he dwells on the foreground rather than great vistas; as the scene for intimate moments it may recall the spirit of Watteau's canvases rather than those of Poussin or Claude. There is nothing sombre or melancholy about Gessner's scenes, no ruins to remind one of the impermanence of human endeavour so beloved of later decades.

His eye for contrasts of light and shade, probably developed by his interest in the visual arts and essential in one who was to devote much of his time to engraving, is apparent in the idylls. A white dress stands out in the moonlight, its shape broken by black branches (V, 131). Ivy twining round a tree becomes clearer when the trunk is light in colour – Gessner calls it white (V, 23). His alertness to such contrasts influences his appreciation of a snow scene, an unusual setting for an idyll; this winter landscape might well be lowland Switzerland:

Lieblich ists, wie aus dem Weissen empor die schwarzen Stämme der Bäume zerstreut stehn, mit ihren krummgeschwungenen unbelaubten Ästen, oder eine braune Hütte mit dem Schnee-bedeckten Dach, oder wenn die schwarzen Zäune von Dorn-Stauden die weisse Ebene durchkreuzen; Schön ists wie die grüne Saat dort über das Feld hin die zarten Spizen aus dem Schnee empor hebt und das Weiss mit sanftem Grün vermischt...(V, 24)

He was fascinated by the shapes cast by shadows; once when ill in bed he was discovered playing with the bedclothes to create shadow patterns in the candlelight.[19] Descriptions of moving shadows in the idylls give an impression of detailed observation. A girl tells of finding her swain asleep under a bush:

der Sonnenschein streute schwebende Schatten der Blätter auf ihn hin: O ich seh
ihn noch, sie hüpften auf seinem schönen Gesicht umher...(V, 46)

The poet describes moonlight flashing on dancing waters (V, 110),
and notes the moving shadows of grasses and meadow flowers
(V, 63). When, in 'Der Wunsch' he dreams of sitting with his note-
book or sketchpad on his knee, he thinks of shadows playing over
the paper.

Such details appeal to the mind's eye, and derive from the
author's observation of nature as well as of art. Gessner spent
much time sketching from nature and was particularly concerned
with the detailed reproduction of intricate forms in rocks, plants
and trees. He was fond of the small wooded gorges or 'Tobel' near
Zurich, where streams rush through rocks and bushes. There is a
hint of such a valley in 'Der feste Vorsatz':

du, sprudelnder Bach, wohin rauschest du, an den unterhöhlten Wurzeln und
durch das wilde Gewebe von Gesträuchen? (V, 58)

But one idyll stands out for detailed observation of nature, and on
this account has been perhaps more admired than any other: 'Die
Gegend im Gras'. It describes a small patch of meadow, with
grasses, flowers and insect life, with enthusiasm and accuracy:

Was für ein liebliches Sumsen schwärmt um mich her? Warum wanken die
Blumen so? Ein Schwarm kleiner Bienen ists...sie schwärmen umher, von Blume
zu Blume, und verbergen nachsuchend die kleinen haarichten Häupter in den
Kelchen der Blumen, oder sie graben sich mühsam hinein, in die noch nicht
offenen Blumen, die Blume schliesset sich wieder, und verbirgt den kleinen
Räuber...Dort auf die hohe Klee-Blume setzt sich ein kleiner Schmetterling, er
schwingt seine bunten Flügel; auf ihrem glänzenden Silber stehn kleine purpurne
Fleken, und ein goldner Saum verliert sich am End der Flügel ins Grüne; Da
sitzt er prächtig und puzt den kleinen Busch der silbernen Federn auf seinem
kleinen Haupt...(V, 64)

Gessner does not pretend to any more scientific knowledge than a
peasant might possess, but no doubt an expert could name the
butterfly, and other insects described in this piece, from the details
given. Gessner was obviously familiar with the countryside. He
lets a girl tell her companion to walk further ahead through the
undergrowth, lest the brambles fly back in her face (V, 118). Yet

he does not attempt to rival Brockes in accurate miniatures, nor indeed does he compare with James Thomson, whose *Seasons* he much admired, in succinct poetic description of plants and animals. Only rarely does Gessner's natural scene strike a completely realistic note without the intrusion of literary convention. Yet his descriptive passages, notably in 'Der Herbstmorgen' and 'Mycon' in the 1772 collection, are exceptionally vivid, and may have had some influence on the young Goethe.[20]

Gessner's landscape is an amalgam of the classical landscape of pictorial art, literary Arcadia, and lowland Switzerland. In many cases it is impossible to determine the source of a detail, in art or in reality. To those who believed that Switzerland housed remnants of the Golden Age the distinction between fiction and reality was, in any case, not very meaningful. The many shady nooks he described, the vines shading a door or window fitted as well into the Swiss scene as into Arcadia, as did the abundance of fruit trees. So, too, bearded peasants and pictures of biblical patriarchs joined to form Gessner's standard aged swain with flowing white beard. But almost always it is the idealised associations that hold sway. The absence of meat from the diet of Gessner's shepherds was not meant to recall the poverty of peasants, rather the largely vegetarian fare corresponds to a fanciful notion of natural simplicity. It does no harm, however, when reading of the shepherds and their flowers, to think of Alpine herdsmen decking themselves with blooms on festive occasions, as when they left for the high pastures in spring.[21] Nor is it entirely inappropriate to link the fictional swains' prayers to Pan with the real need of pastoral peoples for protective deities or saints. For such possible allusions to rural reality did allow Gessner's idylls to appear in some sense realistic to many of his readers.

Convention and reality are mingled. In Gessner's idylls we find nightingales and doves, but also birds more likely to evoke a real landscape, tits, sparrows, wrens and wagtails. Butterflies and bees are joined by frogs, lizards, grasshoppers and crickets. Myrtle trees, olives and vines mix with fir and pine, oak, beech, elm, poplar, willow, apple, pear, cherry, hazel, hawthorn, ash, and brambles. There are lilies, roses, primroses, lilies of the valley, marjoram, honeysuckle, elderflowers, ox-eye daisy, ferns, dog-roses, meadow saffron, pinks, harebells, hollyhocks, scabious, and watercress. In 'Der Wunsch', admittedly an exception in its contemporary rural setting, Gessner describes a country cottage and its garden or yard where there are ducks and chickens. His reading of descriptive nature poetry stood him in good stead.

The 'realism' of Gessner's idylls may be judged by comparison with the description of the Garden of Eden in *Paradise Lost* as translated by Bodmer. Both bring contrasts with the artificial garden, both have grottos veiled by trailing roses, and both mention Pan. But whereas Gessner's scenery is just possible in real terms, Milton's is purely imaginary: roses bear no thorns, streams run over beds of gold and pearls, and nature is not subject to the seasons – plants bear blossoms and fruit at the same time. The comparison with Milton's Paradise is meaningful because so many landscapes in idyllic and pastoral poetry were similarly unreal. In his 'Patriarchaden' Bodmer describes nature after the Fall, but it is still almost paradisical. He dwells on the depth and coolness of shade, pleasant streams, meadows full of flowers, abundance of fruit and healthy herds. Like Gessner, he tells of seeming labyrinths of undergrowth, of bowers and grottos and climbing vines. Apart from the difference in style – Bodmer's rather weak alexandrines with conventional, often Baroque tropes, Gessner's simple prose – there is a definite disparity in descriptive power. Bodmer is not only less realistic, he is also less vivid.

The importance of Gessner's style can scarcely be exaggerated. As befits writings that extol simple feelings and thoughts, his vocabulary is restricted, his imagery unsophisticated, and his syntax lucid and uncomplicated. The repetition of words, the brevity of phrases, the paratactic constructions and the reliance on simple linking adverbs ('dann' or 'itzt') or common conjunctions ('dass' is used in many meanings and replaces 'damit' or 'so dass') may come close to childishness. But in its simplicity the language is appropriate to the characters, and much of the text of the idylls consists of direct speech, indirect discourse being avoided. Gessner gives an impression of spontaneity and intimacy – it is as if the characters were speaking directly to the reader. The poet himself does not adopt a superior pose, but speaks much the same language as his shepherds. Such uncomplicated comments as he offers follow directly and naturally from the situation or action portrayed. The simplicity of style made a great impact, particularly in France. Gessner himself foresaw the probable reaction of his readers when he contrasted his manner with the 'galanterie' of French pastoral poetry. In a sense, therefore, his language was more realistic than that of previous pastoral poetry, because it was less sophisticated. Yet it is not convincingly realistic, nor was it intended to be. Gessner aimed to write a German that was correct, free of dialect, clear, and poetic. He seems to have drawn his inspiration from several poets, classical and contemporary. If there is any attempt in the idylls to reproduce the mannerisms of real Swiss shepherds or to emulate folk poetry, it is not obvious. Yet his contemporaries were willing to believe that his simple language was not too far removed from the speech of real country people.

His descriptions of nature were appreciated most in France, where descriptive nature poetry was not so developed as in Germany or England. One Parisian reviewer declared him superior to any French poet in this sphere.[22] But in any case such descriptions were new to the idyll, and the naming of so many plants, and Gessner's eye for light and shade, colour and shape resulted in quite exact, attractive pictures.

Gessner devotes idylls to the beauties of autumn and winter, not restricting himself to the conventional setting of a warm spring or summer day. Nevertheless, the variations on the 'locus amoenus' are more numerous. In 'Milon' (V, 21) the shepherd looks out from the entrance to a cave shaded by a porch of climbing plants on to a stream flowing through a flowery mead. Plants are named, colours mentioned. But this passage is noteworthy not only for its attention to exact detail, but also for its emotional tone, as Milon repeatedly calls on us to look and see how lovely everything is.

Almost without exception Gessner places more importance on the emotions aroused by nature than on exact description of the scene. The mood depends largely, of course, on the type of scene described.

He occasionally mentions an extensive panorama or a storm that evokes feelings of awe. But more often the scene is an intimate one, with men embraced, as it were, by beautiful nature. Typically, in the idyll 'Mycon', a vivid evocation of noonday heat serves to introduce the delights of cool shade and water:

Mittag wars, und der Sand brannte unsre Solen, und die Sonne die Scheitel; so gerade stand sie über uns, dass die Locken an der Stirne ihre Schatten das ganze Gesicht herunter warfen. Die Eidexe schlich lächzend im Farrenkraut am Weg, und die Grille und die Heuschrecke zwitscherten unter dem Schatten der Blätter im gesengeten Grase. Von jedem Tritt flog heisser Staub auf, und brannte die Augen, und sass auf die gedörreten Lippen. So giengen wir schmachtend: Aber wir verlängerten die Schritte, denn vor uns sahn wir am Wege dicht emporstehende Bäume; schwarz war der Schatten unter ihnen wie Nacht. Mit schauderndem Entzücken traten wir da in die lieblichste Kühlung. Entzückender Ort, der so plötzlich mit jeder Erquickung uns übergoss! Die Bäume umkränzten ein grosses Beth, worein die reinste, die kühleste Quelle sich ergoss. Die Äste hiengen ringsum zu ihr herunter...(V, 104f)

His favourite plants are those that form arches and bowers or climb with a twining and embracing movement. The dream cottage of 'Der Wunsch' stands under arching trees; its garden is enclosed by hedges of hazel, with an arbour in each corner. Close by is a bower on an island in a pond (V, 66f). Seclusion and protection are basic themes. Lycas, who is supposed to create the first garden made by man, diverts a stream so that it surrounds his garden, and further encloses it with a thick prickly hedge (V, 40). Two lovers recall how as children they made a miniature house and garden and surrounded the whole with a hedge of reeds (V, 92). The love for such sheltered, enclosed spots is reflected even in the description of a boat in the novel *Daphnis* (F, 13): it is canopied by an arching mass of flowers and foliage so that it becomes an arbour. In building secluded gardens or bowers the characters are imitating their favourite places in nature. Of their own accord or by human design plants and rocks and waterfalls arch over and around the characters in a gesture of benevolent protection and love. Bower and grotto are almost deliberately confused:

ganz umschliesst uns dichtes Gesträuch; und der Apfelbaum, der vom Ufer über das Wasser hängt, deckt uns mit seinem grünen Gewölbe; in einer grünen Höle sind wir hier eingeschlossen, jedem Auge verborgen. (V, 119)

Even when humans are not directly involved, when a climbing plant embraces a tree or a rock in its folds, or grasses arch over a stream, an impression of loving embrace is given.

Bowers and grottos are the scenes of amorous meetings, but their significance is much wider. Nature itself is revealed as protective, benevolent and loving. In creating secluded nooks or in seeking them in nature the shepherds seek to express their oneness with nature. Perhaps their love of such bowers also points to the contented acceptance of natural limitation that is a dominant theme in the idylls.

Gessner's prime aim and claim to critical attention in his depiction of nature was not detailed realistic description. In this field he was excelled in accuracy and variety by Brockes and Thomson. His descriptions are invariably emotional responses; in this respect his technique is closer to that of his friend Ewald von Kleist than to that of Brockes. In his response to nature Gessner belongs to the era of sensibility and to Pre-Romanticism. Nature was to him pleasant, delightful, wonderful and beautiful; but, more than this, it was benevolent, and inspired man to happiness and virtue. His poetic landscapes, full of secluded nooks, have Rococo features. But they are also like a park that includes hills and valleys, natural streams and groups of trees, pastureland and vineyards and orchards and cornfields. The figures who lend scale, who enjoy, admire and tend this park-like landscape are occasionally amateur naturalists. But more often they are worshippers of Pan, a Pan who is not the god of lust, but of moral sensibility. They are contemporaries of Rousseau.

3 · SENTIMENT

A desire for simplicity and naturalness moved Marie Antoinette to retire to the 'hameau' at Versailles, where she could dress as a shepherdess, milk goats and escape from court convention. Her action, and the popularity of pastoral costume and 'fêtes galantes', reflected a longing to escape boredom and the stranglehold of meaningless rules of behaviour. Gessner was bored with his work in his father's business, and conscious of the restrictions imposed upon him by his position in Zurich. But the value that he, a middle-class townsman, placed upon the countryside and rural existence was not simply that of liberty to follow one's own inclinations. This was immediately recognised by his most important French admirers.

It is surely significant that whereas there is no record that the rationalist Voltaire had anything to say about Gessner's work, both Rousseau and Diderot, those connoisseurs of sentiment, were enthusiastic admirers. Gessner was greatly flattered to learn of Diderot's reaction. He agreed with alacrity when Diderot suggested that Gessner's second collection of idylls should appear, simultaneously in French and German, together with two of his own stories. Diderot was attracted by the moral and sentimental aspects of Gessner's work, in this respect somewhat akin to his own. The belief in the natural goodness of man and the stress on feelings as the source of virtue also appealed directly to Rousseau, who himself experienced, though in a more complex and melancholy way than Gessner, the natural beauties of Switzerland and the attractions of rural life.

Rousseau had received a pre-publication copy of Gessner's first collection of idylls in French translation; no doubt this was part of a promotion campaign. On the 24 December 1761 he wrote to the translator; significantly, in his enthusiasm he scarcely distinguished between Gessner's shepherds and Hirzel's real 'philosophical farmer' Kleinjogg, whose fame had reached his retreat in Monmorency. He was most impressed by the simple language of the idylls:

J'étais, Monsieur, dans un accès du plus cruel des maux du corps, quand je reçus votre lettre et vos idylles. Après avoir lu la lettre, j'ouvris machinalement le livre, comptant le refermer aussitôt; mais je ne le refermai qu'après avoir tout lu, et je le mis à côté de moi pour le relire encore. Voilà l'exacte vérité. Je sens que votre ami Gessner est un homme selon mon coeur; d'où vous pouvez juger de son traducteur et de son ami, par lequel seul il m'est connu. Je vous sais, en particulier, un gré infini d'avoir osé dépouiller notre langue de ce sot et pretentieux jargon qui ôte toute vérité aux images et toute vie aux sentiments. Ceux qui veulent embellir et parer la nature sont des gens sans âme et sans goût, qui n'ont jamais connu ses beautés. Il y a six ans que je coule dans ma retraite une vie assez semblable à celle de Ménalque et d'Amyntas, au bien près, que j'aime comme eux, mais que je ne sais pas faire; et je puis vous protester, monsieur, que j'ai plus vécu durant ces six ans que je n'avais fait dans tout le cours de ma vie. Maintenant vous me faites désirer de revoir encore un printemps, pour faire avec vos charmants pasteurs de nouvelles promenades, pour partager avec eux ma solitude, et pour revoir avec eux des asiles champêtres qui ne sont pas inférieurs à ceux que M. Gessner et vous avez si biens décrits. Saluez-le de ma part, je vous supplie, et recevez aussi mes remerciements et mes salutations. Voulez-vous bien, monsieur, quand vous écrirez à Zurich, faire dire mille choses pour moi à M. Usteri? J'ai reçu de sa part une lettre que je ne me lasse point de relire, et qui contient des relations d'un paysan plus sage, plus vertueux, plus sensé que tous les philosophes de l'univers. Je suis fâché qu'il ne marque pas le nom de cet homme respectable....[1]

The beauties of nature referred to in this letter surely include the sentiments described by Gessner. For nature was understood at the time to include humanity at its supposed best; and Rousseau himself here moves easily from comments on Gessner's nature descriptions to the wisdom and virtue of Kleinjogg. The great novelty of Gessner's idylls, it seemed to the French, was his portrayal of sentiment and virtue. In his foreword to the French translation of 1762, Turgot stressed this point:

Combien les sentiments d'honnêteté et de vertu...ne sont-ils pas préférables aux raffinements mystiques et aux delicatesses puériles que les poètes Italiens et Français ont mis dans la bouche de leurs bergers et de leurs bergères ?[2]

Even before the translation appeared, a Parisian journal, the *Journal des Sçavans*, announced:

Jusqu'ici on n'avoit point que des Bergers, ou aimables par leur simplicité, ou séduisans par leur galanterie ingénieuse. M. Gessner a imaginé de rendre les siens respectables par des vertus généreuses, qui pourtant ne sont point au-dessus de leur portée...[3]

The same journal, reviewing the idylls in 1762, made three main points, of which two concerned the character of Gessner's shepherds and the emotions he portrayed: these aspects clearly seemed more important than his descriptions of natural scenery:

Trois principaux caractères distinguent avantageusement le ton Pastoral de M. Gessner: 1º Les mœurs de ses bergers. À cet egard il est très-supérieur à tous les Auteurs d'Églogues connus...Ils sont aussi respectables qu'aimables, sans cesser d'être simples, d'être Bergers. Ils ne sont pas bornés à l'amour. Ils ont tous les sentiments d'une âme qui sort des mains de la nature. De là une variété infinie dans l'objet et dans l'expression de leur sensibilité...2º Le second caractère ...par lequel il seroit trop fort de dire qu'il surpasse les Anciens, mais par lequel la postérité jugera peut-être qu'il les égale, c'est la richesse de la Poësie et le talent de peindre...Le troisième caractère distinctif des Idylles de M. Gessner est une certaine manière fine, naive et original d'exprimer le sentiment.[4]

But Gessner's shepherds reveal their characters when they sing of the scenery.

The poet of *Die Nacht* experiences 'Entzücken' and 'sanftes Taumeln' (V, 7) as he gazes on the wonders of nature by night. In one of the 1772 idylls the old man Menalkas tells his grandson that there is no pleasure to equal that of doing a good deed; but the standard of comparison is joy in nature:

Die schön aufgehende Sonne, das Abendroth, der volle Mond in einer hellen Nacht, schwellen unsern Busen vor Vergnügen; aber süsser, mein Sohn, süsser ist jene Freude noch. (V, 123)

The first version of 'Die Gegend im Gras' ends as the poet addresses the flowers and insects he has described with such loving enthusiasm: he leaves them to join his girl:

ich eil izt an ihre Seite, ihr Blumen, und ihr, ihr kleinen Bewohner; aber noch oft sollt ihr mir das sanfte Entzücken gewähren, das Entzücken, auch in der kleinsten Verzierung der Natur die Harmonie mit der Schönheit und dem Nuzen ins Unendliche hin in unauflöslicher Umarmung zusehn. (V, 65)

The mention of 'Nuzen' here is rather misleading. Gessner does more than echo Brockes' ever repeated conclusion that nature is both beautiful and useful to man. Gessner's mood is lyrical and emotional rather than philosophical and rational. He does not think, like Brockes, of the practical use to which natural products may be put, but of natural beauty as a reminder that man was created to be happy and virtuous.

Nature teaches man gratitude towards the Creator. In 'Palemon' an old man sums up his reactions to the dawn:

O wie schön ist alles um mich her! Alles was ich höre sind Stimmen der Freude und des Danks. Die Vögel in der Luft und der Hirt auf dem Felde singen ihr Entzücken, auch die Herden brüllen ihre Freude von den grasreichen Hügeln und aus dem durchwässerten Thal...Ist das Entzücken, das meine Zunge nicht stammeln kann, sind meine Freuden-Thränen, ihr Götter! nicht ein zu schwacher Dank? (V, 41)

Although most of Gessner's scenes are peaceful, he occasionally describes nature in a melancholy mood (reflecting the temporary sadness of a character) or an awe-inspiring aspect. The narrator of 'Der feste Vorsatz', wandering in a dark forest, feels 'schauerndes Entzücken' und 'Schwermuth' (V, 58). The title figures of 'Damon. Daphne' witness a thunder storm from the shelter of a cave. They comment on the peace after the storm and the refreshing effect of the rain; they are brought to feel the power and goodness of God. Here Gessner departs from his more usual practice by mentioning one Creator rather than pluralistic gods. His lovers are moved to ecstasy, their thoughts raised far beyond the present time and present circumstances:

O was für Freude durchströmt mich! wie herrlich ist alles um uns her! Welche unerschöpfliche Quelle von Entzücken! Von der belebenden Sonne bis zur kleinsten Pflanze sind alles Wunder! O wie reisst das Entzücken mich hin! wenn ich vom hohen Hügel die weitausgebreitete Gegend übersehe, oder, wenn ich ins Gras hingestrekt, die manigfaltigen Blumen und Kräuter betrachte und ihre kleinen Bewohner; oder wenn ich in nächtlichen Stunden, bey gestirntem Himmel, den Wechsel der Jahreszeiten, oder den Wachsthum der unzählbaren Gewächse – wenn ich die Wunder betrachte, dann schwellt mir die Brust, Gedanken drengen sich dann auf; ich kan sie nicht entwikeln, dann wein' ich und sinke hin und stammle mein Erstaunen dem der die Erde schuf! (V, 32f)

In one of the later idylls, 'Der Sturm', Gessner reveals that he was susceptible to the awe-inspiring aspects of a storm, and could enjoy 'mit Angst gemischte Wollust' (V, 127) aroused by movement and immensity. Yet he seldom plays upon such feelings. The sun setting on the mountains is admired with reverence, but there is little trace of an appreciation of the sublime beauty of the mountains themselves. As distinct from Haller, who sang the grandeurs of the Alps, Gessner evokes a more homely scene. He played but a minor role in the development of the feeling for sublimity that was an important facet of eighteenth-century sensibility. It was Klopstock's 'Frühlingsfeier', not Gessner's very similar 'Damon. Daphne', that inspired Goethe's Werther in his famous reaction to a thunderstorm.

It is usually the peace of nature that inspires Gessner's characters with moral or religious emotions. Several idylls take place in the heat of day, when the swains seek shade and rest, but they sing, too, of other romantic hours, of sunrise, sunset and moonlight; Gessner thus extends the scope of the traditional idyll. More importantly, however, he links the seasons with stages in the life of man. Human existence is seen in parallel with nature, and subject to the same laws, with an unaltering, repetitive progression from day to day, year to year, generation to generation. The realisation that man is in this respect, as in others, one with nature, brings a comforting feeling of stability and continuity to Gessner's shepherds. An old man speaks of his children as trees that he has planted, that now bear fruit and provide shade and protection for his last years ('Palemon', V, 41f). In 'Tityrus. Menalkas' (V, 51) old age is compared with autumn, and death with winter. Aristus in *Daphnis*, also linking a man's life with the course of the seasons, sees death as a natural and peaceful event, like the withering of a flower:

Mein Leben soll hier verfliessen wie ein stiller Bach, sanft soll es verwelken, wie die Rose verwelkt; sie steht da, die welkende Rose, und haucht die letzten Gerüche; ein sanfter Zephyr fährt schmeichelnd über sie hin, die welken Blätter fallen, und die Rose ist nicht mehr. (F, 36f)

This consoling analogy applies if a man has produced fertile seeds or 'fruits', in the form of virtuous children or memorable deeds. Then indeed death is comparable to sleep after a day's work:

Und wie der, der nach den Arbeiten eines schönen Sommertages vergnügt an der Kühlung des Abends sitzt, den Göttern dankt und so den stillen Schlaf erwartet, so waren seine übrigen Tage den Göttern und der Ruhe heilig; denn er hatte gearbeitet und Gutes gethan, und erwartete gelassen und froh den Schlummer in dem Grabe. (V, 122)

The idyllic shepherd is scarcely conscious of historical change. The cyclical patterns of nature remind him that he is part of an eternal system. Palemon looks back over his long life, recalling unhappy interludes, but his overall impression is one of enjoyment and of stability: for him the eternal spring of the Golden Age is a subjective truth:

wenn ich zurük sehe, dann ists, als hätt' ich nur einen langen Frühling gelebt, und meine trüben Stunden waren kurze Gewitter, sie erfrischen die Felder und beleben die Pflanzen. (V, 41)

In this situation progress is meaningless. Any desire to 'improve' oneself materially is condemned as ingratitude towards the gods and a certain cause of tragedy. Two cowherds, having witnessed a shipwreck from the safety of the shore, pray that they may never be tempted by dissatisfaction, nor, like those seeking fortune at sea, desire more than the peace and sufficiency that nature gives them ('Der Sturm'). Of course Gessner's shepherds are sometimes fearful that their love is not returned, and there are occasional mishaps; but always the reader is led to feel that all is for the best. Poverty is no bar to happiness; life itself is a source of joy, and the contented mind overcomes or dismisses slight imperfections or misfortunes: in *Daphnis* the hero echoes the words of his future mother-in-law when he repeats the advice of his own father; and the same sentiments are expressed immediately by his beloved Phillis:

Werde nicht ungeduldig, wenn du unglücklich wirst; mich besuchte auch das Unglück, aber wenn es wegging, wenn das Glück mich wieder umfing, dann fühlt' ich's, dass ich glücklich war. Ja, Daphnis, sagte sie, da wir uns liebten, ohne Hoffnung uns zu finden, da waren wir unglücklich; wie fühlten wir da unser Glück, als wir uns fanden! (F, 53)

Misfortune has a function in the world, for it increases man's appreciation of common happiness; we are close to the argument of Pope's *Essay on Man*. Not only nature, but also virtue is celebrated as an eternal value. Indeed, without a consciousness of virtue, man cannot appreciate nature:

Glücklich ist der, dessen unbeflecktes Gemüth keine begangene Bosheit nagt; der seinen Segen zufrieden geniesst, und, wo er kann, Gutes thut...Jede Schönheit, jede Freude, geniesst sein frohes Gemüthe...(V, 95)

Emotional reactions to nature and to virtue are deliberately linked:

Mich entzückt der thauende Morgen, der kommende Frühling entzükt mich, noch mehr des Redlichen Thaten. (V, 23)

This confession is taken from 'Idas. Mycon', where an oak tree stands as a memorial to Palemon's virtue. Now the tree, Palemon, and virtue are revered by the next generation of shepherds. Living men, too, exercise a stabilising moral influence. An eighty-year-old is an example to his grandchildren (V, 123). A son regards his sleeping father, thinks of his impending death, of his piety and his love for his children, weeps, and resolves to perpetuate his memory by making offerings on his grave and by doing good deeds ('Menalkas und Alexis', V, 26f). 'Daphnis und Micon', in the 1772 collection, tells of a monument to a conqueror who laid waste lands, attacked innocent peoples and lived in pomp and splendour; it now lies in ruins, half submerged in a swamp, and forgotten, but is surrounded by a permanent memorial to virtue – a fertile settlement wrested from a barren stretch of land. Two herdsmen comment on the contrast: the one man, if remembered at all, is remembered with revulsion, and frogs and snails creep over his monument, reflecting, it seems, the attitude of nature herself; the goodness of the other is felt even after his death:

Herrliches Denkmal, womit man Segen und Nahrung auf würdige Nachkommen bringt, und auch nach seinem Tode Gutes thut! (V, 118)

Occasionally Gessner combines his love for the fantastic tales of Ovid's *Metamorphoses* with his desire to show the eternal value of virtue. Palemon dies after a long, virtuous life; he is turned into a cypress that shades the grave of his wife. In death he remains part of nature and transcends time, for although the tree may not stand for ever, it remains in the timeless present of the idyll as a memorial and a reminder:

wer in dem Schatten des Baumes ruht, dem bebt ein heiliges Entzüken durch die Brust, und eine fromme Thräne fällt ihm vom Aug. (V, 43)

Immortality is also vouchsafed the nymph Erythia as a reward for virtue. Pursued by Pan, she cries for help and Diana changes her into a stream ('Erythia', V, 102f).

The connection between innocence and happiness is announced in the idyll that opens the 1756 collection, where Gessner proclaims that he will tell 'von Grossmuth und von Tugend, und von der immer frohen Unschuld' (V, 20). 'Der Wunsch', indeed, ends with the thought that happiness in nature may be an idle dream for the modern townsman, who should concentrate on living virtuously and accepting the place allotted to him in life:

Unser wahres Glük ist die Tugend. Der ist ein Weiser, und glüklich, der willig die Stell' ausfüllt, die der Baumeister, der den Plan des ganzen denkt, ihm bestimmt hat.
(V, 71)

The idylls, it seems, were not intended to promote unrest. Gessner's vocabulary reveals that virtue and piety are almost indistinguishable: it is a 'Tugend', and also 'fromm', to accept life with gratitude and joy. The word 'Redlichkeit' occurs frequently in the idylls: it covers generosity, charity and good will. 'Redlichkeit' was generally thought by Gessner's contemporaries to exist among the middle classes, and was opposed to the egotism of the courts. Something of these associations is present in the idylls, more especially where Gessner expressly contrasts town and country.

'Der Herbstmorgen' (1772) brings a much clearer idealisation of homely middle-class virtues, 'wirtschaftliche Ordnung und Reinlichkeit', 'Geschäftigkeit' and 'häusliche Sicherheit' (V, 96); here we almost feel ourselves transported, with Goethe's Faust, into Gretchen's room. Both Gessner as narrator and his characters have complete faith that the gods will reward virtue:

denn die Götter lassen die Redlichen nicht ungesegnet (V, 31)

Gerne hören die Götter die Gebete der Unschuld (V, 101f)

der Segen ruhet bey der Hütte des Redlichen und bey seiner Scheune (V, 52)

The reward may take the form of justified self-satisfaction, itself construed as the blessing of the gods. Daphne resolves on the grave of her mother to resist the advances of the rich Nicias, and is filled with self-approval (V, 115). Phillis gives two goats to Alexis, who has lost two belonging to his father, and both weep with joy (V, 25). But there are also more tangible proofs of divine benevolence – not just happiness, healthy flocks and plentiful harvests, but near miracles. Palemon prays to Pan for an increase in his small flock, that he might share it with a poor neighbour. His prayer is granted (V, 23). Amyntas saves a young oak from destruction by the waters of a stream; he is offered a reward by the dryad that guards the tree. Although he is himself poor, Amyntas asks that his neighbour should recover from illness. This happens, and Amyntas's flocks and orchards prosper so well that he becomes rich (V, 31). Here pity for plants and charity towards men are linked.

Compassion towards animals is also depicted as a sign of goodness of heart. Menalkas teaches his grandchildren to feel for both men and animals (V, 123). Micon recalls how as a child Daphne, now to be his bride, accidentally tore a leg from a grasshopper, and how she wept with remorse:

Ach wie entzückend war es mir, so gütig dich zu sehn. (V, 93)

Daphne then remembers how she had shed tears of joy when he returned two fledglings to their nest. In another idyll two children are about to sacrifice birds to Pan, praying that their father recover from a serious illness, when a voice cries to them 'würget eure Freunde nicht Kindergen, euer Vater ist gesund!' (V, 102). Gessner's gods do not, however, seem to oppose sacrifices on principle, and offerings of a sheep or goat are mentioned several times.

The reader is expected to be just as moved as the characters by the examples of virtue and by the realisation that good men are happy. One idyll ends as a father embraces his wife and children:

Sie redeten nicht, sie empfanden nur ihr ganzes Glück: Und wer sie da gesehen hätte, würde, durch die ganze Seele gerührt, empfunden haben, dass Tugendhafte glücklich sind. (V, 97)

Since each individual naturally wants to do what is right and good, and there are no problems about what is right and good, no system of laws is required in Gessner's idyllic world – at least none is mentioned. The only political community mentioned is the town that is contrasted with the country. For the shepherds the important unit is the family. In common with many contemporaries Gessner sees the family as the natural basis of life in society. In treating parents' love for children, or filial affection, Gessner again reflects the sensibility of his age. The bonds of love and respect that link parent and child were the pivot of many an eighteenth-century novel or domestic drama. Yet these themes were still fresh when Gessner wrote, and were quite new to the idyll.

The oak that commemorates Palemon's virtue serves as an aid to parents bringing up their children:

es siehet ihn fernher der Hirt, und weist ihn ermahnend dem Sohn; es sieht ihn die zärtliche Mutter, und sagt Palemons Geschichte, dem horchenden Kind auf der Schooss. (V, 23)

One of the most popular of the idylls in the eighteenth century was 'Tityrus. Menalkas', in which a son speaks fondly of his father's piety and goodness. It ends as he kisses his sleeping father's brow, and wakes him gently to take him into the cottage away from the cool of the night. Gessner increases the emotional content of such scenes by stressing the contrast between youth and age: his parents are mostly on the point of death, if not already dead. In the later idylls he celebrates the joys of family life, which he tends to view from the father's point of view. The most vehement expression of the pleasure given by marriage and children is found, in 'Der Herbstmorgen', in the form of a father's lyrical monologue.

Gessner extends the scope of the idyll by writing of married life, but the feelings of lovers, the standard repertoire of the genre, are not neglected. For happy marriage is based on love. Gessner's youngsters are attracted by virtue as well as beauty. Often the lover tells, with tearful admiration, of good deeds done by his loved one. A girl proclaims that if she had not loved her Micon before, she would have fallen in love when he showed his concern for birds (V, 93). Lycas, singing of his feelings for Chloe, submits that she should be attracted to him for his virtue:

wilst du mich nicht auch lieben wie die Götter, weil ich tugendhaft bin? (V, 30)

Love, like the contemplation of virtue or nature, directs the shepherds' thoughts to higher things. They think of the divine providence that brought them together:

O Chloe, wenn du mit thränendem Auge, wenn du mit umschlingendem Arme mir sagst, Daphnis! ich liebe dich! Ach dann seh ich durch den Schatten der Baume hinauf, in den glänzenden Himmel; ihr Götter, seufz ich dann, ach wie kann ich mein Glük euch danken, dass ihr Chloen mir schenkt? (V, 38)

The lovers' emotions have moral and religious dimensions. But this does not prevent them appreciating the sensual attractions of the opposite sex. Indeed, one distinguished scholar declared that Gessner saw love in purely sensuous terms.[5] Shoulders, bosoms and pretty knees are often admired, though the erotic appeal is usually more delicate than in the following passage from *Daphnis* describing a nymph bathing:

wie rund, wie weiss ist dein Busen; wie glänzend, wie weiss deine Hüften; wie hüpfen die Wellen um die runden Kniee, als ob sie versuchten, noch höher zu hüpfen! (F, 23)

In *Die Nacht* a lover is tempted to take liberties with a girl whose charms are enhanced by a diaphanous garment (V, 8f). In the idylls sensual elements were toned down: Gessner had moved closer to Bodmer. Yet it is clear that he did not abandon the belief, formulated in 1752, that love could not be divided into sensual and platonic types, for the senses were the basis of higher feelings. With this argument he characteristically reconciled two opposing attitudes particularly evident in the poetry of his contemporaries; he wrote to a young friend:

Was sagt nun dein Weibgen vom Amor, dünkt er ihr noch ein Kind zu sein, das keine Achtung verdient? findt sie ihn nun nicht liebenswürdig? O er ist es gewiss, trotzt Wieland und der ganzen Platonischen Welt mit Eiskaltem Blut, die Freundschaft reicht ihm gar zu gern die Hand, sie spielt zwar oft ein wenig die Spröde, aber sie zittert und erröthet so oft sie ihn sieht... Das ist doch körperlich gedacht, würde ein kalter Jüngling oder ein Paulus Purganti sagen, allein es ist doch wahr, nehmen nicht fast alle unsere Tugenden meistens aus niedrigen Umstenden ihren Schwung, und sie keimen aus selbigen hervor... sie bleiben doch immer da hocken, wie die Blumen mit den Wurzeln in der Erde, das nöthiget uns Menschen zu bleiben, sonst würden wir ganz leicht zu Engel werden, und das sollen wir jetzt noch nicht seyn.[6]

Gessner's characters react to beauty, virtue and love with 'Entzücken', 'Freudenthränen', 'süsseste Freude', 'Seligkeit' and 'Ströme von Wollust'. Like many of his contemporaries, Gessner worshipped joy. It is a central, perhaps even the basic theme in his idylls. His shepherds experience that state of soul that Shaftesbury called enthusiasm – they feel the joy of living in a benevolent universe. Within Gessner's poetic world joyful man is fulfilling his duty to the Creator, for he is meant to be good and happy. The joy expressed by his shepherds is not simply lighthearted gaiety, and their utterances not the straightforward imitation of Horace that is common in the poetry of the time. Furthermore, Gessner often evokes transitions from sadness to joy, or mixed, bitter-sweet feelings. For when misfortunes occur in the idylls, they serve to heighten subsequent joy. Gessner's standard sentimental episode shows how misfortune is deeply felt or remembered, but superseded by happiness. Chloe swoons in despair, believing her Daphnis drowned, only to find him alive and enjoy raptures of bliss (V, 44f). A lover's jealousy causes him torments that are proved unfounded (V, 129f). Mixed feelings are expressed by a man thinking of his father's impending death, and 'schwermütige Entzückung' by a lover unsure of his sweetheart's attitude (V,

110). The monuments to the pious dead arouse sorrow and joy. Perhaps because of this, such monuments, often trees, were not uncommon in later sentimental literature. In Sophie La Roche's novel *Rosaliens Briefe* (1781) they are intended to recall the religious practices of early Christians. In Gessner's work they have similar associations with simple, or primitive, religious feeling.

Despite the inclusion of sadness and suffering, the world of Gessner's idylls remains harmonious. Elegiac complaint, a regular feature of the traditional idyll, is transformed by the moral that a modicum of suffering may be accepted by a contented mind. Social distinctions mean little in a land where all men are seen as human beings rather than as masters and servants, where a poor orphaned maid is the natural and right choice of wife for her master's son (V, 106f). Even death is not seen as tragic. Only once, in the idylls, does Gessner mention an afterlife ('seligere Gefilde', V, 26); rather death reminds man that he should be happy in life. Yet Gessner's Arcadia, like most, evokes a subtle melancholy, not because passion and death produce inevitable tragedy, but because of the contrast with reality.

Many of the sentimental aspects may be ascribed to the influence of Bodmer, an influence that is much stronger in *Der Tod Abels*. Gessner's foreword to this work, indeed, alludes directly to Bodmer's views on poetry and the biblical epic. Yet he also promises to provide a love interest and implies that his epic is not as unwordly as Klopstock's. In *Der Tod Abels* he tells of violent death, but endeavours to show human goodness and divine providence at work. No doubt the character of Cain gave him most difficulty, since he could not be portrayed as a good man, nor one who is easily converted to the paths of righteousness.

The other characters are cast in the familiar Gessnerian mould. They are pious, virtuous, and each is called 'zärtlich'. They express at length joyful and grateful praise of God, appreciation of nature, and concern about Cain. Gessner invents Mehala and Thirza, sisters and wives to Cain and Abel, and gives them children, in order to provide more sentimental interest. All are concerned about Cain's brooding melancholy. For Cain is unable to recognise the goodness of God or his fellow humans without profound reservations, and is resentful of his brother's contentedness and scornful of his tenderness. Like so many villains in eighteenth-century literature, he finds tears and other exhibitions of emotion distasteful. He is prone to despairing and evil thoughts because he alone is unhappy, yet these thoughts are the cause of his unhappiness. Adam states, with a conviction that echoes that of the author, that Cain is miserable because passion overrides reason within him:

der Herr ruft kein Geschöpfe aus dem Nichts zum Elend hervor. Zwar kann der Mensch elend sein, bei seinem Glücke vorübergehn und elend sein. Wenn die Vernunft unter dem Tumulte tobender Leidenschaften und unreiner, unbeschränkter Begierden erliegt, dann wird der Mensch elend...(F, 112)

Reason is here closely linked with the ability to feel 'naturally', for it is assumed that experience teaches that man is naturally good and destined to be happy on earth. The belief in the innate goodness of man is so strong that Cain himself is shown capable of conversion. Significantly he, the only one not to weep when Adam tells of the first days on earth, breaks into tears when Adam is ill, and again, unrestrainedly, after he has killed his brother. He never defies God, nor does he wish to hurt anyone. He is affectionate towards his wife and children. But he is exasperated by Abel's self-righteousness (understandably perhaps – Gessner does not develop this point since he is intent to show Abel as righteous and kind) and relapses into envy and hatred. At the end of the story he leaves for the wilderness with his family. The signs are that his own remorse and the sympathy of his family will lead him to come to terms with his guilt. Certainly the others hope and believe that he may prove worthy of God's pardon. Although Abel is said to go the Heaven, there is no mention of Hell, but only of the hell of a guilty conscience. An angel proclaims that sinners are punished in life that they may return to the paths of righteousness.

Gessner begins by telling of a temporary reconciliation of the brothers that is celebrated by the whole family. The second canto brings a flashback, Adam's tale of the expulsion from Paradise. This allows Gessner to introduce idyllic motifs, and to explain Adam's pious trust in God: for after the Fall an angel told him of God's presence on earth. Eve is worried about her guilt, but only Cain is overwhelmed by the wrath of God and does not welcome, with joy and gratitude, His mercy and goodness. Cain is tormented by the idea that God's curse is upon him and feels that his prayers are not heard. When Adam is ill, an angel brings a healing herb, not to Cain, but to Abel, and when Cain gives thanks for his father's recovery, his sacrificial altar is destroyed by a sudden storm. But even after he dreams, under the influence of the fallen angel Anamelech, that his children will become slaves to Abel's, Cain does not seek out his brother to kill him. Abel comes to him, solicitous of his state of mind. After the dreadful deed has been done, the last canto portrays horror and sorrow, but is dominated by hope. Cain is to be redeemed by a miracle that is by implication not exceptional, for it depends only on the proper functioning of the human heart as created by God.

The sentiments of *Der Tod Abels* echoed the spirit of the age, and the epic was much appreciated in wide circles. Yet some critics recognised that it was inferior to its illustrious predecessors, Milton's *Paradise Lost* and Klopstock's *Messias*. The high poetic tone, the role of the supernatural powers, and details of setting and cosmic geography bear witness to Gessner's reliance on these works for inspiration. But, like Bodmer in his biblical epics, Gessner falls short of Milton and Klopstock in dramatic interest and powerful religious conviction as well as intensity of poetic utterance. His answers to the theological problems raised by the Fall seem too facile. He did not appear to expect opposition on theological grounds – except from those who would reject any poetic treatment of the Bible.[7] Moreover the characters of *Der Tod Abels* have little individual life, a lack which, in a work of this length, seems particularly glaring to the modern reader who may be able to accept the same fault in the idylls. The simplicity of characterisation is part of the sentimentality that has become a barrier to appreciation. The character-types are established at the outset, and their situations then varied to elicit a series of rather similar tender effusions. Like the idylls, *Der Tod Abels* gives the impression of a static world, an impression that is reinforced by the 'tableaux' that occur as frequently here as in the idylls, marking the awful dramatic as well as the touching moments.

'Ein Gemälde aus der Sündflut', a short work published in 1762, also reflects Gessner's concern with the sentimental aspects of his story rather than its theological interpretation. It tells of the last victims of the Flood, two young lovers awaiting inevitable death on a mountain top. Despite the vistas of horror that surround them, the man, Semin, persuades the girl they should not question God's wisdom and justice. Conscious of their virtuous lives, they look forward to bliss after death. At least one contemporary reviewer could pardon the departure from biblical fact since Gessner portrayed the couple's moving faith in God and the afterlife:

Die Erfindung des Dichters ist kühn, zwo tugendhafte Seelen in dieses Strafgerichte mit einzuflechten, da uns doch die Offenbarung von lauter Gottlosen sagt, die dasselbe betroffen habe. Aber auf der anderen Seite vergiebt man ihm diese Freyheit, wenn man die meisterhafte Wendung siehet, die er dabey gebraucht: er lässt sie diesen gewaltsamen Tod als einen Weg zu reineren und ewigen Freuden betrachten, die sie vereinigt geniessen sollen.[8]

Sentiment again provides the main interest in 'Evander und Alcimna', a pastoral drama in three acts, like *Daphnis*, based loosely on Longus's *Daphnis and Chloe*. It contains humorous scenes with caricatured representatives of the court and artificial society. The only tension arises from the conflict between filial duty and love, the happy outcome is obvious and no suspense created. The inclusion of a love duet and above all the formal balance of many speeches bring the play close to opera. Yet Gessner's prose is here undistinguished. The play is perhaps most interesting for its social criticism, for the satire of degenerate civilisation is more prominent and more outspoken than in any other work by Gessner. The naive lovers expose foolishness and vice, the farce of ceremony and convention, the emptiness of formal learning, and the wickedness of war. Distinctions according to social class and the inheritance of rank and power are rejected, though it is suggested that illegitimate children might form a category apart:

ALCIMNA: [*zornig*] Was ist das! Edle Geburt? Ist nicht jede ehrliche Geburt edel? O! ich versteh' eure witzigen Lehren nicht, die so wenig natürlich sind; und ich will sie auch nicht verstehen.[9]

The one-act play 'Erast' also contains a diatribe against injustice. The servant Simon, insensed by the undeserved sufferings of the family, persuades himself that he is justified in stealing money for their sake:

Nein, beym Himmel! es ist unbillig, dass so viele Schurken mit allem Überfluss durch die Welt schlendern, und mein braver Herr, und Lucinde, und ihre Kinder, und ich sollen indess hülflos und hungrig in dieser Wildniss schmachten. Ha! mir siedet mein Blut, wenn ich sehe, diese Prasser, diese stolzen Ungeheuer, die den Armen und den hülflosen Elenden zum Vieh zählen, und in allen Wollüsten sich wälzen; ihr meist durch andrer Elend erworbenes Gut in Lasterthaten verprassen; indess soll der Arme verhungern, und der Elende verschmachten, und mit heissen Thränen zusehen, wie diese ungerochen in den Gütern dieser Welt schwelgen...[10]

But Simon's master, for whom the crime was committed, orders him to return the money, and the final reward of virtue, and the tearful scene of recognition and reconciliation between Erast and the father who had disinherited him, beat out the family's trust in divine providence and come as little surprise. There is no egalitarianism here. Erast's fears that his children will not, through lack of money, enjoy their proper status in life, are intended to arouse sympathy. In these plays social criticism is included for sentimental effect. Both are fairly typical, though not outstanding, examples of the sentimental comedy of the time. Published after Lessing's first 'bürgerliches Trauerspiel', *Miss Sarah Sampson*, they attracted little attention. 'Erast' was, however, read with considerable emotion by a small circle of aristocrats at Warthausen, the residence of Wieland's patron, Graf Stadion, in 1770; like Gessner's characters, these good men savoured tears shed over innocence, and they prepared to act the play for their own pleasure.[11] Requiring more enthusiasm than expertise from the actors, Gessner's little dramas were best suited for modest amateur performance, but no doubt they conquered more readers than audiences.

The chief distinction of *Der Tod Abels* is its poetic prose. Compared with the idylls, the work contains more metaphor. Its images have biblical or religious associations or recall the epic tradition. Its quite involved syntax, personifications of abstractions, its composita and particularly its use of verbs recall the poetry of Klopstock. Gessner seems to have associated solemnity with present participles used adjectivally and with adjectival constructions replacing a relative clause, for both are characteristic of the style of this epic. Here the high epic style is more appropriate than in *Daphnis*, and individual passages, particularly in the first canto, are impressive.

In one of his speeches, Cain vents his spite and disappointment when Adam gives his blessing to Abel before turning to his elder son. Adam has prayed for Cain's peace of soul. Cain then retires:

itzt ging er aus der Hütte, schlich seitwärts sich in das Dunkel eines Gebüsches, stund da melancholisch still und sprach: Ruhe, ungestörte Ruhe in der Seele – wie kann das – ich; ruhig sein? – Musst' ich nicht den Segen erbitten, der ungebeten von den Lippen floss, da er den Bruder segnete? Zwar, ich bin der Erstgeborene; schöner Vorteil! ich Elender! ich habe das erste Vorrecht auf Elend und Verachtung. Durch ihn hat der Herr geholfen, ihm soll kein Mittel entstehen, ihn vor mir stets geliebter zu machen. Sollen sie mich achten, mich, den der Herr nicht achtet, und den die Engel nicht achten? Mir erscheinen sie nicht, mit Verachtung gehen sie neben mir vorüber, wenn ich auf dem Felde meine Glieder müd' arbeite und der Schweiss von meinem braunen Angesicht fliesst, dann gehen sie mit Verachtung vorüber, ihn zu suchen, der mit zarten Händen in Blumen tändelt, oder bei den Schafen müssig steht, oder aus dem Überfluss seiner Zärtlichkeit einige Thränen weint, weil dort, wo die Sonne untergeht, die Wolken itzt rot sind, oder weil der Tau auf bunten Blumen flimmert. Weh mir, dass ich der Erstgeborne bin; denn wie es scheint, so sollte der Fluch allein, oder doch seine grösseste Last nur den treffen. Ihm lächelt die ganze Natur; ich nur esse mein Brot müd im Schweisse des Angesichts, ich nur bin elend. (F, 144f)

This passage requires to be read with expression and emphasis. The situation, sentiments and rhetoric point forward to Karl Moor's speech at the end of Act II of Schiller's *Die Räuber*. If Cain's words are less dramatic, it is not because of the style, but because his speech does not lead to a dramatic decision, and because Karl Moor is a more vigorous character. For Gessner is able to develop a train of thought so as to give the impression of passionate, disjointed utterance. Seeing Thirza weep over the dead Abel, Cain's first reaction is to flee, but something holds him back:

Ich will fliehen! fort, Verruchter, von der heiligen Scene! fort – ich Elender! warum kann ich nicht? – Drängt euch nicht um mich her, ihr – o! höllische Gestalten sperren die Flucht! Lasst mich – lasst mich fliehen – o lasst von der heiligen Scene mich fliehen, höllische Gestalten! – ich kann nicht fliehen – ich Elender! Wie sie jammert! und ich kann nicht fliehen! – Sie jammert nicht mehr – o Tugend, Tugend! Was für Hoffnungen, was für Trost! für mich, ach! für mich ewig verloren, ach! ohne Hoffnung, entfernteste Hoffnung bin ich elend! – Itzt, itzt fühl' ich's, wie ich elend bin, o was für Qualen! Neue unnennbare Qualen! du Hölle! in deinem tiefesten Abgrund hast du nicht schrecklichere Qualen! – Sie betet – o! sie betet für mich, für mich! – und du hassest mich nicht, und du fluchest mir Elenden nicht! Unaussprechliche Güte! o was empfind' ich, was empfind' ich bei diesem Glanze der Tugend! Mein Elend steht mir fürchterlicher entgegen, dunkel, schwarz, wie tiefe Klüfte am Eingang der Hölle, ich fühl' es stärker, mit höllischen Qualen fühl' ich's, das nagende Verbrechen! ... (F, 182)

In such speeches Gessner may be seen as a forerunner of the style of 'Sturm und Drang'. Indeed he scarcely loses by comparison with Schiller on the score of passion, rhetoric and rhythm. The prose of *Der Tod Abels* was an outstanding means for the expression of violent emotion.

But not all of the epic is of this kind. More predominant in the work is a more balanced rhythm, similar to that of the idylls, for most of the speeches express less frenzied feelings. In these Gessner develops the language of emotion of the earlier idylls.

Usually it is Klopstock, himself influenced by the Swiss school, by Haller, Bodmer, Pyra and Lange, who is recognised as the great innovator in the development of German as a means to express emotion, preparing the way for 'Sturm und Drang'. Gessner's emotive style is, indeed, less extreme than Klopstock's. Inspired less by grandiose beliefs in the creative mission of the poet, and more by ideals of naturalness, Gessner did not imitate many features of Klopstock's language that are foreign to the spoken language: absolute genitives, archaic vocabulary, neologisms, omission of prepositions through peculiar case usage, unusual ellipsis. But he does employ, in a solemn or sentimental context, often in descriptions of nature, compound adjectives similar to those of Klopstock and Bodmer. Adjectives formed from a noun with the suffix 'voll' or 'reich' are used in the same contexts, as are absolute or adjectival participles. Strangely enough, given the religious (Pietistic) origin of these usages, they occur less often in idylls celebrating piety than in those treating love or feeling for nature.

Yet Gessner does make use of water imagery, frequent in Pietist writings, to describe states of soul:

Freude durchströmt mich (V, 32).

Entzüken fliesst aus dir izt mir zu (V, 51)

The concept of 'Stille', the inner peace achieved by the truly pious according to Pietist thought, is also present in Gessner's works in a secularised form. In *Der Tod Abels* it is found in a religious context: 'heilige Stille' refers to the silent awe of nature before God (F, 124). The adjective 'still' is virtually interchangeable with 'sanft' in such a frequent expression as 'stilles Entzücken', where it denotes not a lack of power in the emotion, but rather a harmonious fullness. The tender feelings that hold sway in the idylls contrast with the passions that dominate in 'civilised' society or that torment Cain; the distinction is one of kind rather than of degree. Emotions that satisfy and bring inner peace differ from those that cause unrest and disruption. They are felt equally deeply; nevertheless they are associated with moderation. The very phrase 'stilles Entzücken' expresses, if its verbal noun is understood in its literal sense, a fusion of contrasting feelings typical of 'Empfindsamkeit'. At the same time it suggests that in spiritual, as in material matters, true happiness is to be found in composure. Gessner's vision of idyllic perfection in Greek costume may thus be linked with the idea of 'Mass' in German Classicism.

In the first version of *Die Nacht* Gessner used the word 'heilig' as an emotional intensifier without Christian associations. Later the 'heilige Laube' or 'Heiligthum', dedicated to Bacchus the god of wine, became 'hochgewölbte Laube' or 'Gewölbe'. (Perhaps the arch motifs in the idylls are sometimes intended to suggest ecclesiastical architecture.) After 1753, Gessner used 'heilig' in association with religious feeling only; though since this feeling is often directed towards nature, and classical gods are the most obvious points of reference, some degree of secularisation is involved.

Verbs of motion were already quite firmly established as means to depict love and friendship, and Gessner was not original or daring in applying them to states of soul. Such expressions are, however, characteristic of his style:

reisst das Entzüken mich hin (V, 33)

schwellt mir die Brust (V, 33)

mich durchzittert dann etwas (V, 35)

bebt ein heiliges Entzüken durch die Brust (V, 43)

Whereas Brockes and Haller had described nature as essentially static, Klopstock, and particularly Ewald von Kleist, had begun to use verbs of motion, intensified by a prefix, in descriptions of nature when they did not necessarily correspond to observed movements. Gessner surpasses his contemporaries in registering movements in nature, many of which reflect the emotions of the observer. As opposed to the later poets of 'Sturm und Drang' and Romanticism, Gessner sees movement in small things rather than large masses, and it is more often gentle than violent. It is also often realistic (objectively observable) rather than imaginary. But in a context in which the whole of nature is imbued with feeling, and man and nature are deliberately linked, any verb that could be applied to humans takes on an emotive function, especially when it exaggerates the movement it describes. The emotions ascribed to nature are the same as those depicted in man: joy, love, tenderness and gratitude towards the Creator. Nature itself not only inspires, but also celebrates natural piety and virtue. Nature, natural goodness, tender emotions, an optimistic message that virtue and happiness are interdependent and within the reach of the simplest man: with these contents, presented in a simple, easily readable guise, the idylls could hardly fail to appeal to Gessner's contemporaries. The promotion campaign organised in Paris ensured that they enjoyed success. Their novelty was proclaimed in

France. But their moral was conventional enough, and their criticism of society sufficiently vague and indirect for them to be accepted by the Establishment. Melchior Grimm, a leading man of letters in Paris, expressed a generally held view when he wrote that Gessner's idylls were morally improving.[12]

The sentimentalism of Gessner's work, his restricted repertoire of emotions, gestures and expressions, render it stylised and unreal, and his Arcadia seems to have little connection with practical everyday life. Yet, at a time when only the heartless were expected to refrain from tears of sorrow or joy, his lachrymose characters reflected the conviction that society would be better if men did not fight against tender feeling. When he wrote, political thinkers seriously considered that man would benefit from a return to the countryside and a farming life, or were busy establishing utopian standards against which actual practice might be judged. It was a time of great hope in human nature, when sentiments were confused with the voice of conscience, and when ideal moral behaviour seemed often to have less to do with strength of will than with freedom from exposure to corruption. With due allowance made for the pastoral setting, his idylls could therefore be seen as an expression of a desirable ideal that was not completely beyond the realm of possibility. The difference between his shepherds and the 'philosophical farmer' Kleinjogg was not always apparent. He put forward a belief in common humanity that was uncontroversial and required no commitment to a particular political creed: the revolutionary Robespierre appreciated his work, and so did French aristocrats. The stylisation of the idylls contributed to their success. And sentimentality was not its only aspect. For Gessner did not appeal solely to the hearts of his readers, but also to their fantasy and sense of fun.

4 · CHARM AND INVENTION

With his forehead encircled by roses, the angel who appears to the murderer in Gessner's *Der Tod Abels* (F, 142f) looks suspiciously like the Amor of his *Daphnis*; and when Adam and Eve are allowed a glimpse of the guardian spirits of nature, servants of God, these 'himmlische Jünglinge' (F, 127) have the same graceful appearance as the nymphs and zephyrs of the idylls. They remind us that Gessner's idea of beauty was formed by his exposure to Rococo art and poetry. The classical and sentimental elements in his work are tinged with Rococo grace. His proximity to Bodmer did not cause him to reject altogether the taste of his youth; he never faltered in his admiration for the poetry of Hagedorn and

Gleim, and even after Wieland had broken with Bodmer to become the great poet of German Rococo, Gessner remained his friend. Gessner's lightness of touch recommended him to readers, particularly aristocrats, who would not have accepted so readily moral didacticism and moral sentiment devoid of art and grace.

Two idylls that Gessner first published in his *Schriften* and *Gedichte* of 1762, after *Der Tod Abels*, show no sign of sentimentalism. One, 'Die ybel belohnte Liebe', is an isolated example in his work of imitation of Theocritus's burlesque comedy. It features an ugly satyr in love with a nymph who has countered his unsolicited attentions by trapping him in a net. A faun laughs at the satyr's ungainly discomforture, and is amused even more when he repeats his burlesque love song. With its caricature of immoderate emotion and its lack of elegance the song contrasts with the tone of the other idylls. The satyr sings proudly of an image of Pan he has carved from wood; its Gothic or Baroque expressionism represents all that is tasteless and grotesque in the eyes of a friend of Winckelmann: the satyr and his art lack grace:

Vor meiner Höle steht eine hohe Eiche, und in ihrem Schatten das Bildniss des Pan; ich hab ihn selbst kynstlich aus Eichen-Holz geschnitten; er wcint yber die Nymphe, die ihm in Schilf verwandelt ward. Sein Mund ist weit offen: du könntest einen ganzen Apfel drein legen; so stark hab ich seinen Schmerz ausgedrykt; ja selbst die Thränen, die Thränen selbst hab ich ins Holz geschnitten. (V, 79f)

The wide-open mouth, indeed, seems to be an allusion to Winckelmann's description of the Laocoon group in his *Gedanken über die Nachahmung*, where it is (mistakenly) argued that the half-open mouth shows that Laocoon is sighing, not screaming with pain; a lesser artist would have depicted pain alone, and not endurance and grandeur of soul – and such an artist was Virgil who has his Laocoon scream. The derogatory reference to Virgil, whom he himself had placed behind Theocritus in merit, probably stimulated Gessner to write this parody of ignoble art.

The second idyll, 'Mylon', is a rather silly story. Mylon intends to give a bird to Chloe in exchange for a kiss. He looks forward, in the spirit of Rococo 'Tändelei', to a sweet but superficial pleasure, knowing that his girl is no foolish prude, a type constantly decried in Rococo lyrics. But he allows the bird to escape. Foolish rather than touching in his naiveté, he is an exception among Gessner's shepherds. For much of the charm of the idylls arises from the ambiguity latent in naiveté that may evoke a smile, but may also arouse a nostalgic love of childlike purity. The poet wavers between a playful and a sentimental attitude, adopting now one, now the other, and allowing them to overlap. This ambiguity is never destructive: Gessner is aware of the fragility of his vision of harmony, but its fragility only underlines its value. In 'Die ybel belohnte Liebe' the sentimental interest is lacking; perhaps because of this, as well as because its comedy was rather unrefined, Turgot thought it least likely to appeal to his compatriots.[1] He and Diderot also disapproved of the metamorphosis of Palemon, where Gessner indulged his love for poetic marvels at the expense of direct moral appeal; and Gessner, as always open to advice, deleted the offending last paragraph from his idyll.[2] But Gessner's imagination had not led him astray; his delight in marvels is seen in the most successful and, in his time, most effective of his writings. It is expressed in the childlike wonder of his characters.

Many of them are addressed, almost regardless of their age, as 'Kind'. Even the aged shepherds are not so dulled by experience that they do not savour the variety of life. Their ability to enjoy, their spontaneity makes them all young at heart. His treatment of children constituted an important part of the novelty and the appeal of his idylls. He plays on the overlap of childish naiveté and childlike innocence, and moves easily from a smile to a sigh.

The innocence of Gessner's children may be moving even when they indulge in childish play and make-believe. Micon and Daphne, the couple who recall in sentimental vein their childhood virtues, also recount how they delighted in fashioning and using tiny objects and in imitating in miniature the occupations of their elders. Their games are retold with a delicacy and a stress on diminutives typical of a Rococo mood:

MICON: Weissest du noch? Wir machten Schalen von Kürbis, legten Kirschen und Brombeeren drein, und liessen im Bach wie Schiffe sie schwimmen.
DAPHNE: Weissest du noch? Kleine Schälgen von Haselnüssen, und Schälgen

von Eicheln und der gehölte Kopf der Feuerblume waren unser Hausgerät: Wir
tranken Tröpfgen Milch daraus...
MICON: So ist es...Ach wie süss, wie süss war jede Stunde...(V, 92)

Mylon, in the idyll mentioned above, regards love as a game.
The other lovers of the idylls often revert to childish pranks, not
because they are playing with love, but because they cast inhibi-
tions aside. In *Daphnis* the hero woke as Phillis threw flowers on
to his face and discovered that he was tied and unable to move. He
was released after promising not to kiss her for an hour, though
both soon regretted the promise (F, 14). In the idylls, one Milon
sings of his love for Chloe while, unknown to him, she listens
(V, 21f). Another Milon is cutting the name of Daphne into the
bark of a tree when she slips a garland over his head from behind
(V, 29). Chloe is admiring her reflection in the water when Daphnis
creeps up and tosses flowers over her head (V, 38). Such behaviour
contrasts with that acceptable in a more 'advanced' society.

The young lovers are sometimes portrayed in a teasing light. A
girl teases another for her attachment to a basket woven by a
certain shepherd, or for her enthusiastic praise of the garden
tended by a particular young man (V, 49, 87). Yet these gently
mocking companions are soon moved by the tenderness and artlessness of the lovers' sentiments. The reader is called upon to
sympathise with ingenuousness, with the characters who savour
each moment, however commonplace or trivial it might seem,
with equal freshness and intensity.

Nature, too, seems to share in the sense of fresh joy, a joy which
may be a virtue in itself but is not always directly associated with
moral values. As in the sentimental mood, so in the lighthearted
moments the movements in nature are all important. The light,
effortless movement that characterises Gessner's poetic landscape
is either delightful in itself or an expression of delight. The impression of happy self-sufficiency is strengthened by the use of in-
transitive or imperfective verbs. Fauns, satyrs, tritons and Loves,
zephyrs and breezes, wavelets, spots of light and shade, leaves and
flowers, insects, birds and animals, all 'hüpfen', 'spielen', 'tanzen',
'flattern', 'schwärmen', 'gaukeln', 'zittern', 'wiegen', 'schweben',

'wanken', 'winken'; these verbs indicating pleasant movement, and others describing playful games, occur with amazing frequency in Gessner's work. They, even more than the mythical beings and natural objects that engage in such play, underline the mood of carefree gaiety characteristic of Rococo poetry. Gessner's variations on the classical 'locus amoenus', with their emphasis on light movement, irregular curves and intimacy, become the 'Lieblingsplätzchen' typical of the Rococo landscape in German literature.[3] Indeed Gessner was the leading exponent of this landscape, just as he was superior to all others in exploiting natural scenery to produce sentimental effects that stopped short of drama and pathos.

In 'Die Zephyre' in the 1772 collection of idylls, Gessner recounts how one zephyr persuades another to abandon bathing nymphs in order to carry sweet scents to a virtuous girl who gives charitable help to a poor but pious old woman and her two children. This is a symptomatic, if unimpressive piece: the spirit of Rococo poetry is persuaded to pay tribute to moral sentiment. But Gessner's fictitious creatures are not all converted to the tender love of goodness. A faun, miserable at the loss of his nymph, accepts that flirtation with many nymphs is preferable to the anguish of love and joins in a Bacchic celebration (V, 57). The pursuit of frivolous pleasure is also advocated in 'Der feste Vorsatz': a young man resolves to stop moping about one girl when there are so many pretty lasses in the world.

Rococo prettiness is appreciated by Gessner's shepherds in the decorations of the gourds and cups they possess or make. The descriptions of such artefacts are modelled on the famous depiction of a cup in Theocritus's first idyll. Theocritus describes a cup edged with ivy leaves: a cup in Gessner's *Daphnis* is also bordered with leaves (F, 29). Theocritus's cup is carved with three scenes; so too is the jug or amphora described in Gessner's 'Der zerbrochene Krug'. But whereas the Greek poet's scenes are realistic, Gessner's illustrate Greek myths and are embellished with zephyrs and Loves. Another of his idylls mentions a gourd bottle decorated with figures of Bacchus and Loves (V, 49). Each of the objects described is utilitarian, even if it serves simply as a love token or a toy. This may reflect Gessner's concept of the role of art in natural society, perhaps, too, the interdependence of usefulness and beauty in Enlightenment aesthetics. But the prime significance of the decorations is not so much this, nor the shepherds' belief in classical myth, but their delight in making and cherishing beautiful objects.

The longest of Gessner's descriptions of an artefact, that of the jug in 'Der zerbrochene Krug', is derived from Theocritus, but the framework of the idyll owes something to Virgil. Virgil's sixth eclogue tells how Silenus is released from bonds after singing about the creation of the world. Gessner's faun also sings in order to be set free, but his song has none of the philosophical, religious or mythical pretensions of Virgil's. In adapting a classical pattern, Gessner concentrates on Rococo charm. His faun's song is an elegy to a jug that is broken beyond repair. Yet it was broken in farcical circumstances when the faun collapsed in a drunken stupour. But neither sadness nor comedy prevail. At the end of the idyll the shepherds gaze at the broken pieces in amazement; celebrating the beauty that has been destroyed, the faun recreates this beauty in his song. It seems that the scenes that decorated the jug are indestructible, and that beauty, like virtue, is timeless. It is also appreciated by even the most foolish and grotesque of creatures. Perhaps Gessner had in mind an analogy between himself and the faun as lovers of a lost beauty. The implication that beauty is imperishable becomes clearer if this idyll is compared with the description of the jug in Heinrich von Kleist's comedy *Der zerbrochene Krug*.

The link between Kleist's famous play and Gessner's idyll of the same title is well established. The idea for his comedy occurred to Kleist when he was in Switzerland, dreaming of bucolic bliss, in the company of Gessner's son Heinrich. Rather as Gessner's shepherds engage in singing contests, Kleist agreed to compete with two others writing on the same theme. His description of the broken jug was almost certainly written with Gessner's idyll in mind, although he gives it a dramatic function that has nothing to do with Gessner. The words used by Kleist's character Martha in describing the jug occasionally recall Gessner's. She talks of the historical scenes that adorned the jug. For her these scenes have no reality of their own, they are lost beyond recall and she has no power to recreate them. Her jug, like her daughter's reputation, cannot be made whole again.

Gessner writes of creation rather than destruction. His thunderstorms bring new life to nature; in *Der Tod Abels* he dwells on the wonders of the Creation; and his shepherds create and invent. Some of them, who are said to live in the earliest days of mankind, invent music, a garden, a boat. The shepherd Lycas commemorates his first embrace with Chloe by gathering together plants and flowers in one place, arranging them on the model of his favourite spots in nature, tending them and thus making the first garden (V, 39). A girl, imitating bird song, sings the first songs performed by man (V, 53). The mothers of invention are love, joy in nature, and gratitude towards the gods. These emotions are felt just as intensely by other shepherds, and they too share in the process of creation. The songs handed down from generation to generation point to man's urge and ability to preserve and to re-create what is beautiful and good. Other songs are spontaneous creations, giving to their makers that same joy as is felt by those who fashion beautiful objects.

Gessner was not alone in adapting classical descriptions of artefacts, stories of metamorphoses and inventions to suit eighteenth-century taste. Hagedorn, in his 'Philomen and Baucis', mentions a cup with mythological designs, and another of his poems tells of the supposed origin of dimples.[4] Both Hagedorn and Gessner recount how young lovers learn to kiss from watching birds.[5] Metamorphoses and inventions, and stories of the origins of things (aetiologies) occur throughout Gessner's writings. The earliest examples tend, like Hagedorn's, to involve a condemnation of prudery, whereas the later stories are less frivolous; they are given moral meaning or simply express the shepherds' delight in creation. But all these episodes lack the tragic or heroic aspects present in such stories in Ovid.

Gessner himself was particularly fond of his *Der erste Schiffer*, a longer idyllic narrative first published in 1762. It tells, with some sentiment, but little pathos, and with charm, but little frivolity, of invention and discovery. A young man, longing to meet a girl he has not seen, except in a dream, watches floating logs and water fowl and hits on the idea of making a rudimentary boat from a log and propelling it with 'wooden feet' towards the island where the girl lives. She too embarks into the unknown – the uncharted waters of love. The island is an idyllic retreat, but as she grows up with her widowed mother, Melida begins to feel the lack of something, and wonders why they remain alone while the birds multiply. When the man arrives on the island, she at first thinks him a god. The story is better integrated than *Daphnis*, and less strained and repetitious than *Der Tod Abels*, though its two prose cantos have some epic pretensions. Its style is quite elevated, and the plot involves gods, Amor and Aeolus. They are emasculated by the Rococo approach, though they point to the magic of young love. The characters, models of sensibility, have disturbing thoughts that make them rather more interesting psychologically than the shepherds of the idylls. Melida knows that her longing may be fretfulness and impious discontent, her mother understands her feelings but must pretend not to, and the young man is conscious that his dreams may be foolish. Gessner traces a certain development in their emotions. They do not live in a timeless world: the end points forward to the development of navigation. Yet he leaves on one side anything that would destroy the idyllic mood. He never considers the feelings of the father whose son disappears, apparently never to return.

In *Der erste Fischer* Gessner reveals considerable self-confidence. He makes authorial comments that lay claim to a knowledge of human nature:

denn die Einsamkeit ist phantasiereich (F, 212)

denn wie oft trügt die erhitzte Einbildungskraft die Wünsche derer, welche lieben
(F, 218)

His language is impressive but not solemn. He addresses the reader as the witty poet:

Im Rat der Götter nahm's Amor auf sich. Wer unter den Göttern kann besser ein junges Mädchen beglücken? (F, 216)

There is no moralising element in the sentiment that underlies the whole work and mingles with its charm. As Melida watches the birds and their young her speech stresses diminutiveness; the adjectives 'reinlich', 'süss', 'lieblich', the verbs 'spielen' and 'flattern' help establish a pleasant, joyful mood. But she weeps in sentimental vein, for she yearns for the joys of nature:

...die mannigfaltigen Vögel: Ich sah es und weinte! Dort in der dunkelsten Laube sass ich und bemerkte viele Tage alles. Zween Vögel hatten ein reinliches Nest sich gebaut, dann spielten sie mit süsser Freundlichkeit auf nahen Ästen. O wie sie sich liebten! Bald darauf sah ich Eierchen in dem Neste, die der eine mit sorgfältiger Wache mit seinen Flügeln deckte, indes der andre auf nahen Ästen ihm zur Kurzweile sang. Alle Tage bemerkt' ich's von der Laube. Bald sah ich unbefiederte kleine Vögel, wo die Eier sonst waren, indes dass die grössern mit neuer Freude sie umflatterten und Speise in ihren Schnäbeln den noch unbehilflichen brachten, die mit zwitschernder Freude sie empfingen; nach und nach befiederten sie sich und schwangen die noch schwachen Flügel; aber itzt hoben sie sich aus ihrem kleinen Nest..., die grössern flogen ihnen vor, als wollten sie ihnen Mut geben, ebendasselbe zu wagen. O meine Mutter, wie lieblich war das zu sehen! Sie schwangen oft die Flügel, als wollten sie es wagen; und furchtsam wagten sie es nicht. Da wagt' es der Kühnste und sang vor Freude über die gelungene Sache und schien seinen furchtsamen Gespielen zu rufen; sie wagten es auch, und itzt flatterten sie umher und sangen mit allgemeiner Freude. Ach was wunderliche Gedanken da bei mir entstunden! (F, 214)

In ancient myth the Argo was the first ship. Gessner's first voyage is undertaken for love; it is rather a trivial affair in comparison. His characters are unheroic, they seek quiet contentment. Yet his story has a charm that derives from the harmonious fusion of playfulness and sentiment. He avoids the extremes of both Rococo and 'Empfindsamkeit'; perhaps for this reason he was particularly fond of this work.

A similar charm pervades many of his idylls, where the only hint of real sadness is provided by the reader moved by the fiction of idyllic bliss. Milon, thinking of his girl, sings of the advantages of his person and position in life. He is overheard, and Chloe emerges from the bushes to embrace him. The scene could easily be silly, yet Milon's expressions of contentedness can be moving. His song contains, too, an evocation of a typical idyllic landscape.

Nature is pleasant, fertile and benevolent; the shepherd voices his feelings, but with a light touch, and hints of detailed realism are combined with mention of mythical figures:

Siehe, wie lieblich es ist, auf diesem Hügel in meinem Felsen zu wohnen! sieh wie das kriechende Epheu ein grünes Netz anmuthig um den Felsen herwebt, und wie sein Haupt der Dornstrauch beschattet. Meine Höle ist bequem, und ihre Wände sind mit weichen Fellen behangen, und vor dem Eingang hab' ich Kürbisse gepflanzet, sie kriechen hoch empor und werden zum dämmernden Dach; Sieh wie lieblich die Quell' aus meinem Felsen schäumt, und hell über die Wasserkresse hin durch hohes Gras und Blumen quillt! unten am Hügel sammelt er sich zur kleinen See, mit Schilf-Rohr und Weiden umkränzt, wo die Nymphen bey stillem Mondschein oft nach meiner Flöte tanzen; wenn die hüpfenden Faunen mit ihren Crotalen mir nachklappern. Sieh wie auf dem Hügel die Haselstaude zu grünen Grotten sich wölbt, und wie die Brombeer-Staude mit schwarzer Frucht um mich her kriecht, und wie der Hambutten-Strauch die rothen Beeren empor trägt, und wie die Apfelbäume voll Früchte stehn, vor der kriechenden Reb' umschlungen.

(V, 21)

Make-believe, tender humour, and play on sentiment are merged in this idyll into a picture of harmony, underlined by the balanced rhythm of the phrases. When Chloe responds in tune with Milon's hopes, her words echo the language of Theocritus and round off the idyll with balance and a deliberate poetic flourish:

Milon, du Hirt auf dem Felsen, so sprach sie, ich liebe dich mehr als die Schafe den Klee, mehr als die Vögel den Gesang; führe mich in deine Höle; süsser ist mir dein Kuss als Honig, so lieblich rauscht mir nicht der Bach. (V, 22)

The overlap of moods in Gessner's idylls means that he cannot be ascribed simply to the Rococo or the 'Empfindsamkeit' movement. His work indicates most clearly that they were not mutually exclusive, and is best covered by the term 'empfindsames Rokoko' or perhaps 'rokokohafte Empfindsamkeit'.[6] One sign of this convergence can be found in his vocabulary. He uses words that are usually associated with the Rococo poetry in sentimental contexts and vice versa. The phrase 'angenehme Kühlung' by itself suggests the pleasant 'Lieblingsplätzchen' of the Rococo landscape, but Gessner uses it when evoking religious awe for nature: 'mir schauerts von angenehmer Kühlung' (V, 103). 'Zärtlich' is an adjective common in sentimental passages, it refers, for instance, to the embrace of lovers who have been saved from drowning (V, 45), yet it is also used of the kiss given by a girl who has crept up on her lover and laughs at his surprise (V, 29).

The mixture of two contrasting emotions is typical of the literature of 'Empfindsamkeit'. Yet one mood aroused by Gessner's idylls is a half-smile of indulgence, a feeling of intellectual and emotional superiority that is not a feature of straightforward sentimental literature. And the principle that unites the different moods in the idylls is one that is usually associated with the Rococo movement: it is grace, an important, but very elastic and elusive concept within eighteenth-century aesthetics.[7] Bodmer and Breitinger wrote of grace in poetry and art under the heading of 'Artigkeit', an agreeable prettiness. For the German Anacreontics the central terms were 'Reiz' and 'Zier', the attractions of sensuously pleasing objects. Most writers thought that grace depended on movement, and some considered that it could include teasing and irony, 'Schalkhaftigkeit'. But, following Shaftesbury, grace was also associated with moral goodness, and the term 'Anmut' gradually took on the meaning of moral grace. Winckelmann, writing in 1759, applied the concept of grace or charm to a broad range of attractiveness; he thought it could be most readily found in Greek art and linked it with serious, even sublime subjects and with simplicity and harmony. Moral goodness, serenity, gentleness of spirit: with these associations charm could also be linked with sentimentality. Indeed the French painter Watelet, an admirer of Gessner, associated grace with signs of compassion and sensibility. Grace, in fact, was seen as an aspect of naturalness or naiveté, and was capable of almost as many interpretations as those ideas themselves. Gessner, not given to theoretical distinctions, was inclined, more than most, to exploit the divergent possibilities of a poetic quality that was recognised by all.

The most common figures of speech in Gessner's idylls are also frequent in Anacreontic poetry: they are those based on repetition – anaphora, epiphora, and various kinds of parallel. The German Anacreontics used them mainly for decorative effect, to contribute to the formal gracefulness in which Rococo poets excelled. But the great poet of German 'Empfindsamkeit', Klopstock, also used repetition, reserving it for the expression of intense emotion. Repetition undoubtedly appealed to Gessner because of its simplicity. Herder was later to state that parallelism was natural in emotional speech,[8] and both Klopstock and Gessner modelled their language to some extent on the Psalms, believing them to represent early, and therefore natural poetry. Many of the verbal parallels within Gessner's works recall Gleim rather than Klopstock, their effect is primarily one of charm. But when Milon, describing the natural scene in the passage quoted above, repeats his exhortation, 'Sieh, wie...', the repetition marks the intensity of his feeling. Similarly he expands a sentence, citing various kinds of fruit, to express the rich benevolence of nature. Emotional climax is involved in many such figures of speech in the idylls. Of the following examples, the second occurs in a clearly sentimental situation:

Ich habe dich behorcht, Chloe! dich hab ich behorcht (V, 246)

wann du dann gen Himmel blikest und freudig mich segnest, ach was empfind ich dann, Vater! Ach dann schwellt mir die Brust, und häufige Thränen quillen vom Auge! (V, 26)

In *Der Tod Abels*, too, repetition occurs at moments of emotional and lyrical climax:

Herrlich, herrlich die Schöpfung (F, 106)

itzt – itzt wein' ich vor dir (F, 114)

ich will ihn umarmen...ich will ihn umarmen (F, 109)

ich habe meine ganze Seele, mein ganzes Herz hab ich ausgespäet (F, 109)

The combination of charm and sentiment is one of the distinctions of Gessner's work. Yet the emotional impact of a phrase may be diminished if it is suspected of being mainly decorative in function. Gessner's 'ich liebe dich mehr als die Schafe den Klee, mehr als die Vögel den Gesang' (V, 22) may be compared with a section of Goethe's 'Mailied':

> So liebt die Lerche
> Gesang und Luft,
> Und Morgenblumen
> Den Himmelsduft,

Wie ich dich liebe
Mit warmem Blut...

Goethe has dispensed with the traditional hyperbole, but otherwise the manner of expression is similar. The rhythmical units are
of similar length. The difference in tone, and in effect, is determined by the order of ideas. In Goethe's poem the comparisons
lead to a climax, in Gessner's idyll they conclude a sentence and
seem little more than a pretty poetic flourish. Formal charm is
achieved at the expense of emotional intensity; but Gessner aimed
to touch the heart, rather than to agitate it.

Some idylls end with a different flourish, akin to the 'pointe' of
much Rococo verse, where the poem finishes with a slight surprise
that is never a shock. Gessner often ends his scene with a twist
unforeseen by the main character, or with an appropriately
moving statement or 'tableau'. In each case he shows his skill in
invention or organisation. The stories and songs at the hero's
wedding in *Daphnis* are simply waggish, but have a similar construction. In one of these a girl, arriving late at a rendezvous, her
hair and dress in disarray, tells her alarmed lover that 'der liebe
Damöt' has delayed her. Only when he has vented his anger and
disappointment, believing her unfaithful, does she reveal that
Damöt is a child (F, 55f).

In the foreword to his idylls of 1756 Gessner contrasted his
work with the poetry of wit. Yet wit does clearly play a part in his
writings. It is not the ironic or satirical reflection that is found in
Hagedorn or Wieland, and the shepherds themselves do not score
off one another in verbal interplay; theirs is not the witty dialogue
of comedy. But that wit whose cultivation was central to Rococo
literature was not necessarily comic or even humorous. Rather it
was understood as an attitude of mind, reflecting the superiority of
human intellect. The poet could be 'witty' by revealing his power
of invention and skill in arrangement, by remaining superior to his
creation. Gessner's shepherds entertain by invention: they show
their native wit when singing or creating something previously
unknown. Gessner as poet invents stories and situations, or at
least produces variations on stock situations, which, in so far as

they seemed novel, were taken as products of his wit. In retrospect it appears that his greatest 'invention', and a prime example of his 'wit' as a poet, was his exploitation of the ambiguity latent in his wavering between playful and nostalgic attitudes towards his fiction. Smile at the children of my fancy, he seems to say, for they are unreal; but do not scoff, for this fanciful dream is worthy of respect, not because it is mine, but because it is better than reality.

The 'wit' and grace of Gessner's idylls were noted with approval not only by Gleim and Wieland, but also by Haller. In France, Melchior Grimm commented that Gessner had 'une touche spirituelle et délicate', and had united 'la grâce et le charme avec l'honnêteté.'[9] Formal elegance, indeed, was a prerequisite of recognition in Paris, where a poet thought to be clumsy or pedestrian would have been immediately rejected. But, surely because wit was commonly contrasted with naturalness, French commentators concentrated on the moral and sentimental aspects of Gessner's work, and many reviewers gave the impression that he wrote exclusively about virtue and sensibility. Turgot, however, was interested in the possibilities of prose poetry, and attached great significance to the poetic qualities of Gessner's work. He and others probably believed that the echoes of verse metres and the euphony of Gessner's prose flowed spontaneously from the pen of a natural poet. But it is evident that Gessner to some extent consciously modelled his prose on the language of verse poetry. He aimed at the qualities of elegance and charm cherished by Ramler, Hagedorn, and the majority of poets and readers in the Rococo age. In comparison with Klopstock, or with the French poets of his time, Gessner writes a more natural style; but compared with the poems of Brockes or Haller's *Die Alpen* his idylls are more lyrical.

In their general form, in their limited length, and in crossing barriers between lyric, epic and drama, Gessner's idylls correspond to the overall trends of Rococo literature. The preponderance of direct speech might be compared with the use of letters in eighteenth-century sentimental novels: in each case the author lets his characters speak directly to the reader, creating an impression of spontaneity and intimacy. But extensive use of dialogue is also characteristic of Rococo poetry, with its emphasis on sociability; Gessner's shepherds are sociable beings, eager to communicate: even in their monologues they do not examine themselves with a critical eye, but give way to an uncomplicated desire for self-expression.

In his search for a language at once simple and poetic, Gessner found inspiration in Hagedorn and Gleim as well as Theocritus. In the speeches and songs of his characters, in descriptive and narrative passages alike we find a similar lyrical tone: he subjects his prose to demands usually made of verse at the time, yet, because it was prose, it seemed freer and more natural, and its music was different.

One obvious and fairly consistent means to musicality in Gessner's prose is his avoidance, considered essential to poetic diction at the time, of hiatus and consonantal clash. Final unstressed 'e's are elided, unstressed 'e's inserted between consonants. Yet hiatus does occur in his more realistic nature descriptions where the emphasis is on evocative detail and mood rather than musical sound. He was more concerned with the rhythm of a phrase than with the melodious sound of individual words. For the sake of rhythm he created consonantal clash by shortening adjectives, used either 'gegen' or its poetic replacement 'gen' according to context, and employed the two forms 'sieht' and 'siehet' in the same paragraph of one idyll (V, 23). He seldom imitated Brockes's technique of sound painting, but created sound patterns that are musical but not necessary expressive. Alliteration or assonance in a group of two or three consecutive words is frequent. More subtly, two phrases may be linked by the repetition of the same sound:

sie besch*att*et weit umher, und die kühlen Winde fla*tt*ern da immer (V, 22)

Such repetition is most apparent when the same word – often 'itzt', 'wenn', 'da', or 'dann' – is repeated in a series of clauses or sentences in the manner of anaphora. Gessner thus produces echoes that can bind together a passage of even a whole idyll.

Similar echoes and repetitions are characteristic of Rococo verse. A paragraph from 'Idas. Mycon' (from which the last two examples were drawn) may be cited in this context: the assonance of 'heilig', 'reisst', 'weiss' etc. forms the most obvious pattern:

Die ihr euch über mir wölbt, schlanke Äste, ihr streut mit euerm Schatten, ein heiliges Entzücken auf mich; Ihr Winde, wenn ihr mich kühlt, dann ist's als rauscht' eine Gottheit unsichtbar neben mir hin! Ihr Ziegen und ihr Schafe schonet, o schonet! und reisst das junge Epheu nicht vom weissen Stamm, dass es empor schleiche und grüne Kränze flechte, rings um den weissen Stamm. Kein Donnerkeil, kein reissender Wind soll dir schaden, hoher Baum! Die Götter wollens, du solt der Redlichkeit Denkmal seyn! Hoch steht sein Wipfel empor, es siehet ihn fernher der Hirt, und weist ihn ermahnend dem Sohn; es sieht ihn die zärtliche Mutter, und sagt Palemons Geschichte, dem horchenden Kind auf der Schooss. O pflanzt solche Denkmal' ihr Hirten! dass wir einst voll heilgen Entzükens, in dunkeln Hainen einhergehn. (V, 23)

Like the sound patterns, Gessner's unusual word order recalls the language of verse poetry. Sometimes he displaces a word or phrase for the sake of emphasis:

sah durch die herbstliche Gegend hin, sanft staunend (V, 51)

sometimes for clarity; often, apparently, simply in order to give a poetic flavour. But most often he creates in this way balanced phrases, where a rhythmical cadence follows a verb, or nominal phrases embrace the verb. So, too, he brings a reflexive pronoun, a separable verbal prefix, a participle, infinitive or the finite verb forward in the sentence for the sake of rhythm. In many cases his model seems to have been the Psalms of Luther's Bible.

Gessner's cautious and sparing use of imagery is also typical of most mid-eighteenth century poetry in Germany, where rationalism brought an aversion to the excessive imagery of the Baroque age. Yet the Rococo taste for decoration is evident in his adaptations of Theocritus's simple similes.

In an age when the language of poetry has become quite distinct from that of everyday usage it is difficult to appreciate how close was Gessner's language to normal educated use. In their correspondence Gessner and his friends wrote in a manner not far removed from that of his idylls. His own letters are full of repetition, exclamation, and deliberate digressions that underline his emotional involvement. There was an interplay between poetry and language used for normal communication. But in his idylls Gessner organises his language more consistently. Like the planner of the English garden, he combines art and nature and moulds them into a pleasing pattern, one that is relatively free but none the less deliberate. And, like a gardener, Gessner was continually tempted to make small improvements to the existing pattern; almost every edition of his works brought minor amendments. The first inspired version was not sacred, indeed the original versions had probably been worked over several times before they were printed. Certain principles guided his revisions. He corrected the grammar, standardised Swiss or South-German expressions, and strove for greater clarity and expressiveness. His modifications to the idyll 'Daphne' that heads the first collection indicate that he was most concerned with metre and rhythm. The phrase 'aus deinem holden Aug der Beifall lächle' became the smoother, though metrically identical, 'aus deinem holden Auge Beifall lächle'. The sequence:

seitdem umglänzt ein Sonnenschein von Freude, mein Leben vor mir her, und jeder Tag, gleicht einem hellen Lieder reichen Morgen (V, 19)

became:

seidem seh' ich die Zukunft hell und glänzend, und jeden Tag begleiten Freud' und Wonne.

In the earlier version commas are inserted to mark the division into three sections of five iambic feet, but the section ending with 'Tag' contrasts with the sequence of feminine endings throughout the paragraph. Many alterations affecting rhythm, modifications of punctuation, omission or insertion of unstressed final 'e', do not follow any recognisable pattern. Gessner seems to have been swayed by a personal sense of euphony that changed slightly with time, but in no one clear direction. Yet throughout the arbitrary changes in punctuation he retained parallel punctuation where it marked parallel phrases. After 1777 the phrase 'Ach! sieh wie nett, sieh wie schön' became 'Ach! sieh! wie nett, sieh, wie schön' (V, 49), and verbs in parallel were always altered together: 'durchmischt' followed by 'mischt', in 'Tityrus. Menalkas' of 1756, became, in 1762 and subsequently, 'durchmischet' and 'mischet' (V, 52).

The degree of rhythmic regularity or orchestration varies from idyll to idyll and from passage to passage. At one extreme stand some of the songs in *Daphnis*. Although printed as prose, they could just as well have been presented as rhymeless verses, distinguishable from the best of German Anacreontic poetry by Gessner's inadequate command of prosody. The songs of Daphnis, and Phillis (F, 58) in trochaic dimeters are one example. Another favourite Anacreontic verse form, with lines of three iambic feet is found, disguised as prose, in another song in the pastoral novel; it ends, too, with a typical Anacreontic 'pointe' (F, 59, lines 1–6). One other piece sung at Daphnis's wedding has the refrain and responsion frequent in Anacreontic poetry. It is quite easily divided into metrical lines:

> Ich will nicht lieben,
> so sag' ich immer;
> seh' ich die Vögel
> auf Ästen schnäbeln,
> dann sag' ich immer:
> Ich will nicht lieben... (F, 59)

Each of these songs is a formal piece, performed before an audience, although it is implied that they are spontaneous creations. Since they are no different from his published verses, we assume that he printed them as prose for two reasons. Firstly he did not wish to break up the page into verse and prose: he was much concerned with the visual impact of his work, chose antiqua rather than Gothic print, provided his own engravings and supervised the printing himself. Secondly he wished to obscure the difference between poetry and prose; for his intention was to write a prose as close as possible to verse.

Some of the songs in the idylls, too, are rhymeless verses disguised as prose. Most often they fall into alternating lines of four and three iambs, a form used by Gessner in three of his published verses. One song begins with two lines of blank verse before settling down into the familiar pattern:

> Dem müden Schnitter ist ein frischer Trunk
> nicht halb so süss, als Liebenden ein Kuss;
> viel lieblicher ist sein Geräusch,
> als wann ein kühler Bach,
> wenn uns der schwühle Mittag brennt,
> durch dunkle Schatten fliesst. (V, 34f)

The idyll that opens the 1756 collection, with its echo of Virgil and its summary of the themes of the collection, strikes a more elevated poetic note. It is the only idyll that is metrically regular throughout. With its iambic and trochaic patterns, its division into four stanzas (paragraphs), and its one alexandrine line, it may be compared with the rhymeless verses of Bodmer or Pyra and Lange. The first section is reminiscent of an ode. Some of Gessner's contemporaries noticed the metrical construction of this idyll and of some of the songs elsewhere in the collection; a Zurich reviewer, writing in 1757, noted it with approval:

Wir finden nicht nur eine im wahren Verstande dichterische, sondern auch eine sehr melodische Sprache, und hin und wieder in den Liedern der Schäfer, in der Zuschrift an Daphnen aber durchaus ein abgemessenes Sylbenmaass. Diese Idylle ist daher ungemein wohlklingend, und der Leser, der des natürlichen Falles der Worte wegen nicht glaubet, dass er wirkliche Verse liesst, deren Füsse ohne dem sehr abwechselnd sind, wird auf eine sehr angenehme Art betrogen, und weiss nicht, woher so viel Melodisches kommt. Wir müssten uns sehr irren, wenn es von ungefähr so geflossen wäre, und wollen die Probe hersetzen:

> Nicht den blutbespritzten kühnen Helden,
> Nicht das öde Schlachtfeld singt die frohe Muse...[10]

More influential were Turgot's comments on the metrical patterns and on their expressive function:

Je ne puis...m'empêcher de faire remarquer d'abord l'heureux choix de cet iambe suivi de sept trochées:

> Mein Stab soll mich Greisen
> Vor die Schwelle meiner Hütte führen

pour exprimer la marche lente d'un vieillard, qui, courbé sur son bâton, va gagner la porte de sa cabane...Il y a des parties dans ses ouvrages qu'on peut regarder comme de véritables vers: il y en a d'autres qui ne sortent point du tout de la prose; il y en a un très grand nombre dont l'harmonie mitoyenne entre les deux genres sert à nuancer le passage de l'un à l'autre, et à conserver au ton general une sorte d'ensemble et d'unité.[11]

It is not clear whether Gessner composed his opening idyll and some of the shepherds' songs as verses and then disguised them as prose, or whether, with his ear attuned to verse metre, he simply wrote a regular pattern of stressed and unstressed syllables. In 1752 he was still uncertain whether he should publish his 'Der Frühling' as a prose piece, since he had been unable to transpose it into verse.[12] In December 1755 he wrote to Ramler, rather apologetically announcing that his idylls would be in prose.[13] Ramler, who is supposed to have advised him to write in prose in 1750, wrote in praise of the idylls, but then recast some of them into hexameters. It seems that despite his theoretical approval of poetic prose, Ramler preferred verse. An Italian admirer of Gessner reported that Gessner expressed surprise that Ramler undertook to versify his idylls, since they were already verse poems, if irregular, disguised as prose.[14] It appears, then, that Gessner composed at least some of the idylls as verses, but their measures were so irregular, and he so unsure in his knowledge of prosody and so conscious that he could not achieve the standards set by Ramler and others, that he printed them as prose.

Irregularity, both in metre and in length of line, is indeed apparent in most of the songs of the idylls if we attempt to analyse them as verses in disguise. They are not unlike 'vers libres' or free verse. Where a girl invents a song by imitating the birds, she begins with four iambic lines of three stresses:

> Ihr kleinen frohen Sänger, [so sprach sie mit singenden Worten,]
> wie lieblich tönt euer Lied,
> von hoher Bäume Wipfeln
> und aus dem niedern Strauch! (V, 53)

Then anapaests break into the iambic pattern, the lines become longer, and gradually the song becomes so free in form that any division into lines would be arbitrary. The same tendency to vary a metrical pattern is present in the songs sung at the harvest in *Daphnis*. They begin and end with a hymn to Ceres, performed by all the harvesters in chorus. Then the binders sing, beginning with an iambic pattern:

> Ihr muntern Schnitter, lehnet euch
> nicht auf die krumme Sichel hin,
> dass der, der euch die Garben bindt,
> nicht dürfe müssig stehn. (F, 17)

The reapers reply with another verse of four iambic lines, but freer in line length; the binders' next verse is another variation on this pattern; and the last verse, sung by the reapers, returns to a clearly regular alternation of units of four and three stresses:

> Und wenn du, kühler Abend, kommst,
> findst du das nackte Feld,
> und wir, wir gehn dann mit Gesang
> auf kurzen Stoppeln heim. (F, 18)

On the whole, the more informal, the more personal the songs are, the freer they become. Usually one can note a basic iambic or trochaic pattern, often occasional hexameters, with or without anacrusis, are heard, but this can also be observed of the narrative and descriptive passages of the idylls.

Schiller, in his essay *Über naive und sentimentalische Dichtung*, believing that poetry and prose were fundamentally different and should be kept distinct, castigated Gessner for wavering indecisively between the two. But poetry and prose, as species of one genus, overlap, and the difference between them is one of degree rather than of kind. Certainly this was how the difference was seen in the early eighteenth century.[15] Theorists made no clear distinction between the rhythm of verse and prose. Batteux, on whose work many eighteenth-century aesthetics were based, analysed prose sermons to show that they were made up of verse lines. Gottsched stated that the writer of good prose must be familiar with the rules of prosody, since both verse and prose depended for their effect on patterns of 'long' and 'short' syllables. Ramler attempted to explain the charm of Gessner's prose by isolating verse lines, and one of his terms for poetic prose was 'metrische Prose'. Furthermore, handbooks of rhetoric recommended the use in prose of rhythmical cadences which were very similar, if not identical, to lines of verse. The cadence known as the 'cursus planus' was, for example, the same as the fourth line of a sapphic ode or the last two feet of a hexameter. The echoes of hexameter lines, often noted by Gessner's commentators, are often produced by his use of the 'cursus planus' as a cadence.

Where Gessner seems to follow no regular metrical pattern, his rhythmical cadences often form patterns of repetition which, like the other forms of repetition, establish echoes that unite a sentence, a passage, or even a whole idyll. Milon's song (V, 21) already quoted in part, has several examples of the 'cursus planus' and of other cadences ending with an unstressed syllable (xXx or xXXx). Already in *Die Nacht* there are patterns of cadences, usually the 'cursus planus' (XxxXx) and the choriamb (XxxX):

durch das dichte Gewölb zitternder Blätter, hier am mossigten Stamm, dort auf dem winkenden Gras, oder an zitternden Ästen...(V, 7)

ihr führet den irren Liebhaber zum ängstlich wartenden Mädchen, oder ihr beleuchtet beyden den Weg, wann sie geheime Gebüsche besuchen, oder führet lauschende Verrähter irre, und lasset sie watend im Sumpf. (V, 10)

Since Gessner must have known that cadences were part of Greek style, he doubtless thought of them as natural formal devices.

In printing verse as prose, and in writing prose that had many of the characteristics of verse poetry, Gessner took to their logical conclusion certain trends already present in the earlier eighteenth century as writers searched for freer and more natural forms of expression. One characteristic of German Rococo poetry was the practice of mixing prose and verse within one work, particularly in pastoral pieces. Gessner simply did this without distinguishing typographically between the two. Within the development of verse, Bodmer and the Anacreontics had dispensed with rhyme. A rejection of regular metre was a more fundamental step that had already been taken in theory during the 'querelle des anciens et des modernes' in France. 'Beau désordre' was advocated; some writers favoured considerable variation in the length of lines of verse within a poem, rejecting strict strophic patterns in favour of 'vers libres' and 'stances irrégulières'. In Germany Brockes and Hagedorn both used quite free metrical forms, and the irregular madrigal verse was commonly practised. Klopstock began composing odes in free verse in 1754. Poetry became less rigid in structure, and, particularly where it was infused with a rationalist spirit or when poetic imagery was used sparingly, it came to read more like prose. The opposite development, the practice of poetic prose, again had its roots in France, where Fénélon had drawn attention to the poetic quality of the Psalms and the Song of Songs, and provided stylistic models in his own prose odes and in his novel *Télémaque*. For generations this novel was regarded as the supreme example of prose style and accepted as a 'poem'. Prose odes were common in German periodicals of the 1740s. Shaftesbury's style was another important stimulus to German writers, and in the 1750s both Klopstock and Wieland were experimenting with poetic prose. Wieland looked back to the tradition of Greek prose, and it is possible that he and Gessner gave each other encouragement and advice.[16] But Gessner seems to have been unique in writing a prose whose rhythms copy the metres of verse poetry, although this procedure had been recommended in France by Jean Pierre de Longue in his *Raisonnemens hazardéz sur la poésie françoise* of 1736.[17]

Poetic prose was relatively new to literature and there was no general agreement about what it should be. Yet there are similarities between Gessner's idylls and French prose poems of the early eighteenth century. They arise mainly because prose rhythm was thought of in terms of metre and of balanced clauses. Some writers, notably Houdard de la Motte, heightened their prose by constant use of imagery and rhetorical devices. In concentrating on musicality rather than rhetoric, Gessner was influenced by his subject-matter, and perhaps by some of the idyllic passages in *Télémaque* with their balanced rhythms, simple syntax and short sentences.

The value of poetic prose had been proved by prose renderings of verse originals. Bodmer's translation of *Paradise Lost* almost inevitably retained not only the imagery, but also the formal balance of Milton's poetry. Gessner must have been influenced by this translation, particularly by those passages that have an idyllic flavour. One of Eve's speeches, where she talks of her love for Adam, and of the joys of paradisical nature, is very close indeed, in style and content, to the utterances of Gessner's characters. It is akin to song, has a final 'pointe'-like phrase, much use of parallel and unusual word order:

Lieblich ist die Luft der Morgenstunde, lieblich sein Anbrechen unter dem ver-zükenden Gesange der frühesten Vögel, angenehm die Sonne, wie sie frühe ihre östlichen Strahlen auf dieses anmuthvolle Land ausbreitet, auf Kräuter, Bäume, Früchte, und Bluhmen, die von dem Thau schimmern; wohlriechend der fruchtbare Erdboden nach einem sanften Regen, und lieblich die sanfte Ankunft der Abend-freude, und die stille Nacht, mit diesem ihr geweihten Vogel, und diesem schönen Monden, und diesen Juwelen des Himmels, ihrem Sternengefolge: Aber weder die Luft der Morgenstunde, wenn sie unter dem Gesange der frühesten Vögel anbricht, noch die aufgehende Sonne in diesem ergetzlichen Lande, noch die Kräuter, Früchte und Bluhmen, noch der liebliche Geruch nach einem sanften Regen, noch der milde angenehme Abend, noch die stille Nacht mit diesem ihr geheiligten Vogel, noch das Spazieren beym Monden, oder dem schimmernden Strahlen der Sternen, ist ohne dich lieblich.[18]

The two sentences, strophe and antistrophe in the original, are both characterised by rhythmical cadence. It can hardly be chance that in the second half 'geheiligten Vogel' is part of a sequence of 'cursus planus', whereas in the first part 'geweihten Vogel' is a ditrochaic cadence in the series 'sanften Regen', 'Abendfreude', 'schönen Monden' (both translate Milton's 'solemn bird'). Gessner used less stock poetic imagery (his characters are largely innocent of poetic tradition), and his syntax is simpler. In the last paragraph of 'Damon. Daphne' the parallels between the two speeches recall the strophe-antistrophe pattern, but are less exact and less obviously contrived; it is, after all, natural for the girl to echo her lover:

DAMON: Umarme mich, Daphne! umarme mich!...Welche unerschöpfliche Quelle von Entzucken! Von der belebenden Sonne bis zur kleinsten Pflanze sind alles Wunder!...Gedanken drengen sich dann auf...dann wein' ich und sinke hin und stammle mein Erstaunen dem der die Erde schuf! O Daphne! nichts gleicht dem Entzüken, es sey denn das Entzüken von dir geliebt zu seyn.
DAPHNE: Ach Damon! Auch mich, auch mich entzüken die Wunder! O lass uns in zärtlicher Umarmung...die Wunder betrachten...und unser Erstaunen stammeln; O welch unaussprechliche Freude! wenn dies Entzüken zu dem Entzüken der zärtlichsten Liebe sich mischt. (V, 32f)

Bodmer had also tried his hand at poetic prose in an original work, his *Pygmalion und Elise* of 1749. There, too, the language is full of parallel and repetition, though it does not have the same balance. In trying to render the wonder of an innocent soul Bodmer uses a restricted vocabulary and simple syntax. His Elise, seeing her reflection in the water for the first time, exclaims:

Welch neues Wunder! sagte sie. Hierin sehe ich einen neuen Himmel weit ausgebreitet, und neue Bäume, die unterwerts wachsen. Ich sehe auch eine Gestalt, wie meine ist, mit lachenden Augen, als ob sie sich freute mich hier zu sehen. Steige auf, artiges Ding, und wechsle vernehmliche Reden mit mir. Ich sehe dich wie die Lippen bewegen, die mir zu sagen scheinen, du liebest mich, aber ich kann sie nicht hören. Ich will dir die Hand reichen, reiche mir deine und komm heraus. Mit diesem wolte sie ihr die Hand reichen; das Wasser bewegte sich unter ihrer Hand und das Bild verschwand.[19]

Like Gessner's characters, she compares her emotions to those of animals. Here, as in Gessner, the attempt to portray charming naiveté comes perilously close to silliness. Yet Bodmer's work is punctuated by rationalistic sermons on the benevolence of God. Even further removed from Gessner in tone is J. A. Ebert's prose translation of Edward Young's *Night Thoughts*, a melancholy poem that had great influence in Europe. Ebert aimed to produce 'eine nachdrückliche, feuerige, und doch zugleich harmonische Prosa',[20] and his translation is distinguished by rhythmical balance and conjunctions used in the manner of anaphora. The phrases in Bodmer's *Paradise Lost* and in Ebert's *Night Thoughts*, as in other prose versions of verse originals, are usually balanced in twos or fours; in original prose, in *Télémaque* for example, tripartite sentences are more common. Gessner uses any number of balanced clauses.

Evidently others, apart from Gessner, living in the shadow of Bodmer, were interested in the possibilities of poetic prose. Johann Rudolf Werdmüller, a member of the 'Dienstags-Compagnie', published four prose poems, *Die vier Stufen des menschlichen Alters*, in 1755. Like Gessner, he wrote a predominantly paratactic German, characterised by rhythmical balance, cadences, and an attempt at euphony. But Werdmüller expresses rationalist ideals of life and virtue with an abstractness and earnestness that contrasts with the concreteness and charm of Gessner's idylls.

Although each of the features of Gessner's prose can be found in other writers of the early and mid eighteenth century, together they made something new. With his admiration for the musicality of Gleim's verses, Gessner created a style that was his own. To Winckelmann, himself a distinguished stylist, it appeared quite beautiful, indeed incomparable.[21] Another contemporary, distinguished by birth rather than achievement, the Duchess Philippine Charlotte of Braunschweig-Wolfenbüttel, the King of Prussia's sister, judged that Gessner was the first to show the world that the German language was capable of expressing sentiments with grace.[22] Gessner's language, particularly that of his idylls, was indeed a revelation. Sound and rhythm had become integral parts of style in a musical prose with a musical structure.

Equally remarkable as the music of Gessner's sentences is the orchestration of whole idylls. In so far as their structure depends on content the idylls follow Theocritus and the traditional idyll; some of the more humorous pieces seem to have been inspired by Rococo poems. A song or songs introduced and followed by a short narrative, a monologue that is concluded by a welcome interruption, a scene that brings its own conclusion – whatever the content of an idyll, it is brought to a satisfying end and is complete in itself. But many an idyll has an additional structure. For the repetition, parallel, and formal echoes have a structural as well as stylistic function. Where such a structure is observed, not just in a sentence or a paragraph, but over the whole of a short idyll, that idyll may be called a poem in prose.

The pattern of words, sounds and rhythms in the idylls can be quite complex. Just as regular metre is more common in the formal songs than in emotional utterance, so the overall formal organisation is more apparent in those idylls whose appeal is based on Rococo charm rather than sentimental effusion. It is, perhaps, most obvious in 'Phillis. Chloe' (V, 49), where one girl teases the other about her attachment to a basket woven by a particular shepherd. Although the teasing Phillis respects the tender emotions of the shy Chloe, and ultimately the reader might be touched by the sentiment, this idyll is clearly designed to charm rather than excite. The importance of parallel becomes evident in the first two

sentences: they are almost identical, though one is a half-question
and the other includes an extra syllable (the second 'ja' of Chloe's
line):

PHILLIS: Du, Chloe, immer trägst du dein Körbchen am Arm.
CHLOE: Ja Phillis, ja! immer trag' ich das Körbchen am Arm.

The choriamb cadence established here is now repeated throughout the idyll, sometimes as 'Körbchen am Arm', sometimes, but
not always, with one of these nouns repeated:

Körbchen am Arm...Körbchen so werth...ins Angesicht scheint...hat mirs
geschenkt...trag ichs am Arm...flechten gesehn...eben so schön...gestern mir
sang...zum Körbchen gesagt...Körbchen gemacht...Körbchen am Arm.

Half of these choriambs follow a dactyl to form the pattern
XxxXxxX (the second half of a pentameter), a cadence that was
not recommended for use in prose by handbooks of rhetoric since
it was too reminiscent of a verse line. If Gessner was aware of this,
he ignored the theory and welcomed the pattern because it
sounded like poetry. His use of cadences seems particularly conscious in this idyll. One, 'schon oft geküsst', is echoed at the end
of the following sentence with 'der schönste Hirt'. The trochaic
phrase-ending 'die ich aus dem Körbchen esse' echoes 'die ich in
meinem Körbchen trage' in the same sentence. Between these
stands the 'cursus planus': 'Früchte sind süsser', itself echoing an
earlier phrase in the same sentence, 'dünken mich schöner'. In
another sentence 'Schmiegt euch gehorsam' and 'unter dem
Flechten' alternate with 'bunten Ruthen' and 'Seite hangen'.
Despite these patterns the rhythm is elastic. When a word is
repeated, it usually recurs in a different rhythmical context. The
formal arrangement is not so obvious that an impression of artlessness cannot be given.

'Der zerbrochene Krug' is dominated by the refrain of the faun's
song: 'Er ist zerbrochen, er ist zerbrochen, der schönste Krug, da
liegen die Scherben umher.' The rhythm of this last phrase is
taken up again:

dann sassen wir rings um den Krug...dem Ufer ein trauriges Lied...der Schönen
entblössetes Knie...

and the idyll ends with this cadence and with the repetition of the key word from the refrain: 'bewundernd die Scherben im Gras'.

The structural use of such semantic and rhythmical repetition is peculiar to Gessner's prose and points to the influence of verse poetry on his style. The same technique is characteristic of a poem in free rhythms, of, for example, Klopstock's 'Frühlingsfeier', where, in the absence of rhythm and regular metre, repetition and parallel produce an overall unity.

That the addition of regular metre alone does nothing to improve the poetry of Gessner's prose is shown by a comparison with Ramler's adaptations.[23] He rewrote some of Gessner's idylls as hexameter poems, keeping as close as possible to the original. His choice of hexameters was an obvious one, because Gessner's prose contains so many echoes of this measure that had been used by Theocritus. Ramler did occasionally retain the Anacreontic measures of the songs, but he could not resist the temptation to impose greater regularity. Alexis's song in 'Phillis. Chloe' consists of nine 'lines'; Ramler reduced it to two four-line stanzas, and removed the (unintentional?) rhyme of 'seh' and 'geh'; it was scarcely an improvement. The adaptation of the rest of the idyll posed greater problems. Noticing the repetition of 'Körbchen am Arm', Ramler retained this as 'Körbchen am Arme', but lost the link with the other choriambs. Furthermore, the metre forced him to include additional words and syllables that add nothing to the sense and sometimes read awkwardly:

Ja! wenn sie es werth hält, o wenn sie es werth hielte! wenn sie es oft an ihrer Seite trüge!

became

wenn es ihr würdig scheint – O! schien' es ihr würdig! Trüge sie doch oft es an ihrer Seite!

The expressive power of the original, the rhythm of the lengthening phrases, is lost. Ramler's word order is more artificial, his vocabulary often more traditionally poetic than Gessner's. Indeed, the comparison with Ramler shows just why Gessner's language seemed so natural to his contemporaries. Here are the refrains from 'Der zerbrochene Krug' and 'Mirtil. Thyrsis' in the original and in Ramler's version:

(Gessner) Er ist zerbrochen, er ist zerbrochen, der schönste Krug, da liegen die Scherben umher! (V, 35)

(Ramler) Ach! er ist zerbrochen, der Krüge schönster! da liegen Seine Scherben umher.

(Gessner) Klaget mir nach, ihr Felsenklüfte, traurig töne mein Leid zurük, durch den Hain und vom Ufer! (V, 45)

(Ramler) Klaget mir nach, ihr Felsenklüfte! traurig ertöne Durch den Hain mein Lied und am widerhallenden Ufer!

To have achieved in verse the effects of his prose Gessner would have had to be more gifted than Ramler, that perfectionist in matters of prosody, more than a competent versifier. In terms of organisation, Gessner's idylls are just as much poems as Ramler's metrical adaptations; as vehicles for sentiment and charm they are superior.

Gessner's admirers in his own time did not draw attention to the structural aspects of his art, presumably because they wished to stress the naturalness of his writings. Yet if any attempt is made to define the prose poem as a literary form, the definition must surely correspond in large part to Gessner's practice. And, despite the difference between his rhythms, often based on the rhythms of verse, and those of later heightened prose, his idylls must be regarded as the first prose poems in modern German literature.[24] Like his musical language, this 'invention' of the prose poem may be regarded as an example of his 'wit'. In their combination of art and artlessness his idylls were a unique achievement of great sensitivity and taste.

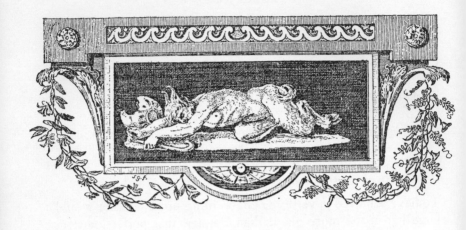

5 · FAMILY, BUSINESS AND ART

In February 1761 Gessner married Judith Heidegger. Six years younger than her husband, and generally admired for her good looks, intelligence and cheerfulness, she bore him five children, three of whom lived beyond infancy: Anna Dorothea, born 1763; Conrad, born 1764, who became a painter and established a reputation as a minor Stubbs, specialising in equestrian portraits; and Heinrich, born 1768, who went into the book trade and, in 1795, married Wieland's daughter Charlotte Luise. Gessner's was a happy marriage. Father and mother were very fond of their children and placed great store by family life, and their home impressed many as a haven of the domestic virtues sung in the idylls.

Through his marriage Gessner entered a very influential Zurich family. His earnings from his writings and from his part in his father's business were not thought adequate to support a family, and in 1761 he left his father, who disapproved of the marriage, to join his brother-in-law, Heinrich Heidegger, as a partner in another distinguished printing and publishing concern. In 1770 this firm, Orell, Gessner & Cie, absorbed its chief rival in Zurich to become Orell, Gessner, Füssli & Cie. Gessner looked after the publishing, Heidegger the printing. The company was astutely run: Wieland complained to Gessner that his novel *Agathon* had been printed in small type on large paper when he was paid by the ream.[1] But it also had a reputation for honesty. Another author and friend of Gessner, J. G. Zimmermann, was agreeably surprised to be paid promptly.[2] The publishers ran some risk in handling Wieland's *Comische Erzählungen* and *Agathon*, works that would not have passed the Zurich censors and were printed with a false place of origin on the title page. They handled most of the important German writers of the time, Bodmer, Wieland, Ewald von Kleist, Gleim, Hirzel, Winckelmann, Mengs, J. C. Füssli, and translations of Shakespeare (by Wieland and Eschenburg), Thomson, Swift, Butler, and others. It was a great era in publishing, and Zurich was renowned for the excellence of its books, its high standard of printing, and above all, for careful and tasteful layout and artistic use of engraved illustrations. Gessner's own interest in beautiful and clear presentation contributed in large part to this success. He became more concerned with business matters. In 1772 he attempted unsuccessfully to establish a formal link between Orell, Gessner, Füssli & Cie and his father's firm. Eventually, in 1775, on the death of his father, he inherited David Gessner Gebrüder.

To his publishing interests he added a stake in a porcelain factory. The manufacture of fine china had such a prestige value that a few citizens of Zurich decided that their state should not lag behind the rest of Europe in this matter. A factory would also provide welcome employment in the canton. One was established just outside the town in 1763. Gessner was not only involved financially; as artistic adviser he also provided some of the designs, and used his contacts throughout Europe to try to boost sales, though to little effect. Despite its quality, Zurich porcelain failed to establish itself in the markets, for competition in this luxury trade was intense, and technical inventiveness was required to create a new fashion, and new demand, at regular intervals. Gessner did not become a Josiah Wedgewood, nor, like Flaxman, make a great impact on the decoration of porcelain.

As his business interests widened, Gessner also took on political responsibilities. On reaching the qualifying age in 1765 he was immediately elected into the 'Grosser Rat' of Zurich. Two years later, largely through the influence of his wife's family (the burgomaster was a Heidegger), he was chosen to serve on the 'Kleiner Rat', the smaller, policy-making assembly of burghers. He did not desire to shine as a public figure, but was proud of his title of 'Ratsherr' and took his duties seriously. In 1768 he was appointed 'Obervogt von Erlenbach', administrator and magistrate of a small rural community on the north shore of Lake Zurich. The union of ecclesiastic and secular authority in the canton could be an embarrassment to a man whose religious views were as liberal as Gessner's; but like many others he did what was expected of him. He cursed and laughed when he had to install a new vicar in Erlenbach in 1776 – as he wrote to Heinrich Meister,[3] who had once been banned from the republic after the publication of his *De l'origine des principes religieux*; that ban was lifted, largely due to Gessner's efforts, in 1772. Slightly more onerous was the post of 'Obervogt von den vier Wächten', a more populous and troublesome district immediately outside the walls of Zurich; Gessner held this position from 1776 until his death. In 1779 he took on a further task, deputising for a friend while he was ill. Two years later, when that man died, Gessner was chosen to succeed to his title and duties as 'Sihlherr'. His function was to administer the forests beside the river Sihl, a few miles outside the town. This duty, too, he performed more than satisfactorily, and was officially commended for dealing effectively with snow damage, striking good bargains with timber merchants, and ensuring an adequate supply of wood to the town. He was able to introduce improvements in forestry, for he now became interested in rural economics and advances in husbandry.

In 1763 Gessner supported J. C. Lavater and J. H. Füssli in securing the dismissal of the 'Landvogt' Felix Grebel who had abused his position of authority in the country district of Grüningen. Gessner worked quite happily within the given political situation, indeed he benefited from it. As 'Sihlherr' he received handsome payment in money and in kind – grain, wine and wood.

The accident of birth and his marriage made him eligible for such positions. But he also worked to help the needy: in the lean 1770s he advised that land held by the municipality should be sold cheaply to the poor; and he persuaded the republic to raise the wages of the forest workers. Without subverting authority he was able to put into practice, to some limited extent, the love and sympathy for his fellow men that he portrayed in his writings. He was no hard governor, aloof from his inferiors, but liked to think of himself as a father to those who were placed under him, trying to realise that relationship of love and respect between high and low that was dear to his age. He rode around the woods, a forester's son perched with him on the saddle, calling on wives and families as well as inspecting the forest and the men at work.

One tragic episode reveals how Gessner and his friends warmed to examples of humanity. In 1771 a twelve-year-old boy was taken in and clothed by the vicar of the village of Wechingen near Nördlingen in southern Germany. He was the only survivor of a family of nine who had emigrated from Schlieren outside Zurich to East Prussia. Driven from the new homeland, mother, father, and six children died on the way back to Switzerland. The orphan was sent on by the vicar, Johann Wilhelm Schlegel, with a letter to other ministers of religion requesting them to assist the boy. He found his way to the house of Hirzel in Zurich, who arranged for him to return to his relatives in Schlieren. Moved by Schlegel's charity, Hirzel and his friends sent him, as a token of respect, a Swiss cheese of monumental proportions. Gessner was entrusted with composing a letter to the German priest, and he wrote of how Providence had led the orphan to a man of feeling and virtue. Thus eighteenth-century sentiment transformed tragedy into a story of natural goodness and divine benevolence.

Switzerland was perhaps less depraved than other countries in Europe, yet the natural morals, so cherished by Gessner and his friends, seemed to be threatened as pomp invaded the country from neighbouring states. Compared with Berne, Zurich was not so prone to ceremony and élitism, but many Swiss intellectuals believed that some common effort, or at least some common concern, was needed to safeguard the Swiss way of life, and to ensure that Swiss democracy was not engulfed by absolutism. So the 'Helvetische Gesellschaft' was formed, with Gessner as a founder member, to discuss political, economic, moral and educational problems. During the sixties and seventies Gessner attended its annual meetings at Schinznach near Baden in Aargau. Serious and highminded were the deliberations, and Gessner was no longer a frivolous youngster, but a family man, businessman and member of the establishment.

He still loved to walk in the countryside, but not too far, for he had grown rather fat. Yet he was still a man of gaiety, delighting his friends with his humour, occasionally lapsing into buffoonery. Once, walking to Schinznach, he subsided by the roadside, groaning with fatigue, much to the merriment of his companions. In the spring of 1765 some fifty prominent Swiss attended the meeting of the 'Helvetische Gesellschaft'. Their two guests, Prince Eugen Ludwig of Württemberg and the 'philosophical' farmer Kleinjogg, walked arm in arm, a symbol of the hopes for the future of mankind that filled the hearts of those present. After food and drink the company grew more boisterous, and called on Gessner to regale them with a comic turn or a character impersonation. At first he was reluctant, but then surpassed all expectations and had to be restrained lest his audience choke with laughter. Gessner commented philosophically on this foolery in a letter to J. G. Zimmermann: at least they had intended to make fools of themselves as distinct from the majority of men, blind to their own stupidity:

Freylich kommen wir Philosophen in Schinznach zusammen, um Narren zu seyn. Aber...das ist allemal so, wo die Art Thiere auf einen Fleck zusammen laufen, die auf zwei Beinen gehn und eine Perrücke oder ihr eigen Haar tragen (diese Definition gibt Linnaeus, wenn mich mein Gedächtniss nicht trügt), man heisse dann dieses: Zusammengelauf, Gesellschaft, Akademie, Magistrat oder Kirchengemeinde...Wir zweyen haben zuweilen den Narren gemacht, weil wir ihn machen wollten, und das soll uns nicht gereuen...[4]

The puritanical attitudes prevailing in Zurich and the self-importance of its burghers must have aggravated as well as amused Gessner. Yet he did not allow such things, or business worries and public responsibilities to weigh him down. Trips to Schinznach, visits to friends and occasional journeys to other parts of Switzerland made a welcome break, even from the demands of parenthood. For he took his duties towards his children very seriously. His letters to his son Conrad, who left home to study art in Dresden and Rome, are full of conscientious, common-sense advice on the importance of healthy exercise and hard work. Family life imposed restrictions, but gave joy. Gessner's domestic life, however, attracted many who would have liked to enjoy it as a public spectacle. He was not too fond of the numerous, often uninvited, visitors who came to see him in Zurich. Many were aristocratic and wealthy nonentities, stopping off on their way to Italy. But others must have been interesting, if sometimes expensive, to entertain. They included the future Czar of Russia, Paul I, the Mozart family (the twelve-year-old Wolfgang Amadeus played the piano), a number of painters, mostly French, including Vernet and Claude-Henri Watelet, but also Tischbein; the English traveller William Coxe, the Swedish scientist Björnståhl, and the Duke Karl August of Weimar. Others were poets and writers: notably the Counts Stolberg, Wilhelm Heinse, Matthison, the historian Johannes von Müller – and Goethe. But Goethe studiously avoided mention of Gessner's work, and spoke about Wieland's *Oberon*. Most visitors were impressed by Gessner's wit and good humour, admired the tasteful simplicity of his home and the spirit of domestic harmony that reigned there. For even if, like Mme de Genlis, they were not quite prepared to find an ordinary middle-class household (and one caller thought Gessner himself looked like an idiot), they found something of the spirit of his idylls in his house. Some were determined enough to seek him out in the house that he occupied as 'Sihlherr' in the summer months, in the beautiful Sihl valley below wooded mountains. At least one aristocratic lady, however, gave up on finding that the road was unfit for a carriage. Those who arrived were as enthusiastic about the beauties of nature there as any Gessnerian shepherd in Arcadia.

In 1787 a friend of Gessner's went to visit him in Sihlwald. He lunched in the nearest village and was shown the track to Gessner's house by an obliging woman, 'recht patriarchalisch' as he thought. Finally he saw the house, among meadows and orchards, not far from the head forester's cottage. Wooded slopes crowded down on each side towards the rocky banks, crowned by larch and fir, of the river that curved through the valley and was crossed by a rustic bridge. The visitor climbed to the crest of the Albis range above Sihlwald and gazed at the Alps in the distance. The scenery so excited him that he was unable to sleep that night and looked from the window of Gessner's house on to 'eine schauerlich schöne Landschaft' in the moonlight. His account shows how Gessner's feeling for nature inspired others and moved them to Romantic awe.[5] Another visitor, indeed, summed up his impression with the word 'romantic', though he, too, did not fail to mention the association of simplicity with the Old Testament patriarchs:

Sihlwald, den 9. August 1786. Nachts: Romantischer lässt sich nichts denken als der Aufenthalt in dieser angenehmen Eremitage mit einer Familie wie die Gessnerische...Diese liebe Familie...nahm mich mit einer Herzlichkeit auf, die mich an die patriarchalischen Zeiten erinnerte...[6]

The domestic scene affected visitors just as much as the natural setting. Sophie La Roche was delighted by the living room; it was 'einfach, aber ganz poetisch verziert', with vines around the windows, its tables, chairs, mirror all carved 'in dem niedlichsten Geschmack', the white furniture contrasting with the green silk of the cushions that matched the green of the walls. Gessner had himself painted Graces over the mirror. The simplicity struck one who was used to the ostentation of aristocratic houses, yet greater taste was evident here than in many a middle-class home. Sophie La Roche hoped that her two daughters would one day enjoy such a home, so conducive to domestic bliss.[7]

Sihlwald in summer was an idyllic spot. One visitor noted in 1786 how Gessner's love of his family and of nature, his character that combined the warmth of youth with the serenity of maturity, could best be appreciated during these months he spent each year in the country.[8] Gessner was cheerful and gay, and belied his languid appearance by striding purposefully up and down hill and taking part in skittles and target-shooting. His immediate family admired the spirit in which he turned Sihlwald into an Arcadia.[9]

Despite the general acclaim accorded to his idylls and *Der Tod Abels* throughout Europe in the 1760s, Gessner had some disappointments. In 1762 he attempted to win the patronage of Queen Charlotte of England by writing an ode on the birth of the Prince of Wales, later George IV, and by dedicating his *Schriften* to the Queen. She did not acknowledge the tribute, and in 1769, when dedicating the idyll 'Die Zephyre' to the Princess Auguste Friederike of Brunswick, the Queen of England's sister, he recalled how hurt he had been.[10] For he liked praise and recognition. He hoped, too, through his writings to break down barriers of class and nationality.

During a holiday in the country, in the summer and autumn of 1770, some time before he became 'Sihlherr', he was inspired to write most of the idylls that appeared in the *Neue Idyllen* of 1772. In 1769 he had been seriously ill and unable to cope with business or public administration for a few months. He had problems with his eyesight, and regularly paid visits to spas not far from Zurich. If life was not entirely blissful, it only served to increase his capacity to appreciate joy and beauty. The holiday, and the idylls, were an escape into a better existence. He could also count on a lively interest, particularly in France, in any new works he might publish. Herder's critical attack on his earlier idylls, made in 1766, was as yet an isolated instance, and Gessner had no reason to doubt the probability of success or to alter his style. In the spring of 1770, still recovering from his illness, he began to write again. In April he reported to Ramler that he had written 'ein paar Kleinigkeiten' and asked if he should continue with more.[11] His letter included early versions of 'Die Zephyre', 'Das Gelübd' and the poem 'An den Amor'. 'Die Zephyre' appeared in the *Göttinger Musenalmanach* and in the *Almanach der deutschen Musen* of 1771. He was evidently not expecting to write enough pieces to make a new collection. The products of this spring were Rococo in manner, marking a return to his earliest writings. But later that year he found unexpected inspiration: 'wie ein Fieber wandelte es mich

wieder an', he told Nicolai.[12] Now he felt that he had struck a new
note:

Musse und die schönste Natur um mich her thaten ihre ganze Würkung...und
solte man nicht etwa hier und da Spuren finden, dass ich die Natur mehr in der
Nähe gesehen habe, als ein und andrer unserer Dichter? Mich dünkt, ich empfinde
selbst, dass diese letzten Idyllen, in ihrem Charakter und vielleicht auch im Thon
etwas andres haben als die ersten.[13]

As before, he hoped to have his opinion confirmed by others. The
joys of marriage and parenthood brought a new theme. But the
second collection is less even in quality than the first; besides very
slight pieces it also includes some of his best idylls, and ones that
describe nature with a vigour and vividness not surpassed before.
The openings of 'Der Herbstmorgen', 'Mycon' and 'Daphnis'
represent a climax in Gessner's nature poetry. Other idylls appeal
to the readers' sentiments and proclaim a moral with a more con-
fident single-mindedness than was evident in the 1756 collection.
And in 'Daphnis' his prose style is as musical and polished as ever,
yet shows a new restraint.

The new idylls, together with two stories by Diderot translated
into German by Gessner himself, were published in 1772, under
the title *Moralische Erzählungen und Idyllen von Diderot und S.
Gessner*. Two French editions, *Contes moraux et nouvelles idylles de
D...et Gessner*, followed in 1773. Diderot's stories supplement
Gessner's idylls in sentiment and morality, but otherwise stand in
contrast to them. To many the two writers seemed strangely
paired, so far is the disturbed world of Diderot's narratives removed from the harmony of the idylls. Yet the contrast is not inappropriate, for it underlines the function of the idylls as a foil to
reality. The year's delay between publication of the German and
French edition was caused by Gessner's anxieties about the French
translation, for they were intended to appear simultaneously.
Huber, who had helped Gessner to fame in France ten years
before, did a version; but since he had left Paris and moved to
Leipzig, Gessner felt that he might be out of touch with the finer
nuances of French and called upon Heinrich Meister, then in exile
in Paris, to revise the translation. Turgot, probably offended that

he had not been asked to collaborate again, judged the published translation less exact than that of 1762. More recent critics have often stated that, in comparison with the earlier idylls, the second collection brings nothing new and that Gessner never refound his original inspiration. The new idylls, indeed, represented variations on the earlier themes rather than a striking innovation.

After his marriage Gessner wrote very little: apart from these idylls, only the ode to the Prince of Wales in 1762, a foreword to the second edition of Gleim's pastoral play *Der blöde Schäfer* published by the Gessner firm in 1767, and the *Brief über die Landschaftsmahlerey* of 1770. In 1760 he had ceased to edit the *Montags-Zeitung*, for which he had been responsible, with his father, since 1750; he took over this weekly paper again in 1772, but gave it up in 1780 when it became the *Zürcher Zeitung*. After 1780 his only literary work was to edit the annual *Helvetischer Kalender*. It seems that he did not spend too much time on business matters either, for his wife was quite capable of running the publishing business, and ready to do so, particularly after his illness in 1769. He was therefore able to devote more and more of his energies to his real interest, which was now etching and painting. Many of his visitors bought a painting from him, and Gessner tried to use his fame as a poet to create a demand for his pictures.

Painting, was, however, an activity that he began in earnest only relatively late in life. From 1760 to 1780 he concentrated on etching. The progression from etching to painting, from vignette to landscape, was not unlike that from idyll to epic: neither was entirely successful, for Gessner's talents were best suited to works small in scale, whether in literature or the visual arts.

The etcher draws his picture much as he would make a pencil drawing, and leaves the acid to cut the plate. This technique is perhaps easier to master than that of engraving proper, where the artist's hand must be firmer. Etching was the favourite technique of the age and a fashionable pastime too: in France almost anyone at all interested in art, including Mme de Pompadour, experimented with the etching needle. More professional practitioners decorated and illustrated every conceivable kind of book. Prints were the chief means of promoting knowledge of painting, architecture and sculpture, and answered a public demand for copies of works of art, representations of picturesque manners, and for illustrations of scientific and technical discoveries. It was partly because the etcher was so useful to the publisher that Gessner applied himself to this art after his marriage. Indeed, the combination of printed word and engraved illustration in the editions of his own works proved extremely popular.

The earliest etching known to be his is a vignette in Bodmer's *Noah* of 1752; its Baroque heaviness is perhaps not an inappropriate accompaniment to a work by the admirer of Milton. The title-page to Gessner's *Idyllen* of 1756 (Plate 3) is quite different. Here Gessner leaves a large area within the oblong frame blank, and finds a Rococo style that was to characterise most of his etchings. The basically rectilinear frame consists of numerous small c-shaped curves, and further movement of line is provided by the musical instruments associated with the pastoral muse, the vine tendrils, fruits, flowers and leaves that enliven the frame. Low down within the frame is a child-shepherd resting by a sheep; here, too, asymmetrically balanced curves determine the composition. The dividing line between sheep and bush is indistinct; frame, pastoral scene and the plinth below that bears the publisher's name are each separate designs with their own functions, but also blend into one overall design. It is a stylised evocation of the spirit of the idylls.

Between 1750 and 1760 Gessner produced some fifty engravings. During the following twenty years he did more than three hundred and fifty. In the early 1760s, too, his interest in Greek and Roman art began to influence his etchings. The change may be attributed to the impact of Winckelmann, the father of Neo-Classicism, and to the general artistic climate. Daniel Webb's *Enquiry into the Beauties of Painting* (1760) which also drew attention to Greek and Roman art, was widely known; Gessner did the title vignette for a translation of Webb published in Zurich in 1766. There was a 'Dactylothek', a collection of plaster casts of classical gems and coins, in Zurich. Already the title-pages of Gessner's

Schriften of 1762 (Plates 5 and 6) show a new clarity and solidarity of disposition. In one, Cain, standing in despair over the body of his brother, appears as if done in relief on a stone tablet. Each element, the outline of the tablet, the oval frame and the fields containing title and illustration are now clearly separate. From now on Gessner favoured heavy frames of regular geometrical shape, frequently used classical temples, shrines and statues as motifs in his designs, and modelled his figures on classical sculptures and reliefs. Indeed, many readers must have seen a classical statue reproduced for the first time in his works.

But Gessner did not altogether forsake the light movement and ambiguous compositions of the Rococo manner, for the greater weight and clarity of neo-classical forms did not entirely correspond to his vision of nature. Often his classical monuments sit awkwardly in the natural scene. The clash between the classical linear style and the more painterly Rococo technique is even more obvious where he sets nude figures in nature. His figures are inept, lifeless and unlifelike, lacking proportion though modelled on ancient sculpture; he regretted never having studied anatomy, and had no opportunity to draw from nude models. Yet when he drew a figured relief or a vase the result was often entrancing. In a vignette etched in 1773, as an illustration to the idyll 'Daphnis und Micon' (see p. 29), the marble relief of a battle scene is nicely contrasted with the movement of the marsh plants that grow around and half conceal it. Another vignette, dating from 1777, an illustration to 'Die ybel belohnte Liebe' (see p. 75), shows a vase decorated in relief with a faun teaching a goat to dance; the vine tendrils that hang over the vase add to the movement. In these and similar attractive etchings Gessner treats a classical motif with Rococo delicacy, sometimes a touch of humour.

Other delightful vignettes are purely Rococo in spirit. One, from his *Werke* of 1762, shows a faun and two putti seated on willow stumps (see p. 53); the boat-like curve of the trunks and the darker foliage above form a restful oval, and the whole is a pleasing visual counterpart to the arbours of the idylls. Another good example, from his *Oeuvres* of 1777, portrays two young tritons chasing a duck among the reeds (see p. 160). Fantasy is nicely combined with realism here, as in a vignette from the idylls of 1772, where a chubby infant, no doubt the spirit of the spring, pours water from an ewer over his head into a cool, damp corner of nature. Each plant, each leaf, seems identifiable. Gessner spent much time sketching local flora, noting the measurements of plants and their favourite habitat with scientific exactness. In his etchings their natural forms are arranged into pleasing patterns; and, as in his poetic descriptions, he was particularly fond of creeping, climbing and trailing plants.

Gessner's full-page etchings are less successful, particularly when they include, as they usually do, nude figures or classical monuments. An illustration to *Der erste Schiffer*, from the *Oeuvres* of 1777, shows the young heroine leaning against a rock face, lost in melancholy longing. She is unconvincing in her postured dreaminess. Yet Gessner could capture sentiment, especially when it was more dramatic. In his illustration to Diderot's *Les deux amis de Bourbonne*, etched in 1772, distress and horror are written on the faces and expressed in the posture of the characters. Here dramatic expression approaches caricature, a sphere in which Gessner might have rivalled his contemporaries Daniel Chodowiecki and William Hogarth, had he produced more. His humorous sketches are, however, small in number, and were mostly intended as illustrations of the work of other writers. A scene from *Henry IV, Part II* (Plate 8), with Falstaff and in his friends in dispute with Mistress Quickly, reveals Gessner's talent as a comic realist. Equally effective, particularly in the stance of the donkey, is an illustration to Butler's *Hudribras*. Gentle humour, rather than caricature, is seen in Gessner's frontispiece to J. J. Hottinger's *Briefe von Selkof an Welmar* (Plate 7), an epistolary novel published in 1777. A fashionable young man seated among meadow flowers greets an older man passing by. The relaxed amiability of the young man meets with the disapproval of his rotund and dignified elder. The contrast is carried over into the natural setting, the soft luscious flowers, the bent fence-posts and the gnarled branches of the trees. Here Gessner makes more use of light and dark areas than is usual in his etchings: the older man is about to cast a shadow over the youth. In the smaller vignettes there is normally only one plane, so that shading is not required to create a sense of recession. Their lightness of touch corresponds to the mood of the idylls that they illustrate. In the larger landscape etchings, trees in the middle ground or beyond are drawn indistinctively to give the impression of distance, yet an intricate pattern of lines suggests the play of light on the foliage.

For, besides producing title-pages, illustrations and vignettes for editions of his own works, and for many other books – by Bodmer, Wieland, J. G. Zimmermann and Lavater, translations of Swift, Butler, Thomson, Shakespeare and Sophocles – Gessner etched three series of full-page landscapes to be published in book form. They do not possess the same charm as the less pretentious miniatures. His best vignettes do not betray the amateur, but the more ambitious his engravings, the more obvious is his lack of technical skill and his failure at large-scale composition. Zurich was not an outstanding centre for the visual arts. Its best painters in the eighteenth century, Anton Graff and Henry Fuseli (Johann Heinrich Füssli), left the town in order to develop their talents. Gessner himself sent his son Conrad to Dresden and to Rome for his artistic training. Yet there were in Zurich a number of men actively interested in painting and etching, including several other members of the Füssli family. And collections of landscape engravings were something of a Zurich speciality. Gessner's own father-in-law was an art-collector, and in his house Gessner studied prints of Dutch, Italian and French paintings, and plaster casts of classical gems and cameos. In his *Brief über die Landschafts-mahlerey*, written in 1770, he related how he had taught himself as an artist. Only late in his development did he realise the importance of composition, so concerned was he with the accurate representation of detail. By 1768 art had become the passion of his life; as he admitted in letters of April of that year, he now considered himself more than an amateur and his ambition was to be recognised as an artist of repute. He sought the advice and encouragement of other artists and art-lovers – Anton Graff, the leading portrait painter in Germany, Christian Ludwig von Hagedorn, the brother of the poet Hagedorn, and Adrian Zingg. He was familiar with the art theory and criticism of his time. The letter on landscape painting contains references to Gérard de Lairesse, a follower of Poussin and author of an influential treatise on art published in 1716; to Christian von Hagedorn's *Betrachtungen über die Mahlerei* of 1762; Webbs *Enquiry into the Beauties of Painting*; to the *Collection of Prints* with commentaries by Benjamin Ralph published by Boydell in 1763; to Winckelmann; Anton Raphael Meng's *Gedanken über die Schönheit* of 1765; and to Adam Oeser, artist and sculptor, friend of Winckelmann and Goethe. Gessner was much moved by enthusiastic descriptions of Meng's altar piece, *Himmelfahrt Christi*, in Dresden. He dedicated some of his etchings to Watelet, whose poem 'Sur l'art de peindre' was greatly esteemed at the time. From these names, and even more clearly from the *Brief über die Landschaftsmahlerey* itself, it is evident that Gessner subscribed to neo-classical aesthetics. He admitted that a purely naturalistic painting might please, if executed with great skill, but aspired to the art that contained an idea. He wished to overcome his own liking for unusual and picturesque aspects of nature, and to reproduce what was great and noble:

Aber bey dieser Art die Natur zu studieren, muss ich mich hüten, dass mich der Hang zum bloss Wunderbaren nicht hinreisse; immer muss ich mehr auf das edle und schöne sehen, sonst kann ich leicht in meinen Zusammensetzungen ins Abentheurliche fallen, und wunderbare Formen allzusehr häufen.[14]

He believed that taste for beauty and grandeur in nature could be formed by studying the masters of landscape painting and by reading poetry, particularly Thomson, and, to a lesser extent, Brockes. Art and poetry were, he thought, interrelated. In the late 1760s he discovered that his ideal was to be found in the works of Poussin and Claude, the seventeenth-century French painters who were the models and the inspiration for the great tradition of the classical or ideal landscape. In the work of Nicolas Poussin (and in that of his adopted son, Gaspard, for Gessner was interested in compositional effect rather than overall quality) he found nature portrayed as great and noble:

sie versetzen uns in jene Zeiten, für die uns die Geschichte und die Dichter mit Ehrfurcht erfüllen, und in Länder, wo unter dem glücklichen Clima jedes Gewächse seine gesundeste Vollkommenheit erreicht.[15]

In Claude he admired the spirit of charm and peace, 'Sanftheit und Ruhe':

Seine Landschaften sind Aussichten in ein glückliches Land, das seinen Bewohnern Überfluss liefert.[16]

Drawing inspiration from these painters, Gessner aimed to give expression to the vision of Arcadia that had fired much of his poetic writing, but a vision that was now less playfully Rococo, more firmly neo-classical.

Prior to the discovery that composition and overall effect were the most important factors in a landscape picture, Gessner studied and copied from nature and from engravings of earlier landscape artists, mostly seventeenth-century Dutch works. His method was eclectic. For trees he took as his models Antonie Waterloo, Herman van Swanefeld, and Nicolaes Berchem; for rocks Berchem, Salvator Rosa, the seventeenth-century Nuremberg artist J. F. Ermels, the Swiss Felix Meyer, and J. P. Hackert, a contemporary whose ideal landscapes were admired by Goethe. From Philip Wouwermann and Claude he learnt how to render distance, stretches of meadow and rolling hills. Gessner's desire to be true to nature, and the availability of prints in Zurich, explain his predilection for the Dutch landscapes. But he aimed at more than realism, and rejected both Dürer and Rubens as models for the painter seeking beauty.

Gessner's three series of landscape etchings were, in 1772, and several times subsequently, issued together as *Paysages dessinés et gravés par Gessner*. The first, ten *Landschaften in Waterloos Geschmack*, was dedicated to Watelet. The second, published two years later in 1768, consists of twelve *Landschaften im antiken Geschmack*. Ten *Landschaften mit mythologischen Figuren* followed in 1771. There was some improvement in composition over these years, and an increase in the use of contrast as well as a change of subject. Gessner began with pictures based on natural details observed in the vicinity of Zurich, but so composed that their local origin is all but unrecognisable, and featuring picturesque thatched cottages and crumbling towers, Dutch trappings that were later replaced by classical motifs. Although his hand was less inhibited in the later series, the technique remained poor, and the figures often appalling. Never did he approach the quality of Poussin or Claude. Nevertheless, he did capture the mood of peace that he wished to express. Even in these larger views, despite his intention to concentrate on the whole, his love for individual forms in leaves and rocks is seen in the carefully executed detail. His eye for the variety of leaf forms is evident, too, in the full-page illustrations he did for his works in the 1770s, where again the mood of harmony prevails.

Where Gessner was tempted to portray grandeur, heroic or sublime vistas rather than restful corners of gardens and woodland glades, his feeling was a less certain guide. Perhaps for this reason, but also because he relied largely on engravings done by Swiss predecessors and contemporaries, his Alpine views are not very impressive. These Swiss views he etched, six each year from 1780 to 1788, for the *Helvetischer Kalender*. Their small size made both richness of detail and the creation of a bold mood impossible, and because they were so tiny the picturesque elements, glaciers, waterfalls, chasms and curious geological formations could not be effectively rendered.

These views did not reach a large public, although only a few years later, as Switzerland and the Alps became synonymous with sublime and picturesque scenery, many such scenes, etched by others, sold throughout Europe. But it was as writer, rather than artist, that Gessner prepared the way for this vogue, simply by fostering the belief that nature was to be seen at its best in his homeland. His *Brief über die Landschaftsmahlerey* was very widely read, and, despite its emphasis on learning to paint from paintings rather than from nature, also encouraged contemporaries to associate Switzerland with feeling for natural beauty.

Although he relied on other artists (and his figures recall Italian Renaissance art as well as classical statues and reliefs), Gessner never ceased to study nature. Nor did he forget to say, in his

1   Anton Graff, *Portrait of Salomon Gessner* (oils, 1766)

2　Salomon Gessner, *Alpine stream with fisherman: right, on the bank,
a peasant house; in the background, mountains* (oils, 1786)

3   Title-page from Gessner's *Idyllen* (1756)

Nicht den blutbesprizten kühnen Helden, nicht
das öde Schlachtfeld singt die frohe Muse ; sanft
und schüchtern flieht sie das Gewühl, die leichte
Flöt' in ihrer Hand.

Gelokt durch kühler Bäche rieselndes Geschwa-
ze und durch der heilgen Wälder dunkeln Schatten, irrt sie an dem beschilften Ufer, oder geht
auf Blumen , in grüngewölbten Gängen hoher
Bäume , und ruht im weichen Gras , und sinnt
auf Lieder, für dich, für dich nur, schönste Daphne !

4   Vignette and beginning of the first idyll
in Gessner's *Idyllen* (1756)

5 Title-page of Part I of Gessner's *Schriften* (1762)

6   Title-page of Part III of Gessner's *Schriften* (1762)

7   Frontispiece to J. J. Hottinger's novel,
Briefe von Selkof an Welmar (1777)

8   Three vignettes in J. J. Eschenburg's translation of Shakespeare
(13 vols., 1775–82): scenes from *The Winter's Tale, Macbeth* and *2 Henry IV*

essay on landscape painting, that imitation should not destroy originality. His landscapes are, indeed, unique. They breathe a charm and freshness, and express, if somewhat awkwardly, an almost religious awe of nature. Less grand and heroic than the ideal landscapes of Poussin and Claude, Gessner's scenes have a Rococo delicacy, but no sign of the melancholy characteristic of Watteau. In their feeling for nature, his etchings might be compared with the work of William Blake and Samuel Palmer; but Gessner's lines are less bold and less fluid, there is a certain fussiness about the detail that detracts from the overall effect.

When Gessner used colour, the links between his work and Romantic art become clearer. His oil paintings are exceedingly rare, for he preferred, in common with many contemporaries, the softer tones of gouache. Less numerous than his etchings, his gouache landscapes also waver between the painterly Rococo and the linear classical styles. They often represent the same scenes as the etchings, being either studies for, or copies of them. They include ideal landscapes with classical buildings, views of Italy probably copied from prints, intimate woodland scenes and studies from nature. Most of the more finished pictures, with their classical temples, nymphs or Arcadian shepherds, clearly portray an imaginary world. Their mood of serenity without grandeur might link them with the work of Gainsborough, yet Gessner was not only a lesser artist, but also rarely attempted to equate ideal nature with observed reality. The staffage figures in his landscapes are nymphs rather than peasants.

He had begun to paint in Berlin, and as soon as he returned to Zurich, in the early 1750s, following a local tradition, he decorated interior walls with murals. Immediately after his marriage he concentrated on drawing, doing pen and wash sketches and watercolour studies, mostly as preparations for etched works. When in 1768 he sent a collection of drawings, etchings and gouaches to Melchior Grimm in Paris, they could not be sold. In that same year Watelet advised him that his work was spoilt by wealth of detail. He endeavoured to remedy this fault, and a certain improvement did come after 1780, when he turned from etching to painting. Nevertheless, his pictures are relatively small, and so rich in detail that they have to be seen at close quarters. Neither detail nor composition is clear from a distance. Delicacy and intimacy are characteristic of his subject-matter, too. He painted arbours with stone busts, trellisses covered by climbing and trailing plants, homely corners of a Rococo garden that has escaped the spirit of regimentation and might be inhabited by Ariel or bourgeois lovers. After 1780 he reduced the size of his figures until they became dwarfed by the landscape. Then his feeling for nature was expressed in an almost Romantic manner, but still with a touch of delicate sentiment and love of intimacy. His woodland glade scenes, with their evocation of mood, an inviting green coolness, point forward to the French Barbizon school. But two pieces, entitled *Die Träumerin* and *Daphne* (both 1780), are suffused with an extraordinary reddish glow, and elsewhere his rocks are an almost grotesque yellow. These are not, however, the nightmarish visions of Henry Fuseli, but pictures of idyllic warmth, in which the emotions of the artist are translated into colour. The occasional picturesque aspect and the contrasts of light and shade are subordinated to a sense of harmonious beauty. The nature he portrays is healthy, almost luxuriant; trees and plants seem to flourish in an ideal climate.

The mixture of classical composition and Romantic feeling for nature evident in Gessner's paintings is also characteristic of the landscapes of his contemporary Joseph Anton Koch. Another self-taught artist, Koch has been variously described as the greatest classical and the first Romantic landscape painter in Germany. Koch and Gessner both show how Pre-Romantic feeling for nature was beginning to break away from traditional technique and theory, but in very different ways. Koch painted sublime vistas, whose many planes and points of interest suggested the magnificence and variety of nature. Gessner's preference was for secluded corners, and the variety he saw was much smaller in scale, in the forms of stalks and leaves. He was very conscious of the play of light on foliage. His greens vary from brown to yellow, and he used an almost pointilliste technique in indicating touches of colour in masses of green leaf. In these respects his work points forward to nineteenth-century Realism; in total effect, indeed, some of his paintings are not too far removed from the pastoral scenes of Ludwig Richter, the sentimental post-Romantic illustrator and painter who admired Gessner's work.

Gessner's studies in pencil and wash, mostly done in the 1760s, reveal perhaps the most attractive aspects of his artistic talent. His sketches of trees are remarkably convincing in their detailed accuracy. Before retiring to his room to compose a picture, he spent many hours sketching in his favourite spots in nature; indeed, he seems to have gained most pleasure from this preparatory work. One or two of his monochrome sketches of local scenes are executed with a fluency and concentration on broad effect that are lacking in the gouache landscapes.

As a painter Gessner was an experimenter, unable to combine successfully the tradition of the ideal landscape with the realism of the Dutch school and his own Rococo and pre-Romantic sensibilities. His merit lies in his intention rather than his achievement. Nevertheless, his most characteristic landscapes are both charming and expressive. Had he belonged to a school of artists, or had talented disciples, his paintings might have become better known. Several passed into private collections, and a few hang in the 'Kunsthaus' in Zurich, but the majority of his works remain unframed, kept in folders in the municipal collections of his home town. They are striking in their originality. He was one of the first to turn to drawing and silhouette in a painterly age, yet his paintings are most remarkable for their colouring and suggestiveness. When Wilhelm Kolbe, a leading engraver of the early nineteenth century, etched some of Gessner's landscapes between 1805 and 1811, his superior technique and more definitely classical manner resulted in a loss of this characteristic suggestiveness and of Gessner's feeling for nature.

Gessner's conception of originality was not that of the 'Sturm und Drang'. He respected rules and decorum, and in the last year of his life was urgently warning his son Conrad against the cult of originality as it flourished among Germans in Rome:

Welch ein Unsinn, nichts anders hören zu wollen, als seine eigene Überzeugung und sein eigen Gefühl. Wer seinen Stolz auf den Grad treiben kann, ist auf dem sichersten Wege, zum Narrn zu werden. Wie leicht kann mein Gefühl falsch seyn, wie leicht mein Geschmack ausarten, wenn ich mich über kalter Untersuchung des Lobes und Tadels anderer, und über ihre Einsichten und Meynungen wegsetze. Daraus entstehen denn freylich jene originalen Feuerköpfe, die in ihrem eigenen Rauche dampfen, alles zu gross oder zu klein, alles schief, verschoben und gespenstermässig ansehen. Um's Himmelswillen! Lass Dich nicht mit hinreissen! Diese Leute haben freylich etwas Bezauberndes in ihrem Geschwätze, und können Menschen warmen Herzens und Kopfs, die nicht jedesmal untersuchen, leicht betäuben. Lass diese Herren auf ihren hochtrabenden Eseln über gesunde Vernunft und über Alles weggaloppieren...Bleibe Du auf dem Wege des gesunden Menschenverstandes; lass Fieberhafte Phantasie Dich nie von demselben abführen ...Wahre Vernunft und Grösse sind immer bescheiden...ich musste Dich warnen, vor dem fieberhaften Zustande von Männern denen man sonst Genie und Talente nicht absprechen kann.[17]

Earlier developments in German literature had not pleased Gessner. No longer was he a man unsure of himself, anxious to hear the opinions of others before committing himself, and eager to enjoy almost everything and anything in contemporary poetry. The respected 'Ratsherr' and internationally famous writer was, by 1770, well read in aesthetics and poetics, and his taste was formed. Johann Heinrich Füssli chose Gessner as his fictitious spokesman through whom to draw a picture of Zurich and Switzerland, and this Gessner speaks with wide knowledge and authority.[18] The real Gessner knew that he was opposed to anything that challenged the broad basis of Enlightenment morality and neo-classical aesthetics, and his acquaintances agreed with him. Ramler was bound to confirm his criticism of the bardic fashion in German literature; in a letter to his friend in Berlin, Gessner began with a rhetorical question:

Aber was sagen sie zu dem jezigen Modeton in Deutschland? Was zu den honig-süssen sentimentalen Säckelgen, die einem unter der Nase vergehn, ehe man sie eingeschlukt hat? Was zu dem eigenthümlich Nationalen Barden Ton? Müssen wir Sitten und Sprache und Mythologie aus den Zeiten holen, wo unsre Nation Wilde waren? Haben die Griechen ihren Geschmack nach jenen Zeiten geformt, da die Griechen mit den Schweinen noch um die Eicheln sich balgten? Was sagen sie zu der Abentheurlichen Hieroglyphischen Helden-Sprache, in der Klopstock und Herder jezt Sachen sagen, die schon oft ganz deutlich in Menschen-Sprache gesagt worden...Sehen sie, mein bester Freund! das Ding macht mich ein wenig unwillig, sonst bin ich ganz ruhig...[19]

He was now corresponding with the staunch rationalist Nicolai in Berlin, whom he complimented on his sequel to Goethe's *Werther* in which the hero is brought to realise the folly of passion. Gessner recognised the artistry of Goethe's novel, but deplored its lack of moral message:

Ich kan Ihnen nicht ausdrüken, mein theuerster Freund, wie sehr Ihr 'Werther' in Zürich gefallen hat...Wie viel wahrer, gesunder Verstand, mit dem Sie das wieder zurecht stellen, was Werther verderbt hat, oder verderben könte...Ich bewundere ihn [Goethe], wie er die Sache auszuführen gewusst hat; viele Situationen sind unverbesserlich und ganz Natur, aber er hätt' uns doch bey alle dem sollen merken lassen, dass Werther ein Narr ist, dass er sich so in diese Situationen hinein wirft und sich nicht mit gesunder Vernunft herausschleppt, das doch mit Menschenverstand ganz wol zu machen war.

Nicolai provided, in Gessner's opinion, 'die Haupt-Apotheke gegen diese Seuche' of 'Sturm und Drang'.[20]

There were enough opponents of 'Sturm und Drang' for Gessner to hope that it was a passing phase. Particularly flattering and encouraging were the respect and adulation accorded to him by many young writers. One became his acknowledged disciple. Franz Xavier Bronner, who had been an enthusiastic reader of Gessner's idylls and *Der Tod Abels* at school, fled from a monastery and found his way to Zurich, where he hoped to escape the clutches of the Catholic church and find greater humanity. He took a job as trainee compositor with Orell, Gessner, Füssli & Cie., and thus made contact with Gessner. Bronner felt greatly honoured to be invited to Gessner's house, and noted the goodness and humanity of the man that confirmed the impression given by his writings. He made friends with Heinrich Gessner; together they read the morning hymn from *Der Tod Abels* while watching the sun rise from the crest of the Uetliberg outside Zurich. At that moment Bronner began to compose an idyll, and admitted that this was not his first: he had written several while in the monastery in southern Germany, and was now persuaded to read them to Gessner, and to write more. Gessner, with great tact, made suggestions for improvements: he was mainly concerned with euphony, clarity and expressiveness:

Überhaupt kritisierte er einen Aufsatz niemals förmlich; sondern hielt etwa im lauten Lesen ein, wenn der Ausdruck nicht rund genug war; oder wiederholte die Stelle, um mich Horchenden aufmerksam darauf machen; oder brachte sein Bedenken als eine unschuldige Frage vor, wie diess oder jenes gemeynt sei? ob es nicht jemand missverstehen könnte? ob das Ganze, auf diese Art gestellt, wohl die beste Wirkung thun werde?[21]

Bronner's idylls were published in 1787 with a foreword by Gessner.

Gessner died on 2 March 1788 after suffering a stroke a few days before. His son reported that he died with a smile on his lips. His death was apparently as serene as his life – but allowance must be made for the understandable tendency of his family, friends and acquaintances to transfer idyllic qualities from his work to his life. For all knew that life in general was not wholly idyllic, and wished to see Gessner as an exception and an example. His widow was left in considerable financial difficulties, arising mainly from the failure of the porcelain factory; and his son Heinrich was not happy to cooperate with Judith Gessner and his father's friends and business associates, and started his own bookshop in Berne. But such problems were not noted in the many obituaries and short lives that appeared in magazines throughout Europe, and Gessner's first biographer, a young friend of the family, J. J. Hottinger, also stressed the harmony and contentedness of the poet's personality and life. All seemed to need a reassurance that the world was not of necessity a hard and unhappy place.

6 · THE GESSNER CULT

The cult of Gessner in France, started by Huber and Turgot in 1760, lasted for more than twenty years, until the eve of the Revolution. During this time Gessner was, it has been claimed, more popular than any French classic. Certainly the French were indiscriminate in their enthusiasm initially. In 1761 *Inkel und Yariko* was praised as a notable product of his genius,[1] and in 1766 *Die Nacht, Ein Gemälde aus der Sündflut* and his two plays were all translated. *La Mort d'Abel* was rendered into Latin hexameters, made into an epic of ten cantos, a three-act play, and given a sequel. Operas, ballets, dramas, and designs for Sèvres porcelain represented scenes from his life and works.[2] He himself became a legend, for he was thought to be a product of nature, almost uneducated, but good and wise. Many a Frenchman believed that the Swiss and the Germans lived idyllic lives in rural surroundings:

Contemple ces Germains, aujourd'hui nos modèles,
De la simple raison interprètes fidèles...
Ils habitent en paix la campagne et les bois.[3]

This picture of an Arcadian Germany was not created by Gessner alone, but he played an important part in its formation. Similarly many readers owed in large part to him an attitude towards nature and their fellow men that became general in the second half of the eighteenth century. His influence mingled with and was modified by that of others to encourage the development of a tender-hearted appreciation of human goodness, of domesticity and of simple rural pleasures. Ordinary readers, indeed, continued to appreciate Gessner's moral sentiments even after he was no longer fashionable in literary circles; he was widely read until the middle of the nineteenth century. For the rational optimism and the moral sensibility of the Enlightenment retained their hold on the minds of the middle classes throughout the Romantic period. A critic writing in the *Journal des Débats* of 1807 declared that Gessner would be a writer of international significance when Klopstock and Schiller had been forgotten.[4] Gessner's works were used in French educational institutions sixty years after his death. Although critics and writers preferred his idylls, *La Mort d'Abel* had a more lasting popular appeal; it was read more than any other German book in the late eighteenth and early nineteenth centuries.

Until the late 1780s French poets and writers, some distinguished in their own time, drew inspiration from Gessner. In many cases they did little more than translate him into verse or ransack his stories for material. Such paraphrases throw some light on the conception of natural poetry that held sway in French literary circles. Gessner was too advanced for the average French poet, as opposed to the average reader. For despite the enthusiasm of leading critics, many thought that his work suffered from lack of taste. Literary patriotism had not been entirely swamped by the tide of cosmopolitanism and xenomania. Good taste, part of the French heritage, could, it was thought, be applied with benefit to Gessner's naturalness. This attitude combined with his popularity to encourage second- and third-rate French writers to improve on his work. In the short term their imitations and adaptations, often travesties of the original, added to his fame. But ultimately they also contributed to the rejection of his work as artificial, for they were produced in a spirit of sophistication that looked to the past rather than the future. His French imitators were drawn to his sentiments, but they were more often inspired by *Daphnis* than by *Der Tod Abels*. Prettiness with a touch of sentiment was preferred to pathos, and Gessner's combination of Rococo and sentimental moods, translated and adapted to suit traditional French taste, became more 'précieux'.

Nicolas Germain Léonard, a creole from Guadeloupe, minor diplomat and a poet of some standing at the time, wrote a pastoral novel *Alexis* (1787) based on *Daphnis*, with a few episodes taken from Gessner's idylls. In his sentiments, his praise of virtue and domestic bliss, Léonard echoes Gessner quite faithfully. But he uses a more traditionally poetic language, whilst retaining something comparable to Gessner's balanced rhythms and simple syntax. The harvest scene from *Daphnis* is transmuted by consistently poetic diction:

L'été penchait vers sa fin; l'instrument de Cérès faisait tomber les épis, et l'air retentissait des chansons du moissoneur. On le voyait promener la faucille, ou ramasser les gerbes et dresser la meule dorée.[5]

Léonard's verse idylls, published in 1766 and 1771 and reissued in enlarged editions in 1775 and 1782, are as unoriginal as his *Alexis*. They were finally arranged in five books, each of ten to twelve idylls, of which six in the first book, five in the second, three in the third and two in the fourth are paraphrases of Gessner's idylls or of sections from his *Daphnis*. Most of the rest are derived from classical idyllic poets; that he looks to Virgil and the Hellenistic poet Bion rather than Theocritus is indicative of his taste. In these verse idylls, too, Léonard translates Gessner into more orthodox poetic language. Gessner's winter scene (V, 24):

Lieblich ists, wie aus dem Weissen empor die schwarzen Stämme der Bäume zerstreut stehn, mit ihren krummgeschwungenen unbelaubten Ästen...Schön ists wie die grüne Saat dort über das Feld hin die zarten Spizen aus dem Schnee empor hebt...

becomes:

> Quel beau mélange offrent ces grains
> Dont la pointe paraît à peine –
> Ces noirs souches de sapins
> Coupant la blancheur de la plaine...[6]

When imitating 'Der Wunsch' in his 'Le Bonheur', Léonard replaces Gessner's favourite contemporary German poets by the French classics, and sits in his dream habitation with La Bruyère on his knee. Léonard's works were well received, and only Melchior Grimm thought him quite unworthy of comparison with Gessner:

Gessner est un poète divin, et M. Léonard un honnête enfant, si vous voulez, et plus sûrement un pauvre diable.[7]

Generally, Léonard was highly regarded as a poet who, guided by Gessner, had discovered an exciting new field of idyllic poetry that promised much for the future of French literature.

A. Berquin, a popular writer of children's tales and a minor poet who revered Léonard, also in his idylls (1775) plundered Gessner for situations; for, as he admitted, he was not deterred by the number of imitations already published, since he believed that Gessner offered 'une abondante récolte à copier'.[8] His adaptations are even more 'précieux' than Léonard's. In his 'Les deux tombeaux', based on Gessner's 'Daphnis und Micon', Berquin omits the croaking frogs, and, where Gessner had foliage brushing a girl's face, he makes sure that we do not imagine brambles by naming the plant as a lilac in flower. Gessner's Daphnis comes to his girl's dwelling (V, 110):

In stiller Nacht hatte Daphnis sich zu seines Mädgens Hütte geschlichen; denn die Liebe macht schlaflos. Hell schimmerten die Sterne durch den ganzen Himmel gesäet; sanft glänzte der Mond durch die schwarzen Schatten der Bäume; still und düstern war alles; jede Geschäftigkeit schlief, und jedes Licht war erloschen.

Berquin elevates the tone and destroys the picturesqueness of the original:

> L'Amour connoît-il le repos ?
> Au tems où le sommeil, d'une urne bienfaisante,
> Verse à tous les mortels l'oubli de leurs travaux
> Daphnis veilloit au seuil du toit de son Amante.

> Et sur la plaine, et dans les airs,
> Regnoit profondément un amoureux silence.
> Phoebé, discret témoin, l'Écho des champs déserts,
> Étoient seuls dans sa confidence . . . [9]

Even more symptomatic of the way in which Gessner was appropriated in France is Blin de Sainmore's version of the opening of 'Milon'; Gessner wrote (V, 26):

Bey stillem Abend hatte Mirtil noch den Mond-beglänzten Sumpf besucht, die stille Gegend im Mondschein und das Lied der Nachtigal hatten ihn in stillem Entzüken aufgehalten.

His imitator translates freely:

> Sur le bord d'un canal, dont l'onde transparente
> De la soeur du soleil répétoit la clarté,
> L'heureux Idas avoit goûté
> De la fin d'un beau jour la fraicheur séduisante. [10]

Other writers chose to imitate Gessner in poetic prose rather than in sophisticated madrigal verse. J. B. Leclerc, an academic and politician, who also wrote verse idylls in the manner of Fontenelle, untouched by Gessnerian influence, produced variations on themes and situations from Gessner in his prose poems (1786).[11] In style he follows the tradition of heightened French prose; like Gessner, Leclerc mixes sentiment with charm, but unlike him he introduces moral comments, and underlines the elegiac tone by writing of the idyllic world as past beyond recall. Prose idylls, indeed, became fashionable after Gessner, but writers drew inspiration not only from him, but also from the French tradition, particularly Fénélon's *Télémaque*. The artificial diction of French poetry that Rousseau contrasted with Gessner's style is still very evident in Gessner's imitators, as can be seen again in Mlle de Levesque's prose idylls (1786) whose themes are virtue and compassion. She has a girl appear on an animal whose base name could be indicated by periphrasis only: it is 'un de ces animaux, qui, sans avoir la noblesse du cheval superbe, ne nous rendent pas des services moins précieux'.[12]

This same lady wrote an idyllic epic in prose, *Lise et Alexis*, that owes a great deal to *Daphnis*. But it includes more melodrama:

here the wicked rival does not simply deceive the lovers, he attempts to murder the hero. At his trial, Alexis appeals for clemency, and the criminal is so moved that he promises to live in self-imposed banishment, as indeed he does, until he dies happy in the knowledge that Alexis and Lise are blissfully united in marriage.

In *Le Lévite d'Éphraïm*, that much more distinguished admirer of Gessner, Rousseau, told a story of atrocity culminating in the final triumph of virtue. In his *Confessions*, Rousseau relates that he attempted to treat the biblical story in the manner of Gessner. Its horrors were to be alleviated by sentimentality and a simple style, 'une plus antique simplicité en toute chose'.[13] The idyllic and sentimental episodes, the references to the simple ways of the Israelites, and above all Rousseau's poetic prose in this minor work do, indeed, recall Gessner's idylls. The epic pretensions of *Le Lévite d'Éphraïm*, its division into cantos, derive from *Der Tod Abels*.

Another author who wrote under the influence of Gessner, but with rather more originality than most of his imitators, was J. P. Florian. With his pastoral novel *Estelle* (1788) he produced an extremely popular work that was itself to give great impetus to the type of literature encouraged by Gessner's success; but it also marked a move away from the Arcadian idyll towards more realism and more excitement. In an essay on pastoral that prefaces *Estelle*,[14] Florian paid tribute to Gessner's sentiments, and the novel echoes Gessner in its moral and sentimental attitudes. But Florian also argued that a pastoral novel could be more interesting than an idyll, and his admiration for Longus's *Daphnis and Chloe* is reflected in the complications of the plot and the exciting adventures of *Estelle*. Florian puts greater emphasis than Gessner on action, and is less selective in his portrayal of rural life: he describes not only the countryside beside the river Garonne, but also – quite exactly – the practical business of sheep-shearing.

Since Gessner aroused or renewed interest in pastoral or idyllic literature in France, in poetic prose, and in morally satisfying episodes, the estimate that more than one hundred and fifty works in French were in some sense imitations of Gessner may not be totally unrealistic.[15] He certainly influenced the development of sentiment, both in literature and in life. But he did not invent it, nor is it likely that French literature would have evolved in a fundamentally different way had he not been famous. Distinguished works have been linked with his name. Yet one of these, Bernardin de St Pierre's *Paul et Virginie*, shares with Gessner only a general interest in simplicity and innocence and the use of poetic prose; and André Chénier's idylls are similar to Gessner's only in their exaltation of virtue and nature. Nevertheless, since Gessner played such an important part in the rise of sentimentality and Neo-Classicism, and since his name was so familiar to writers and readers, it is right that he should be remembered in this context even when his direct detailed influence cannot be established. Indirectly, through the spirit of the age, Gessner's impact on the course of French literature and on the development of taste was very significant, more significant than his influence on second-rate writers of verse and prose and his kindling of new interest in pastoral poetry. He could not have pleased the mass of readers more, even if he had deliberately aimed at popular success. His sentiments, his descriptions of nature, and his simple language seemed new, particularly when included in the idyllic genre. He was one of the first foreign writers to come to the notice of an increasingly cosmopolitan age, and this added to his novelty at first. But he also expressed ideals of naturalness that created a more lasting response. In France, and more particularly in England, he contributed to the revival of religious feeling that was to culminate in the Romantic era.

The story of Gessner's reception in England shows even more clearly that his main appeal was to the ordinary reader. For English critics and authors of standing were far less enthusiastic than the French. There was less interest in the idyll as a genre. Gessner's 'realism' did not make much impression, for he gave less local colour than Ambrose Philips and his nature descriptions were not so detailed as Thomson's. His sentimental scenes of virtue and affection scarcely represented anything new in the land of

Richardson and the domestic drama. Whereas the French contrasted Gessner's style with traditional poetic diction, any contrast
with Augustan poetry did not strike the English so forcibly. *Der
Tod Abels* suffered from direct comparison with Milton. Even
Gessner's poetic prose seemed of little consequence when
measured against the more dramatic development of 'natural'
poetic diction represented by Macpherson's *Ossian*. It has been
claimed[16] that Macpherson's rhythmical prose was influenced by
Gessner. The Scotsman was, indeed, influenced and encouraged
by Hugh Blair, one of the most distinguished of Gessner's admirer's
in Britain. But, as we shall see, Blair refrained from pronouncing
on Gessner's style; and, in any case, Macpherson had shown the
first of his bardic poems to John Hume in 1759, and his *Fragments
of Ancient Poetry* were published in 1760, a year before Gessner
appeared in English. There is no evidence that Macpherson knew
German, and it seems that his measured prose was inspired by
Lowth's ideas on Hebrew poetry, also propagated by Blair. The
dark tones of *Ossian* are nowhere paralleled in Gessner, and any
very general similarities of style between the two derive from
their common inspiration, the Bible. *Ossian* and Gessner represent
very different attempts to capture the simplicity of natural poetry.

The Scot Blair was, it seems, the only leading critic or academic
in Britain to judge that Gessner's idylls marked an exciting new
venture. In his *Lectures on Rhetoric and Belles Lettres* (1783) he
remarked on the insipidity of pastoral poetry, but asked whether
the repetition of commonplaces was inevitable in the genre.
Could not the range of pastoral be widened to include more sentiment in tune with modern sensibility? Once he had seen Gessner's
idylls in English translation, he concluded that Gessner had fully
exploited these possibilities:

The above observations on the barrenness of the common eclogue were written
before any translation from the German had made us acquainted in this country with
Gessner's Idyls, in which the ideas that had occurred to me for the improvement
of pastoral poetry, are fully realised...Of all the moderns, M. Gesner, a poet of
Switzerland, has been the most successful in his pastoral compositions. He had
introduced to his Idyls (as he entitles them) many new ideas. His rural scenery is
often striking, and his descriptions are lively. He presents pastoral life to us, with

all the embellishments of which it is susceptible; but without any excess of refinement. What forms the chief merit of this poet is, that he writes to the heart; and has enriched the subject of his Idyls with incidents that give rise to much tender sentiment. Scenes of domestic felicity are beautifully painted. The mutual affection of husbands and wives, of parents and children, as well as of lovers, are displayed in a pleasing and touching manner. From not understanding the language in which M. Gessner writes, I can be no judge of the poetry of his style; but, in the subject and conduct of his pastorals, he appears to me to have outdone all the moderns.[17]

Blair's hesitation about Gessner's style may be explained by the quality of the English translation. Three different renderings of the idylls were published in 1762, of which the most successful was a verse paraphrase by a certain A. Penny. Based on the French of Huber, they were a direct consequence of Gessner's fame in France. But critical attention was concentrated on *The Death of Abel*. Mrs Mary Collyer's translation that appeared in 1761 was neither inspired nor painstakingly exact. Huber's translation was remarkably faithful to the original, but, in using it, Mrs Collyer followed the then much more usual technique of paraphrase rather than of literal translation. She exaggerated the rhetoric and pathos, following the tradition of Miltonian English, and thus destroyed much of the flavour and picturesqueness of the original. By 1803 John Aikin was in a position to note that *The Death of Abel* did not appeal to 'persons of a refined literary taste' because of the 'turgid and affected style in which it had been drest by the English translator',[18] but the early reviewers echoed the judgements of French critics, listing over and over again the qualities of simplicity or naiveté, touching sentiments and pathos, moral propriety and lively descriptions of nature. Without the French they would have had little or nothing to say. These English reviewers of Gessner impress by their facility of style rather than by knowledge of their subject; they were mostly hacks who did not always distinguish between the biblical epic and the idylls. Yet the number of these reviews, and, above all, the many editions of *The Death of Abel* (eighteen between 1761 and 1782) show that Gessner was widely read. The painter Henry Fuseli (Gessner's godson Johann Heinrich Füssli) noted in 1765 that Gessner was almost the only German poet known in England; he doubted whether the idylls would appeal to the robust character of the English.[19] Another German visitor to Britain, the writer Carl Philip Moritz, observed in 1782 that *The Death of Abel* was the only German work to have made any great impression there; indeed, it had been reissued more often in England than in Germany.[20] Gessner's biblical epic was extraordinarily popular, and remained so well into the nineteenth century. When William Taylor, the champion of German literature in England, translated Goethe's *Iphigenie auf Tauris* in 1793, it sold one hundred and fifty copies in a year; Bürger's *Lenore* was even less successful as a publishing venture.[21] But *The Death of Abel* was to be found, alongside *Pilgrim's Progress* and *Robinson Crusoe*, in the bookshops of small towns and at country fairs.[22] Short lives of Gessner, based on Hottinger's biography, were printed in periodicals in 1796 and 1797 in response to public interest. To the ordinary reader aesthetic judgements were largely irrelevant. What mattered was the content of the book. It was considered morally and religiously edifying. An anonymous admirer of Gessner wrote in 1766 that *The Death of Abel*, 'whose characteristic distinction is devotion', should be read by the whole family, and particularly by 'the young person, who will gradually find herself able to write and to discourse, to live and to die, like a Christian'.[23] Critics writing in the early nineteenth century confirm that Gessner's work was regarded as a 'good book' and appealed to readers of a religious turn of mind because of its scriptural subject and its morality. In 1810 it was still 'the wonder and delight of the young and the pious in humbler classes of society',[24] and translations continued to be published for some time after that.

Gessner's success in England must be understood in the context of the 'Great Awakening'. In 1761, when *The Death of Abel* first appeared, Wesley's Methodism had become a movement or great strength, and the Moravians were at the height of their popularity. The climate was favourable for the reception of the 'German stories', among them Klopstock's *Messias* and Bodmer's *Noah*. Gessner's work was the first of this type to be translated, and the most successful, probably because it was relatively short and its religious attitudes more 'modern'. Containing little dogma, it was acceptable to most varieties of religious belief, and, while depicting the sufferings of a sinner, it proclaimed the goodness of God and man. The belief that Gessner was a simple man, and Switzerland an idyllic, and Protestant, land, also facilitated his adoption in wide circles.

English imitators of Gessner followed the pathos of *Der Tod Abels* rather than the charm of his idylls. But, like their French equivalents, they were doubtful about the simplicity of his language, in so far as this was betrayed in the translations. They chose a higher poetic tone, a flowery and rhetorical prose, emulating the grandeur of Milton.

The Death of Cain, in five books after the manner of The Death of Abel, by a Lady (London, 1789, pp.vf.) claimed to be 'in all its parts fashioned to the modulation of the much admired symmetry of the plaintive Swiss projector, whose harmonious numbers agreeably entertain and smoothly strike the ear with a pleasing symphony'. This sequel to Gessner's work tells of Cain's suffering, repentance and peaceful death. Sublime and terrible emotions are expressed in long rhetorical speeches accompanied by exaggerated gestures. The style is deliberately highflown. Later a certain W. H. Hall claimed this epic as his own and republished it in an even wordier version.[25] In 1821 another *Death of Cain*, ostensibly by a John Macgowan, in reality a slightly amended reissue of Hall's work, was published with a new translation of *The Death of Abel*.[26] An abridged *Death of Cain*, by G. Stephens, appeared in 1810.

The English idyll in the late eighteenth century, as represented by William Richardson, John Scott and John Cunningham, seems to have been untouched by Gessner's influence. But great claims have been made by one student of Gessner's reception and influence in England. By assuming that almost any emotional reaction to nature, children or animals, any portrayal of domestic bliss, and any idyllic episodes in Blake, Cowper, Wordsworth, Coleridge and Byron must have been indebted to Gessner, Bertha Reed[27] claimed that he had a very significant impact on the English

Romantics. But this was to confuse Gessner with a broad tendency in literary history of which he was but one representative. The extent to which the English Romantics followed or reacted against a conception of nature that they associated with Gessner must remain obscure. Where they mentioned his name, they often did so with scorn. Yet most of them were familiar with his work to some extent, and he did influence Coleridge and Byron in a very minor way.

In 1798 Coleridge suggested to Wordsworth that they should together write a sequel to *The Death of Abel* to be called *The Wanderings of Cain*. Wordsworth was to write the first canto: it did not materialise. Coleridge, however, did compose the second canto, which is modelled on Gessner in several respects. The innocent child, Cain's son, is introduced as a sentimental contrast to the wretchedness of his father; his innocence is linked with the carefree play of animals. Coleridge's prose, with its concentration on direct speech, its repetitions and inversions, biblical phrases, and spirit of childlike simplicity, his use of 'tableaux' to balance wild gestures and expressions of pain and despair recall *Der Tod Abels*. The repentant Cain was to find the God of Mercy; this consoling conclusion had been suggested by Gessner himself and appears in all the sequels to his biblical epic. In concept and form, the fragment of *The Wanderings of Cain* is closest to the model and the most readable of the imitations. Though it is not counted among Coleridge's greatest achievements, it is less verbose and flowery than the other stories of Cain mentioned above, simpler in language, indeed, than *Der Tod Abels* itself.

Some three or four years later, Coleridge was still occupied with Gessner. In 1802 he published a poem entitled 'The Picture, or the Lover's Resolution', which is a free imitation of Gessner's 'Der feste Vorsatz'. Coleridge's reluctant lover is converted from scorn of females, not by the footprint of an unknown maiden, but by the discovery of a picture done by his sweetheart on 'birchen bark' with the juice of whortleberries. Coleridge does not follow Gessner's Rococo conception of love as amusement, but reflects on its folly. The setting is clearly English, and its picturesque elements more clearly established. Yet, besides the general plan of the poem, Coleridge takes many descriptive details from Gessner. There are similar touches of charm in both. But the English poet describes the same, or similar, natural features much more vividly. In 1802, too, he was planning to translate *Der erste Schiffer* into English verse. He liked the general idea of Gessner's work, but had doubts about the way it had been executed. The heroine's thoughts seemed to Coleridge to lack real innocence, and the intervention of the classical deities to lack seriousness.[28] A few days later he decided that it was not the psychology, but the dramatic organisation of the story that was deficient.[29] He reported to Sotheby that he had translated the work, but no more was ever heard of it; and in 1811 he was toying with the idea of writing a quite different version of the invention of the first boat,[30] but this plan, too, came to nothing.

Robert Southey's 'English Eclogues' were written immediately after his meeting with William Taylor, when he was infected by Taylor's enthusiasm for German literature. But Southey's knowledge of Gessner's work was apparently extremely slight, and his poems show no sign of indebtedness to him.

Nor was Lord Byron's *Cain* (1821) yet another sequel to Gessner's epic. Byron's hero is a Faustian rebel. Byron had read Gessner at school; and, no doubt, his choice of subject was influenced by his memories of *The Death of Abel*. He follows Gessner in some details: he provides Cain with a wife and children in order to create sentimental episodes, and the pious speeches of Adam and Abel sometimes recall Gessner's tone. The conspicuous use of repetition and parallel might also owe something to Gessner.

Although William Blake's strange genius as revealed in his pictorial art and poetry shares some elements with Gessner, his *The Ghost of Abel* was probably occasioned by Byron's *Cain*, and has nothing in common with *Der Tod Abels*. The young Blake did, however, experiment with rhythmical prose in the manner of Gessner.

Thomas Hood mentions *The Death of Abel* in his 'The Dream of Eugene Aram, the Murderer' (1829). The conscience-stricken schoolmaster finds one of his pupils reading Gessner's work. This testifies to the popularity of the book, but nothing in Hood's poem reveals Gessner's influence.

Coleridge was not the only English Romantic who, in contrast to the general public reaction, prized the charm as much as the moral and religious sentiments of Gessner. The minor Romantic poetess Mrs Felicia Hemans (who wrote the original of 'The boy stood on the burning deck') did a verse translation of Gessner's 'Morgenlied';[31] it is a poor rendering of a poor original. She was conversant with much of German literature, but Herder, Schiller and the German Romantics made a greater impression on her than did Gessner.

As in France, the story of Gessner's success in Britain represents a significant chapter in the history of taste, but, despite the interest shown in him by major writers, a minor episode in the history of literature. In America, too, he was popular until about 1820, as a religious writer.

The nations of Europe came to know Gessner's work as a result of his fame in France. Although the full spate of translations ended in 1788, he continued to be rendered into every conceivable European language, including Modern Greek and Welsh, until well into the next century. The Danes, exceptionally, were introduced to Gessner, not through Huber's translation, but by the German poet Gerstenberg. Gessner was translated into Swedish and Dutch in 1762, into Danish in 1763, Polish in 1768, Portuguese in 1778 and Spanish in 1785. The Italians seemed to have rivalled the French in their enthusiasm, indeed outdid them in the number of translations produced. In Italy Gessner gave new life to pastoral (most imitations were written in verse), and had some influence on writers of the Romantic era, on Girolama Pompei, Pindemonte and Leopardi. His greatest champion there was Bertola, an enthusiast for German poetry. In Spain, on the other hand, his influence was restricted to the Pre-Romantic generation, and was partly occasioned by the writings of the Scot, Hugh Blair, who was held in great esteem. In Romania, Gessner's period of fame came between 1830 and 1840; there the rise of nationalist literature brought an abrupt end to his success. The story of his reception in

Sweden, where he was championed by Gjörwell, who introduced his compatriots to much foreign literature, is more typical. Gjörwell did not think Gessner's writings unrealistic, rather he tried to relive, with his family and friends, a life of pastoral innocence. Gessner was one of the first German authors to find a public in Sweden at a time when that country was dominated by French taste, yet he also appealed to those who rejected French standards. There were several translations and imitations of Gessner in Swedish, mostly between 1765 and 1795. Most of those who wrote in the manner of Gessner are now forgotten, and his influence on two important poets, Thorild and Lidner, did not extend beyond their early works. Thorild developed Swedish prose as a poetic medium, but *Ossian* soon replaced Gessner as his inspiration. Gessner's greatest success was with ordinary readers, especially women.

Each nation, each individual, found something slightly different to admire and love in Gessner's work. Yet one aspect dominated the story of his reception: his sentimentality. Whether the emphasis was on aesthetic, moral or religious considerations, the idea of naiveté, innocence and simplicity, appealed everywhere. When the reaction against Gessner came, it took different forms, varying from contempt to indifference, but everywhere it accompanied the development of new ideas of naturalness.

In England critics rejected sentimentality associated with sustained pathos and rhetoric. Early commentators had not been entirely happy with Gessner's style, but placed most, if not all of the blame on his translator. But by the mid nineteenth century condemnation became general. The *Encyclopaedia Britannica* of 1856 reflected a general view in calling his works repetitious and tiresome.[32] In 1897 *The Eclectic Review* declared *The Death of Abel* unreadable, a dreary and mechanical performance.[33] Gessner's work was neither anchored in reality, not acceptable as an ideal. This criticism echoed that made earlier in Germany, where the reaction against Gessner was expressed with greater vehemence.

7 · GERMAN REACTIONS

Gessner's poetic writings were widely read and remained popular with the general reading public in Germany until well into the nineteenth century. *Der Tod Abels* was not quite such a singular success here as in England, but it was issued in ten editions between 1758 and 1800 and was universally known. It was, of course, a major part of Gessner's *Schriften*, and these appeared in nineteen editions between 1762 and 1839. But, from about 1770, there developed a great gulf between the taste of the general public and that of leading critics and writers, who reacted against Gessner rather earlier than their colleagues in other countries, and with greater incisiveness. The fervour with which they attacked him reflects the degree of his success. But critics, as distinct from the public, had no doubts that his idylls represented his real claim to fame. His detractors included men of great genius, so well known today that it is often forgotten how isolated they were from general opinion. They tended, in their consciousness of their isolation, to overstate their case. But there were other reasons, apart from exasperation, that determined their dismissal of Gessner. Those who read him in the original could not blame the translator, or a different national taste, for his supposed weaknesses. Furthermore, Gessner's success abroad was not, in the long run, helpful to his reputation in Germany: men who were passionately concerned that German poetry should free itself from the tutelage of French taste had misgivings about a writer whose fame was made in Paris. Besides, literary developments in Germany moved very quickly during the latter part of Gessner's lifetime, with a violence not paralleled in other countries, and he was associated with trends and personalities that soon fell into disrepute: with the Anacreontics, with descriptive poetry, and with Bodmer. The 'Sturm und Drang' generation, for which he had so little sympathy, advanced ideas of nature and of poetic genius quite different from his. The younger writers were attracted to the theme of family strife as found in *Der Tod Abels*, and not averse to sentiment, but they were much more interested in stark tragedy and horror. They began to link nature with passion, and to stress fate rather than providence. From the new standpoint it was easy to dismiss Gessner as an imitator who lacked creative genius, or one who misunderstood those classics whom he claimed to follow. In France he was proclaimed as the herald of a new age of poetry; this was not felt so strongly in Germany, where the more extreme revolutionary spirit of Klopstock exerted a greater fascination. When Gessner congratulated Nicolai on his sequel to Goethe's *Werther*, he expressed his solidarity with members of the older generation and adherents of established values, who, whatever their differences, came closer together in their rejection of 'Sturm und Drang'. The rationalistic, sentimental and Rococo tendencies of mid-eighteenth-century literature belonged to one cultural scene; this cultural tradition lived on in the late Enlightenment, and retained its hold on the mass of the reading public, despite 'Sturm und Drang', Weimar Classicism, and German Romanticism, well into the next century. Among its representatives we find the admirers and defenders of Gessner until 1800. After that date its values were seen to be represented, in the sphere of idyllic poetry, by Voss rather than by Gessner. Neither sales of Gessner's works, nor positive appraisals of his poetic achievement ceased dramatically as soon as Herder and Goethe threw doubts on his genius. In any case these first important attacks on him were not as destructive in intent as was later assumed.

The comments of Gessner's German admirers between 1760 and 1790 reflect the broad basis of his appeal in that age. They add little to what was said in France, indeed often seem to derive from the observations of French critics, reminding us once again of the cultural unity of Europe at that time and of the general respect for French opinion in matters of taste. These German commentators were proud that Gessner's achievement had been recognised in Paris. They drew attention to his melodic language, natural style, his descriptions of nature, touching sentiments and situations, and edifying examples of moral attitudes and behaviour.

In the second edition (1762) of his adaptation of Batteux's aesthetics, Ramler ranked Gessner beside Theocritus, and stated that he had captured the spirit of the Ancients.[1] J. G. Sulzer, the associate of Bodmer, in his *Allgemeine Theorie der schönen Künste* of 1771, an important compendium of Enlightenment views on art and poetry, placed Gessner first in merit among modern writers of pastoral or idyllic poetry, surpassed only by Theocritus and Virgil. He believed that his idylls could do more than Rousseau's rhetoric to bring men to a life of virtue.[2] J. J. Eschenburg expressed, in his *Entwurf einer Theorie und Literatur der schönen Wissenschaften* (1783), patriotic pride in Gessner:

Fast in keiner Dichtungsart haben die Deutschen so unstreitigen Vorzug vor den Ausländern, als in dieser [the idyll]. Sie verdanken ihn vornehmlich der so glück-lichen und originalen Schäfermuse Gessner's [sic.][3]

When, in 1788, Eschenburg published a collection of texts to illustrate his theoretical work, he included idyllic writings chosen, it seems, to show Gessner's influence; examples of Gessner's work were not included, but simply because they were so well known.[4] Even as late as 1804, in another theory of literature, J. J. Schlegel's *Anfangsgründe einer Theorie der Dichtungsarten*, we find an expression of uncompromising admiration for Gessner:

Das Ideal, das sich unser Gessner von der Idylle geschaffen, ist unverbesserlich.[5]

It is, perhaps, significant that these positive appraisals of Gessner's literary merit mostly emanated from Berlin, the centre of the late Enlightenment in Germany.

These theorists did not agree on all matters. Sulzer wrote that idylls could only be written in idyllic situations and implied that Gessner's works corresponded to Swiss reality, whereas Eschenburg thought that the idyll, and Gessner, portrayed an ideal Golden Age. Nevertheless, all tended to define the genre according to their own interpretation of Gessner. Before 1756, J. A. Schlegel had distinguished between bucolic and pastoral poetry and declared descriptive passages inappropriate in the latter. In 1759, almost certainly in order to accommodate Gessner, he revised his argument and admitted description to pastoral. J. A. Schlegel did not believe that comic elements could be integrated into an idyll. This traditional view was also revised as a result of Gessner's success: Moses Mendelssohn, attacking Schlegel in the *Literaturbriefe* of 1762,[6] used Gessner to illustrate his own theory of the idyll, according to which the manner, not the subject-matter, made the genre. Thus he could justify some supposedly non-idyllic, comic and even near-tragic aspects in Gessner. Otherwise Mendelssohn's views were quite conventional: Gessner had struck the right balance of ideal and real components and could be compared with Theocritus and Virgil. Yet, in suggesting that approach rather than subject made an idyll, he heralded a new development in poetics and opened the way for the non-pastoral idyll that was, a few years later, to replace the Gessnerian model.

There were a few voices dissenting from the general admiration, raised by those who might be called reactionary in their literary views. Frederick the Great of Prussia, in his essay on German literature, written to emphasise its defects when compared with French poetry, admitted only reluctantly that some thought highly of Gessner; since these included, as we have seen, his own sister, he said no more.[7] Joseph Freiherr von Penkler, in an uninspired and eclectic *Abhandlung vom Schäfergedichte* (1767), echoed pre-Gessnerian theory and the standpoint of Fontenelle, and criticised Gessner for not idealising his characters enough.[8]

Gessner received many letters from admiring readers. They show that it was his depiction of sentiment and virtue that made the greatest impression. Christian Felix Weisse, dramatist and friend of Lessing, wrote to Gessner in 1764 to acknowledge the emotional effect of his writings:

Ihre Schriften sind meiner Frau und meine süsseste Unterhaltung auf dem Lande: wie oft wünschen wir uns da den zärtlichen Dichter persönlich kennen zu lernen, der solche Empfindungen einflösst, die wir uns alsdann in der feurigsten Umarmung vorstammeln.[9]

Even young men associated with the 'Sturm und Drang' movement were among his admirers, and this after Herder had led the attack against Gessner's reputation as a poet: J. H. Merck and F. M. Leuchsenring wrote to Gessner in February 1772 to praise the power of his works.[10] The contemporary cult of sentiment coloured many such individual tributes. In 1780 Johann Lorenz Benzler, who had included idylls by Gessner in a collection of stories for children that he had edited, wrote to the author to tell him how much he admired his work and how he owed his moral education to him.[11] Some of these exuberant expressions of praise and gratitude prefaced a request that Gessner should look through the unknown letter-writer's own poetic attempts. They were not necessarily insincere on that account. A certain Franz Xavier Beckert of Freiburg simply coveted a reply from Gessner that he might treasure; he wrote in 1774, the year Goethe's *Werther* was published, and his letter is couched in the emotional manner of that time, not so very different from the epistolary style of Goethe's hero:

Erschrecken Sie nicht. Sie empfangen einen Brief von einem Menschen, der Sie von Person gar nicht kennt. Aber wie? sollte ich Sie nicht durch Ihre vortrefflichen Schriften kennen, welchen die gelehrteWelt ihren Beyfall schenkt. Wie Gessner, der göttliche Gessner! soll mir unbekannt seyn? Allein es ist nicht meine Absicht, Sie zu loben. Man wird dadurch zu ausschweifend, und scheint zu schmeicheln. Wie viel müsste man hersetzen, mein Gessner, bis man Sie so loben würde, wie es Ihre seltenen Vorzüge verdienen!

Ich bitte Sie, Hochzuehrender Herr, um Ihre Freundschaft. Um alles, was ich bitten kann, bitte ich Sie darum. Und o! wie glücklich werde ich mich schätzen, wenn Sie mir selbe schenken! – Schon bin ich ganz ausser mir. Ich traume, mein Gessner, ich träume. Schon stammle ich den Namen, den süssen und reitzenden Namen, dass ich Ihr Freund bin. Ihnen schwöre ich meine Liebe auf ewig zu. Gott! wie heilig ist dieser Schwur! Entzückt schau' ich mich in Ihren holden Umarmungen. Der Himmel selbst lächelt auf uns herab und billigt unsere Verbindung...Verzeihn Sie, wenn ich den Trieben des Herzens zu viel nachgehangen habe. Ich bitte Sie endlich, und um was? Um Ihre Briefe bitte ich Sie: denn warum schreiben Sie so schön?...[12]

Eight years previously, in 1766, came the first serious questioning of Gessner's claim to fame. It was contained in an essay, 'Theokrit und Gessner',[13] by Johann Gottfried Herder, that brilliant, if erratic, critic and thinker who heralded or introduced new attitudes towards poetry and life. Haller and Wieland had already pointed out that there were differences between Theocritus and Gessner. Nevertheless, Gessner was often called 'the German Theocritus', for it was fashionable to thus affectionately or reverently raise modern poets to the classical Parnassus. Herder attacked the equation of Theocritus and Gessner, not so much to discredit Gessner, though this he did in large part, as to dismiss previous critical practice and the idea that a modern poet could ever write just as the Ancients had done. He also rejected the theory that the idyll should represent an ideal world. Like Gessner, Herder took Theocritus as his model in defining the genre, but he dismissed the Golden Age as a figment of the imagination.

Theocritus, he said, did not portray an ideal, but made reality poetically beautiful. His characters had moral deficiencies, he depicted a real world; Gessner's characters were perfect, his idyllic world was completely imagined and therefore unconvincing. Gessner's naiveté was artificial, Theocritus was natural. The idyll, wrote Herder, should produce an illusion of reality, it should please, but not aim to describe perfection nor to be morally instructive. Gessner had misunderstood the function of idyllic poetry.

Herder's rejection of Gessner's idylls as models of the genre and of his claim to naturalness was to have profound consequences. So influential were his remarks, and so new in their basic assumptions, that it is easy to overlook those passages in which Herder spoke in praise of Gessner. He particularly admired his descriptions of nature, although he contended that they were only incidental to the idylls: Herder was more concerned with his definition of the genre than with understanding the spirit of Gessner's work. He called Gessner a consummate artist in prose and a source of moral inspiration greatly welcome in the modern world. He regretted that he had to compare him with a poet so totally different as Theocritus. Yet the basic point had been made: Gessner's poetry was artificial, and not true poetry because not based on real experience.

Herder later completely revised his opinion. In his *Briefe zur Beförderung der Humanität* (1796) he wrote an unambiguously positive tribute to Gessner, perhaps the greatest that has ever been paid:

Warum ist *Gessner* von allen Nationen, die ihn kennen lernten, mit Liebe empfangen worden? Er ist bei der feinsten Kunst *Einfalt, Natur und Wahrheit*. In Darstellung einer reinen Humanität sollte ihn selbst das Sylbenmaas nicht binden; wie auf einem Faden, der in der Luft schwebt, lässet er sich in seiner poetischen Prose oder prosaischen Poesie jetzt auf blühende Fluren hinab, jetzt schwinget er sich in die goldenen Wolken der Abend- und Morgenröthe, bleibt aber immer in unserm blauen Horizont gesellig, froh und glücklich. Mit Kindern ward er ein Kind, mit den ersten Menschen Einer der ersten Schuldlosen Menschen, liebend mit den Liebenden und selbst geliebt von der ganzen Natur, die ihm in seiner Unschuld ihren Schleier wegzog. Gerade der einfachste Dichter, dessen ganze Manier Verbergung der Kunst war, ist unser berühmteste Dichter worden, und hat manche Ausländer mit dem süssen Wahne getäuscht, als sei alle unsere Poesie *reine Humanität, Einfalt, Liebe und Wahrheit*.[14]

By linking him with 'Humanität', the conception of human goodness and perfectibility cherished by the German Classics, Herder reminds us that Gessner's characters are not so far removed from Goethe's Iphigenie and Schiller's 'schöne Seelen'. But his generous recantation of his earlier verdict found little echo, apart from astonishment, in influential circles.

Goethe's review of Gessner's idylls of 1772,[15] published in the *Frankfurter gelehrte Anzeigen* of 1773, complements Herder's essay of 1766. Goethe, too, could appreciate Gessner's nature descriptions; he thought them extraordinarily precise, evocative and persuasive and, unlike Herder, he recognised that they were an integral part of his idylls. He also praised his descriptions of characters, but since there is little physical description of the persons in the idylls, Goethe must have provided details through his own imagination, nurtured by classical art (he says Gessner's figures recall antiquity), or have been thinking of Gessner's engraved illustrations. Goethe modified Herder's praise of the structure of the idylls: he found the longer pieces lacking in organisation. And he expanded on Herder's point about their unreality and lack of variety: Gessner brought no dramatic interest, no contrast or conflict between characters. Goethe, too, had a different conception of idyllic poetry. He preferred more realistic idylls, and this determined his liking for Gessner's 'Das hölzerne Bein'.

'Das hölzerne Bein', in the 1772 collection, tells of virtue in just the same way as the other idylls. But there is one difference: the scene is set in Switzerland and there is reference to an historical event, the battle of Näfels in 1388. This scarcely makes it realistic, but it was enough to cause Goethe to regret that Gessner had not written more Swiss idylls with a 'Nationalinteresse'. We may assume that Goethe also preferred this idyll because it suggested that harmony could be won, or might have to be defended, by heroic action.

Gessner's reputation among leading German poets never recovered after these attacks by Herder and Goethe. Indeed, some twenty years later there were signs of total rejection. Schiller, in his essay 'Über naive und sentimentalische Dichtung' (1795), had nothing good to say of him. He condemned poetic prose outright, and denied that Gessner's idylls represented an acceptable ideal of humanity. Gessner's vision of perfection was too limited, the ideal should, in any case, be placed in the future, not the past, if it was to spur men on to moral progress. Perhaps because he was so interested in the possibilities of idyllic poetry himself, Schiller did not allow Gessner as a worthy representative of the genre. August Wilhelm Schlegel, a leader of early Romantic thought in Germany, was equally scornful. Reviewing Hottinger's biography of Gessner in 1796,[16] he repeated all the adverse criticisms of Gessner made by Herder, Goethe and Schiller; he took particular exception to his lack of appeal to the Swiss or German reader looking for specifically local interest. This point was telling in the years that saw the rise of nationalist feeling in Germany. The contribution of Herder, Goethe, Schiller and A. W. Schlegel to German literature and their standing as critics meant that their condemnation became almost definitive for later generations. Yet they did not convince all their contemporaries, and Gessner was not so completely forgotten in the nineteenth century as has often been assumed.

These decisive attacks on Gessner were also attacks on his imitators. For in the 1760s and 1770s a spate of idylls in the Gessnerian manner were produced, mostly just as lacking in inspiration as their equivalents in France and the sequels to *Der Tod Abels* in England.

Many of the idylls written at this time were verse poems. The Rococo tradition in pastoral poetry survived, sometimes untouched by Gessnerian influence, without sentiment or moral. Translations of classical idyllic poets, Theocritus, Virgil, Bion and Moschus appeared in great numbers. The fashion for poetic prose started by Gessner was felt in all genres; in his autobiography, Goethe commented on the enormous influence of Gessner on German prose in the 1760s.[17] Many authors were inspired by Klopstock's experiments in poetic prose too. Within pastoral or idyllic writings Gessner's influence was most obvious and direct.

The best verse idylls of the period immediately after 1756 were those of Gessner's friend Ewald von Kleist. Before 1756 Kleist had written two idylls, rather conventional lover's complaints. Then, in 1757, he dedicated the idyll 'Cephis' to Gessner: it tells of a tree that stands as a monument to virtue; its 'heilig Rauschen' and the moral of the poem ('Der Himmel segnet stets die Redlichkeit' in the first version) point to Gessner's influence. Kleist evidently introduced moving morality into his idylls as a result of reading Gessner. In another idyll, 'Irin', he again echoed his friend in writing of the beauty of nature, the pleasure it gives to the virtuous man, and in comparing a long life to a day in spring. Kleist has his own characteristic tone and cannot be called a slavish imitator of Gessner. Yet Gessner's influence on a poet who was highly re-garded could only encourage minor poets to pillage Gessner's works for material.

One such third-rate writer was K. C. Reckert, whose idylls (1771) are based on situations described by Gessner.[18] In his open-ing idyll Reckert follows his model so closely that he almost equals Gessner's achievement as a writer of poetic prose. But elsewhere, despite abundant repetition, parallel and iambic sequences, his language falls far short of Gessner's stylistic stan-dard. Reckert shows no real feeling for nature, nor any excellence as a writer. A similar imitator, Hektor Wilhelm Freiherr von Günderode, was only sixteen when he published his Versuch in Idyllen (Karlsruhe, 1771). He was particularly attracted to Gess-ner's aetiological idylls, and copied them. Yet he had no more success than Reckert in fashioning a satisfying whole from pieces taken from his model and rearranged arbitrarily into a 'new' pattern.

A cross-section of the idylls of this time is given in an anthology, Idyllen der Deutschen (1774), edited by Klamer Schmidt. With seven idylls in this selection, Gessner is a clear favourite; next come Kleist, with four, and Rost, with three. Klamer Schmidt, whose Rococo leanings are evident from the choice of texts, describes the now forgotten Andreas Grader as the most promising idyllic poet since Gessner and Kleist. But he admits that Grader's prose style is not equal to Gessner's. Grader copied Gessner in trying to combine Rococo and sentimental elements. The fashion for biblical idylls, in which Klopstock's stylistic influence was strong, and for idylls set in the Middle East after the pattern of the English poet, William Collins (*Persian Eclogues*, 1742), also determined Schmidt's choice of texts.

The poets associated with the 'Göttinger Hainbund', with their patriotic leanings and worship of Klopstock, tended in their idyllic poetry, strangely enough, to continue the tradition of pastoral song as found in the work of Gleim and Kleist. Hölty's 'Das Feuer im Walde' may well, however, have been an attempt to surpass Gessner's 'Das hölzerne Bein' by introducing more realism. Hölty tells of a one-legged Prussian veteran who is reduced to begging but stirs patriotic feelings in two country lads. Closer to Gessner in their mixture of sentiment and charm are the idylls by Ernst Theodor Brückner published in the *Göttinger Musenalmanach* and in Voss's *Musenalmanach*. They mostly tell of children, and were intended to teach Christian values to young readers. Brückner regarded Gessner as one of his masters, but neither he, nor the other members of the 'Göttinger Hain' in the early 1770s could be called imitators of Gessner. They seemed to have no common programme for the idyll, and only Hölty and J. M. Miller introduced a new note of greater realism.

Equally vacillating in his approach to the idyll was the anonymous author of the *Neue Idyllen eines Schweizers* of 1780. The title of the collection is a tribute to Gessner, and the poet admits modestly that he cannot compete with his predecessor. His poetic prose follows the Gessnerian manner, but in subject he mixes two quite distinct modes, the sentiment and morality of Gessner and the amoral wit and sensuality of Rost: they are not happy bedfellows. Sometimes the tone is more realistic than Gessner's, sometimes more solemnly poetic. 'Sturm und Drang' influence is evident in passages of breathless emotion.

The idylls of Gessner's protégé, Franz Xavier Bronner, were published in 1787. Gessner himself, in the foreword to these *Fischergedichte und Erzählungen*, commended Bronner, though he expressed some reservations about the wealth of realistic detail in his descriptions. Watching life along a river, Bronner had the idea of emulating Gessner, but following Theocritus's fisher-idyll rather than the pastoral tradition. In 1794 he wrote in defence of fisher-idylls by reference to the classics. His taste for beauty in nature was not so firmly regulated as Gessner's: he describes tadpoles wriggling in a muddy pool and insects being devoured by fish and lizards. Yet such was his enthusiasm for nature that he integrates these details into the idyllic pattern. The characters, and the world they live in, are less than perfect, but Bronner treats imperfections with humour, and suggests that human goodness can overcome the problems of poverty and vice. In his style he learned much from Gessner. He concentrated on direct speech, and captured better than any other writer the rhythms of Gessner's prose: not surprisingly perhaps, since Gessner himself advised on the preparation of the texts. Bronner also followed Gessner's lead in writing stories of inventions and origins, including an imitation of *Der erste Schiffer*. But he failed to harmonise the Rococo charm and the use of classical myth with his realistic tendencies. Despite their Greek names his characters clearly belong to a northern landscape. Nor could he avoid sudden changes from sublimity to prettiness, as in this description of a sunrise:

Itzt standen sie auf einem Hügel am Ufer des Meeres stille, und sahen, wie sich im Osten die blässern Dünste allgemach färbten, itzt leichteres Roth in glänzende Feuerfarbe übergieng, und itzt sich zur blendenden Glut erhöhte....Kleine krystallhelle Tröpchen auf allen Kräutern schimmerten schöner als Perlen in der offenen Muschel. Junge spielende Weste jagten kleine röthlichverbrämte Wellchen ans Ufer...[19]

Like many of Gessner's followers, Bronner wanted to expand the scope of each idyll and was not satisfied to restrict each piece to one theme. Consequently his idylls often lack unity. But had they appeared twenty years earlier, the inclusion of greater realism, and the reference to social problems, combined with a humorous approach, would have been of greater importance for the history of the genre.

For in the early 1770s two poets began to set their idylls more firmly in reality, so developing the genre in a manner more likely to avoid Herder's strictures of Gessner. Both Maler Müller and

Voss devoted much of their creative energy to writing idylls, and their move away from the Gessnerian pattern marked a turning-point in the history of the genre in Germany.

Friedrich or Maler Müller was associated with the 'Sturm und Drang' movement. The best known of his idylls, *Die Schafschur* (1775), is based firmly in the everyday life of villagers in the Palatinate. The dialogue is colloquial. The central character, the farmer Walter, attacks the pastorals favoured by the ridiculous schoolmaster:

wo giebts denn Schäfer wie diese ? Was ? das Schäfer, das sind mir curiose Leute, die weiss der Henker wie leben, fühlen nicht wie wir andre Menschen Hitze oder Kälte; hungern oder dürsten nicht; leben nur vom Rosenthau und Blumen und was des schönen süssen Zeugs noch mehr ist...alles im Traume nur, schwätzen wie die Schulmeisters von Grossmuth und hundert Sachen, die einem Schäfersmann nichts angehn, und das, Herr, was uns alle Tage vor Augen kommt, und ans Herz geht, davon pipst sie kein Wort.[20]

Understandably, this passage was taken as an attack on Gessner. Both *Die Schafschur* and its companion piece *Das Nusskernen* portray an intimate world of good sense, an island of relative harmony within a world that is anything but idyllic. The parents are worried about the development of their children, there is talk of an unjust local administrator, and the characters sing folk-songs and ballads (the poetry preferred by Walter) that tell of tragedy. Both works are cast in the form of one-act dramas. There is a good deal of comedy, and the characters are more individual and lifelike than Gessner's. They have no time for Rococo prettiness, and know that a certain strength of mind is required to withstand the rigours of existence.

Müller clearly rejected Gessner's conception of naturalness. His style is not mellifluous, but forceful, his prose rhythms often broken, and, in complete contrast to Gessner, he deals with syntax in a cavalier fashion and is completely unconcerned about linguistic correctness. His language reflects a desire to portray an extract from reality that is idyllic, but vigorous. The stylisation that transmutes reality into an idyll is provided by humour and comic touches, rather than by gracefulness and sentimentality.

Yet Müller insisted that he admired and respected Gessner's

work.[21] It seems that his enthusiasm for Gessner predated his interest in Klopstock, *Ossian* and Shakespeare. He left Gessner behind when he found his own manner. But several of his short prose idylls and Arcadian fragments that probably belong to his earliest writings bear witness to his interest in Rococo and sentimental poetry and in Gessner. One fragment, entitled 'Idylle',[22] is modelled on Gessner's 'Der zerbrochene Krug'. Another fragment with the same title[23] mixes sentiment, humour and morality and ends happily much in the Gessnerian manner. Gessner's influence can also be seen in the 'tableaux', repetition and parallels, and occasional echoes of hexameters in these early fragments. Müller's 'Micon – Theron, eine Idylle' brings the song of a man close to death. He faces death with equanimity, for it is seen as the natural end to life, and he recalls the joys found in nature and the pleasures of family life. When he compares his children with trees, the echo of Gessner's 'Palemon' seems unmistakable:

welche Freude, als mit meinem wachsenden alter meine kinder und Enkel wie ein wald um mich herwuchsen! wie ein wald, in dem rossen gebüsche und tausend blümger blühen, standen Sie um mich oft her und begleiteten meine tritte mit ihrem segnenden lallen.[24]

With rather more gusto Müller develops that isolated example of grotesque comedy in Gessner's work, 'Die übel belohnte Liebe'. 'Der Satyr Mopsus, eine Idylle in drei Gesängen'[25] retells Gessner's story and then relates how the satyr and his friends try to take vengeance on the nymph. Müller's satyr has been trapped, not in a net, but more painfully in a thornbush. The story becomes more grotesque and more farcical. Mopsus indulges in wild imaginings of sensual excitement. Here, as in his biblical idylls, Müller's prose owes more to Klopstock than to Gessner. Yet these biblical idylls seem to have been inspired by *Der Tod Abels* and here, too, 'tableaux', sentimental scenes and idyllic motifs recall Gessner, although Müller's characters are less idealised and the nature he describes is full of violent movement. There is, too, a strong awareness of the power of time, so that when Müller's Cain is reconciled with his family the happy outcome seems temporary rather than final.

As his name implies, Maler Müller was a painter as well as poet, and he may well have been influenced by genre painting in his conception of the idyll. Both *Die Schafschur* and *Das Nusskernen* suggest genre pictures. But as long as the genre picture portrayed peace and contentment, or unpleasant features were stylised by gentle humour, the idyllic mood could be preserved. Müller adapts typical features of the Gessnerian and pastoral idyll to suit his own purpose. *Die Schafschur*, built around songs whose merits are discussed, is a variation on the singing contest. Riddles, and their solution, provide an element of wit. Walter's idea of happiness is not so far removed from that found in Gessner's works: certain folksongs, says Walter, remind one of a garden in spring:

...einer meynen sollte, wenn mans so singen hört, stünd einer in seinem Garten im Frühjahr wenn die liebe Herrgotts-Sonne nieder auf die Welt scheint und die blühende Bäume – und die Vögel in der Luft und des Singens und Gejubel in der fröhlichen Zeit, dass wieder warm ist und einem ein laues Lüftgen in die Ohren surrt, wenn man so über Gottes jung grüne Wiesen hingeht...[26]

One song makes him recall how he fell in love with his wife: it was a Sunday evening, in an old castle; he heard the 'zarte Stimmen' of the girls and the sound of the echo; he admired the sunset – again the mood is not so very different from that of many an idyll by Gessner. And, like Gessner, Müller shows love and the family to be the bases of happiness and stability.

Müller's move towards an idyll set in a familiar world was paralleled by that of Johann Heinrich Voss, who was more influential and, indeed, replaced Gessner as the idyllic prototype in Germany. Voss, at first associated with the 'Göttinger Hain' and then, particularly as translator of Homer, with Weimar Classicism, never found direct inspiration in Gessner. His first idylls were modelled on Klopstock. A pair sharing the title 'Die Leibeigenschaft', written in 1775, describe the injustices of serfdom with some bitterness and then celebrate the freeing of serfs with a visionary hymn to liberty. Alone, the first part could not be called an idyll. More directly than Müller, Voss contrasts the ideal with the deficiencies of reality, and shows that idyllic harmony has to be won. His hexameters, the Homeric touches in his language and his tendency to make his characters into types remove these poems from the level of simple realism. Manner or style has become more important than subject-matter in determining the idyllic quality of these pieces.

Voss's best idylls, and the most influential, *Luise* (1783–4) and *Der siebzigste Geburtstag* (1781), concern family relationships and are closer to Gessner in sentiment. Neither hexameter poem reveals indebtedness to Gessner in detail, although the epic length of *Luise*, three long idylls joined together, may owe something to the example of *Der erste Fischer*. Voss describes interiors, food and clothes with the love that Gessner had dedicated to the portrayal of nature, steering the idyll decisively away from pastoral towards the spirit of genre painting. He places his domesticities in a middle-class milieu. The stylisation necessary to an idyll takes the form of a gentle humour that is applied even to sentimentality. The contrast between poetic diction and ordinariness of subject contributes to the humorous tone, yet there is no denigration of the values of harmony, virtue, love, and trust in God. Voss seems to have responded to Herder's demand that an idyll should make reality beautiful, not portray an ideal. Schiller, and ensuing generations, preferred Voss to Gessner for this reason.

The gentle humour, and the settings of a country parsonage and schoolhouse found in *Luise* and *Der siebzigste Geburtstag* set a new fashion in idyllic writing; encouraged by the popularity of Goldsmith's *Vicar of Wakefield*, it lasted well into the nineteenth century. *Luise* and Goethe's *Hermann und Dorothea*, which follows Voss in its touches or humour and epic dimensions, and Homer in its heroic tone, became the starting point of a new tradition.

Another tendency that marked not only a break with the Gessnerian idyll, but also encouraged a turn away from the idyll as a specific genre began with Goethe's *Werther* (1774).

At the beginning of this novel Goethe skilfully draws on idyllic associations as his hero thinks he finds peace and happiness in the countryside. Some of the themes, happiness in nature and love for the innocence of children, may be linked with Gessner; to these Goethe joins references to biblical patriarchs and Homer, for both, it seems to Werther, lived or portrayed a more natural existence. There is little doubt that Gessner was in Goethe's mind when he wrote *Werther*.[27] He reviewed Gessner's *Neue Idyllen* in 1773, sent a copy of the fifth volume of Gessner's works to Gleim in April of that year, and knew that Jerusalem, whose tragic end formed the basis for the story of the novel, was an admirer and collector of Gessner's etchings. The clearest link with Gessner in Goethe's text is found in the famous letter of 10 May 1771 describing rapturous union with nature. The similarity with Gessner's 'Damon. Daphne' and 'Die Gegend im Gras' extends to the language as well as the subject of enthusiastic joy in nature and wonder at the myriads of tiny plants and insects. Gessner's Damon says that he cannot express his rapture coherently; Werther claims that he cannot formulate his feelings adequately. Both address their partner in conversation or correspondence with an ejaculation at a moment of climax marked by the word 'dann' that follows a series of 'wenn' clauses. There are, of course, significant differences in style and tone. Werther's outburst is presented as the expression of an intensely personal, almost unique experience; his correspondent Wilhelm is unlikely to share his feelings. Damon's emotions are shared by his companion and are by implication typical or universal. Gessner stresses the harmonious order of nature; Goethe its creative energy. Damon's mood is wholly pleasant, Werther's includes a touch of despair. Damon's speech is more obviously arranged into a pattern, Werther's letter has a more flowing rhythm. Paradoxically, though Goethe's language is more sophisticated, it seems more natural than Gessner's; Gessner's style is more graceful, Goethe's more expressive. Yet later in the novel, in the letter of 10 August, when Werther recalls his former closeness to nature, the details of the landscape and the 'wenn' clauses again seem to echo Gessner.

A series of parallel 'wenn' clauses leading to a climax broken by 'dann' became, after *Werther*, a favourite pattern in passages of heightened prose marking sublime moments or thoughts. Did Gessner start this mannerism? Klopstock, too, used the same technique in his verse, to evoke imagined situations in the conditional tense, and it is possible that Goethe learnt from him.[28] But, given the connections between *Werther* and Gessner, that Gessner was describing a 'real' experience, and that he also showed how certain features of verse poetry could be used in poetic prose, his claim to be the instigator of the technique must be equally strong.

Just as the idyll in Germany broke with the Gessnerian pattern, so, following *Werther*, did poetic prose. Euphony, cadence, parallel remained fundamental elements, but Gessner's reliance on metrical patterns was abandoned.

Goethe's *Werther*, and before that Rousseau, had suggested that the mind of the individual, rather than circumstances, made an idyll. Subsequent writers began to show that idyllic contentment of spirit was not given to everyone. When it was, the writer might question, as did Jean Paul in his *Leben des vergnügten Schulmeisterlein Maria Wutz in Auenthal* (1793) and elsewhere in his voluminous work, whether the idyllic mind did not involve a lack of sensitivity towards the problems of suffering and mortality. Whereas Gessner had been content to hint that we might smile at naiveté in so far as it was foolish, Jean Paul wondered whether the person who saw only harmony in the world should be admired, or pitied, or despised. The early Romantics did not believe that man's longing for happiness and fulfilment could be satisfied by anything as limited as the experience portrayed in the idylls of Gessner or Voss. But the idyll could not be destroyed. It lived on as an episode in a novel, or in any literary genre, profoundly modified by its function within the greater whole. It survived, its content changed by new attitudes to nature, in the lyric. In the 'Biedermeier' period the ideal of modest acceptance of life encouraged new forms of idyllic literature; the idyllic short story became almost a genre in itself, and new themes were developed: even warfare, if treated in the right way, could become idyllic.[29] Gessner had been overtaken, but not forgotten.

CONCLUSION

About Gessner's achievement with the etching needle there has been little controversy. To state that he was a master of the art of Rococo book decoration, however, gives but little idea of the attractiveness of his etchings that played a large part in popularising his poetic works and in shaping public taste. They encouraged men to open their minds to the delights and wonders of nature, and also, through their depiction of classical subjects, contributed to the rise of Neo-Classicism. The combination of Antiquity and nature took possession of the European imagination. The delicacy and charm of his vignettes still exerts an appeal. These Rococo characteristics, and the sentimental poses of some of his figures, less pleasing today, made his pictures of innocence and simplicity more acceptable to generations not yet attuned to a stricter Classicism. Expression evidently meant more than technical perfection to a public whose members were not greatly disturbed by his inability to draw figures of convincing anatomical proportions. In Gessner's paintings this failure is even more evident, but so, too, is his sensitivity to nature. Because they were not so widely known, his works in gouache were less influential than his etchings, but his use of colour to render moods of nature foreshadowed developments in the Romantic era. In concentrating on intimate corners of nature he began to break away from the tradition of the ideal landscape. His love of nature also led him to depict detail with an exactness that points forward to nineteenth-century Realism. In his landscapes he achieved originality and was a leading amateur of his time.

Subject-matter, it appears, determines reactions to the visual arts rather less than to literature. Certainly pastoral paintings do not suffer from the same prejudice as pastoral poetry. Gessner's excellence as a writer is disputed, even though here he displayed more technical skill than in his etchings. His mastery of a literary style has scarcely been challenged, except by fanatical opponents of poetic prose. We have been able to outline some aspects of his artistry as a writer that have been ignored or underestimated in the past. Yet his tendency to mannerism cannot be overlooked. Despite a certain variety, the restrictedness of his manner remains; it can scarcely be separated from the narrowness of his subject-matter. The lyrics of Eichendorff, one of the greatest and most popular of German poets, are hardly wider in range than Gessner's idylls. But even when we read these idylls as we would a collection of lyric poems – one or two at a time – there are still obstacles to enjoyment. Rococo charm and wit are often regarded with suspicion, as signs of 'decadence' and lack of seriousness. Gessner's sentimentality and pathos are further problems: together with many of his contemporaries, he is suspected of indulging in sweet sentiment as an escape from more earnest matters. His apparently naive optimism adds to the barrier to sympathetic reading. An understanding of eighteenth-century sensibility can reduce these difficulties. Nevertheless, Gessner's sentimentality seems a greater deterrent than its equivalent, also applied to nature, children and family life, in, say, the work of Blake, Wordsworth or Victor Hugo. It appears that a major part of the problem is the idyll itself, and not just the Gessnerian idyll.

The criticisms directed against the unreality of Gessner's idylls, by Goethe, Schiller and many others, were levelled less at their use of Greek costume and lack of individual characterisation than at their lack of variety. The Romantic writer Tieck, often a seismograph of contemporary opinion, summed up the objections to Gessner when he called for 'mehr Wolf' in the idyll[1] – more danger, more strife, more conflict and more life. The variety that exists in Gessner's work is not the whole variety of life. But the idyll must portray harmony, it must select from and stylise reality. The more 'realistic' idylls that followed Gessner did not escape this restriction, except in so far as they included non-idyllic, or 'un-idyllicised', elements. Jean Paul, perhaps the greatest experimenter with the description and evocation of happiness in narrative prose, remarked that it could not be made as interesting as misfortune, for it could not be seen to have so many degrees and divisions:

Freylich ermüdet die Augen leicht die Darstellung des Glücks, aber nur darum, weil es bald zu wachsen nachlässt. Die vorgedichteten Schmerzen hingegen unterhalten lange, weil der Dichter, wie leider das Schicksal, sie lange steigern kann; die Freude hat nicht viele Stufen, nur der Schmerz so viele.[2]

The call for greater realism in the idyll was basically misfounded, for an idyll is essentially a vision contrasted with reality. Schiller was right to classify Gessner as a 'sentimental' writer, one who seeks nature as an idea and contrasts observed reality with the ideal. Gessner portrayed an idea of naturalness, as relative as that conception of naturalness by which we might now measure his work. To many of his contemporaries his idylls seemed natural – and so did the English garden, the clothes of the English country gentleman, and the 'robe en chemise' by comparison with the Baroque garden and French court costume. If we understand this, and see Gessner's idylls as expressing a longing for nature, a 'Romantic' yearning for the unobtainable, we may come closer to appreciating his work.

Few will find the idylls convincing as the expression of an ideal. For, as Schiller also argued, Gessner's ideal is too restricted to appeal to us as the ultimate goal of mankind; it omits too many aspects of existence and puts too little emphasis on effort and endeavour. Yet few would reject the virtues of love, charity and contentedness associated with Gessner's ideal. As not too binding a reminder, a partial expression of a dream of perfection, his idylls can still appeal wherever ideals of harmony and natural goodness have not been totally rejected, more particularly, perhaps, where men are disillusioned with politics and advanced civilisation but still have faith in humanity and the possibilities of life in society.

Gessner claimed to describe a Golden Age that had once existed; but there are indications in the idylls that he was conscious of its unreality. Contradictions or paradoxes in critical reactions to Gessner have arisen from an ambiguity in his work, as well as from differing conceptions of the function of the idyll – as escapism or indirect satire, a poetic picture of bucolic reality, representation of an ideal, past, present, future, or outside time, a fiction serving as a spur to moral improvement. Gessner's idylls were all these things; they were also intended to delight and amuse. One of the last great examples of pastoral poetry in Europe, they flourished in an atmosphere of continuity of artistic purpose, claiming to mark a return to the beginnings of a timeless genre; but they were so impregnated with the ideas of their own age that they represented an innovation that stimulated new definitions and new departures. Their wit and formalism, and the pastoral convention itself, create a distance between the writer and his subject, a framework for impersonal poetry that does not wish to improve or convert and needs no justification outside its own aesthetic system; yet their sentiment functions in the opposite direction, calling for sympathy and involvement and aiming at moral refinement or correction. They show characters who shy away from excessive passion and abstract thought, but are alive to sensations and beauty, whose freedom from care has little to do with concepts of political or social liberty, but involves some notion of fraternity and equality; their world is both an escape from reality and a lesson in the joy of living. Because of these 'complications', the story of his influence, as well as his reception, has several strands.

Gessner's impact on foreign poets has sometimes been exaggerated. There is no doubt that he helped form a taste for beauty in nature, for simplicity of manners, moral sentiments and domestic affections, and that his contribution in preparing the way for Romanticism, and in encouraging religious revivals, especially in England, outweighed his detailed influence on important poets abroad. Equally, his success shows that he fostered tendencies that already existed, not least in Paris where artificiality, irreligion and immorality were supposedly most rife (the more his idylls contrasted with reality, the greater their impact). His influence in Germany was of the same kind, but has usually been underestimated, largely because Germans themselves have not wished to acknowledge a debt to writings that, it was thought, bore no relation to the national spirit. Without Gessner, idyllic literature would hardly have figured so prominently in German culture. He triggered a reaction, but one that brought the development of possibilities already suggested in his work. The new idyllic tradition that started with Voss was a continuation of the tradition represented, and largely created, by Gessner. The development of poetic prose in German, the pathos of 'Sturm und Drang', the idealisation of Greece and the concepts of 'Mass' and 'Humanität' of German Classicism, were all influenced by his work. Indeed, in no other German author do we find, in so small an *œuvre*, so many facets of eighteenth-century culture reflected in such a way that their interrelation is so clear. From Gessner's work we can see that rationalistic optimism, moral and religious sentimentality, Rococo formalism and frivolity, and Rousseauistic feeling for nature and criticism of civilisation, Enlightenment, Pre-Romanticism and Neo-Classicism were not necessarily mutually exclusive, but interrelated aspects of one age.

Gessner's ability to reconcile apparent contradictions both enabled him to conceive his poetic vision of idyllic harmony and recommended this vision to men of divergent interests and opinions in many lands. Never before had a German work of fiction captured the imagination of Europe as did his writings, and few since have enjoyed such fame and popularity. Gessner's work contains a sophisticated (though not over-complex) fusion of detachment and involvement, convention and invention, seriousness and fancy; its art lies in its deceptive simplicity.

NOTES

I. TOWARDS A SYNTHESIS

1 Mme (S. F. Brulart) de Genlis, *Les Souvenirs de Félicie L*...(Paris, 1804), pp. 225f.

2 See J. J. Hottinger, *S. Gessner* (Zurich, 1796), p. 19.

3 See H. Brunner, 'Kinderbuch und Idylle', *Jahrbuch der Jean-Paul-Gesellschaft* 2 (1967), pp. 86f.

4 See Hottinger, pp. 147f.

5 See Hottinger, p. 43.

6 See William Coxe, *Travels in Switzerland*, third edition (London, 1794), Vol. 1, p. 66.

7 H. Wölfflin, *S. Gessner* (Frauenfeld, 1889), p. 150 – to J. G. Schulthess, 5 May 1752.

8 See Wölfflin, p. 158 – to Schulthess, 28 Oct. 1752.

9 See Wölfflin, p. 156 – to Schulthess, 12 July 1752.

10 See E. v. Kleist, *Werke*, edited by A. Sauer (Berlin, 1881), Vol. 2, letter no. 129.

11 J. Bächtold, *Geschichte der deutschen Literatur in der Schweiz* (Frauenfeld, 1892). p. 172, and E. T. Voss, *S. Gessner, Idyllen* (Stuttgart, 1973), p. 153: both ascribe 'Die Viole', published in *Das Angenehme mit dem Nüzlichen* (1756), p. 80, to Gessner.

12 Gessner, 'Werke', edited by A. Frey, *Deutsche National Litteratur*, Vol. 41 (1) (Berlin and Stuttgart, no date), pp. 196f; this edition is referred to below as F. Frey used late editions of Gessner and modernised the spelling. The texts of the first editions are given in the *Idyllen* edited by Voss (see note 11), referred to subsequently as V.

13 See Wölfflin, p. 153 – letter dated 19 May 1752.

14 Kleist, Vol. 2, letter no. 129.

15 See F. Bergemann, *S. Gessner* (Munich, 1913), p. 103.

16 V, p. 11; Bodmer was inspired by J. A. Schlegel's 'Choriambische Ode an Herrn K.', *Bremer Beiträge* (1748) – see V, pp. 229f.

17 See Bergemann, p. 51, p. 103.

18 See *Briefe der Schweizer Bodmer, Sulzer, Gessner*, edited by W. Körte (Zurich, 1804), p. 217 – to Gleim, 29 Nov. 1754.

19 See Hottinger, p. 62.

20 A. v. Haller, *Die Alpen*, lines 261ff.

21 *Briefe der Schweizer*, p. 130 – Feb. 1755.

22 See J. Mörikofer, *Die schweizerische Literatur des 18. Jahrhunderts* (Leipzig, 1861), p. 290.

23 Unpublished letter to Ramler, 23 Dec. 1755 (Zentralbibliothek Zürich); letters of 24 Jan. 1755, 5 Apr. 1755, in *Briefe der Schweizer*.

24 *Briefe der Schweizer*, pp. 248f – 2 Oct. 1755.

25 See C. M. Wieland, *Ausgewählte Briefe 1751–1810* (Zurich, 1815), Vol. 1, pp. 150f.

26 C. F. Gellert, *Fabeln und Erzählungen* (Leipzig, 1746).
27 Cited by P. Usteri, 'Inkel und Yariko', *Archiv für das Studium der neueren Sprachen und Literaturen* 122 (1909), p. 359.
28 See *Briefe der Schweizer*, pp. 246f. – 2 Oct. 1755.
29 See *Briefe der Schweizer*, p. 218 – 29 Nov. 1754.
30 *Briefe der Schweizer*, pp. 216f. – 29 Nov. 1754.
31 See R. Böschenstein, *Idylle* (Stuttgart, 1967), p. 42.

2. A TASTE OF NATURE

1 *Freymüthige Nachrichten* (1757), pp. 218f.
2 A. v. Haller, *Tagebuch* (Berne, 1787), pp. 296f.
3 C. M. Wieland, *Gesammelte Schriften*, 'Erste Abteilung', Vol. 4 (Berlin, 1916), p. 702.
4 *Le Journal des Sçavans* (June 1760), pp. 326f.
5 A. R. J. Turgot, *Oeuvres*, edited by G. Schelle (Paris, 1913), Vol. 1, pp. 666f.
6 Unpublished letter to Ramler, 23 Dec. 1755 (Zentralbibliothek Zürich).
7 See C. Schüddekopf, 'Aus dem Briefwechsel zwischen Gessner und Ramler', *Zeitschrift für vergleichende Litteraturgeschichte* Neue Folge 5 (1892) – to Ramler, 1 Apr. 1765.
8 J. C. Gottsched, *Versuch einer kritischen Dichtkunst* (Leipzig, 1730), pp. 382f.
9 J. J. Bodmer, *Neue Critische Briefe* (Zurich, 1749), p. 300.
10 Bodmer, *Pygmalion und Elise* (Zurich, 1749), p. 4.
11 *Das Angenehme mit dem Nüzlichen* (1755), pp. 137f.
12 *Briefe der Schweizer*, p. 217 – to Gleim, 29 Nov. 1754.
13 See Schüddekopf, p. 101 – Ramler to Gessner, 16 Oct. 1755.
14 *Briefe der Schweizer*, p. 218 – to Gleim, 29 Nov. 1754.
15 Cited by G. Waniek, *Gottsched und die deutsche Literatur seiner Zeit* (Leipzig, 1897), p. 163.
16 Undated letter to Michele de Sorgo in Ragusa, cited in *Neue Zürcher Zeitung* (7 Dec. 1924).
17 W. Coxe, Vol. 1, p. 32.
18 See Böschenstein, pp. 2f.
19 See P. Leemann-van Elck, *S. Gessner* (Zurich, 1930), p. 69.
20 See V., p. 278.
21 See C. V. v. Bonstetten, 'Briefe über ein schweitzerisches Hirtenland', *Der teutsche Merkur* (1781), p. 192.
22 Fréron – see T. Süpfle, *Geschichte des deutschen Kultureinflusses auf Frankreich* (Gotha, 1886), Vol. 1, p. 191.

3. SENTIMENT

1 Cited by F. Baldensperger, 'L'Épisode de Gessner dans la littérature européenne', *S. Gessner 1730–1930* (Zurich, 1930), pp. 98f.
2 Turgot, Vol. I, p. 667.
3 *Le Journal des Sçavans* (June 1760), pp. 326f.

4 *Le Journal des Sçavans* (Feb. 1762), pp. 116f.
5 P. Kluckhohn, *Die Auffassung der Liebe in der Literatur des 18. Jahrhunderts und in der deutschen Romantik*, third edition (Tübingen, 1966), p. 163.
6 To Schulthess, 28 Oct. 1752, Wölfflin, pp. 157f.
7 See Preface to *Der Tod Abels*, F., pp. 102f.
8 *Freymüthige Nachrichten* (1762), p. 93.
9 'Evander und Alcimna', Act III, scene 3, Gessner, *Schriften*, Vol. 2 (Zurich 1817), p. 189.
10 'Erast', scene 5, *Schriften*, Vol. 2 (Zurich, 1817), p. 212.
11 See P. Leemann-van Elck, 'S. Gessners Beziehungen zu Zeitgenossen', *Zürcher Taschenbuch* (1931), pp. 166f.
12 M. Grimm, *Correspondence littéraire* (Paris, 1812), Vol. 2, p. 427.

4. CHARM AND INVENTION

1 Turgot, Vol. I, p. 669.
2 See V, p. 241; Turgot, Vol. 1, p. 669.
3 See A. Anger, 'Landschaftsstil des Rokoko', *Euphorion* 51 (1957), p. 162.
4 F. v. Hagedorn, 'Der Ursprung des Grübchens im Kinne', *Gedichte*, edited by A. Anger (Stuttgart, 1968), p. 102.
5 Hagedorn, 'Die Vögel', *Gedichte*, p. 11; V, p. 34.
6 See A. Anger, *Deutsche Rokoko-Dichtung* (Stuttgart, 1963), p. 65.
7 See F. Pomezny, *Grazie und Grazien in der deutschen Literatur des 18. Jahrhunderts* (Hamburg and Leipzig, 1900).
8 See A. Langen, *Dialogisches Spiel. Formen und Wandlungen des Wechselgesangs in der deutschen Dichtung 1600–1900* (Heidelberg, 1966), p. 38.
9 M. Grimm, Vol. 2, p. 427.
10 *Freymüthige Nachrichten* (1757), p. 219.
11 Turgot, Vol. 1, p. 660, p. 662.
12 See Leemann-van Elck, *S. Gessner*, p. 16.
13 Unpublished letter, 23 Dec. 1755.
14 See Abbé Giorgi d'Bertola, *Lobrede auf Gessner* (Zurich, 1789), p. 44.
15 See E. Blackall, *The Emergence of German as a Literary Language 1700–1775* (Cambridge, 1959), p. 212.
16 See F. Sengle, *C. M. Wieland* (Stuttgart, 1949), pp. 79f.
17 See V. Clayton, *The Prose Poem in French Literature of the 18th Century* (New York, 1936), pp. 161ff.
18 J. J. Bodmer, *Johann Miltons Episches Gedichte von dem Verlohrenen Paradiese* (Zurich, 1742), pp. 175f.
19 Bodmer, *Pygmalion und Elise* (Zurich, 1749), p. 41.
20 J. A. Ebert, *Edward Youngs Klagen oder Nachtgedanken* (Braunschweig and Hildesheim, 1751), Vol. 1, 'Vorbericht des Übersetzers'.
21 See Leemann-van Elck, *S. Gessner*, pp. 35f.
22 See Leemann-van Elck, 'S. Gessners Beziehungen zu Zeitgenossen', *Zürcher Taschenbuch* (1931), p. 155.
23 K. W. Ramler, *S. Gessners auserlesene Idyllen in Verse gebracht* (Berlin, 1787).
24 See U. Fülleborn, *Das deutsche Prosagedicht* (Munich, 1970), p. 58.

5. FAMILY, BUSINESS AND ART

1 See Wieland's letter (20 Sept. 1763) cited P. Leemann-van Elck, 'Ungedruckte Briefe von Wieland an Gessner und Orell, Gessner & Cie', *Zürcher Monats-Chronik* (1934).

2 See M. Rychner, 'S. Gessner als Verleger', *Gessner 1730–1930* (Zurich, 1930), pp. 130f.

3 See P. Usteri, 'Briefwechsel S. Gessners mit Heinrich Meister', *Archiv für das Studium der neueren Sprachen und Litteraturen* 120 (1908), p. 369.

4 Letter (22 June 1765) cited E. Bodemann, *J. G. Zimmermann* (Hannover, 1878), pp. 193f.

5 See O. Pestalozzi, 'Ein Besuch bei S. Gessner', *Zürcher Taschenbuch* (1924), p. 167.

6 Cited Leemann-van Elck, *Gessner*, p. 123.

7 Cited Leemann-van Elck, *Gessner*, p. 50.

8 See Leemann-van Elck, *Gessner*, p. 123.

9 See *Salomon Gessners Briefwechsel mit seinem Sohne* (Bern and Zurich, 1801), p. 55.

10 'Briefe von S. Gessner an J. G. Zimmermann', *Zürcher Taschenbuch* (1862), pp. 164f.

11 F. Wilhelm, 'Briefe an Ramler', *Vierteljahrschrift für Litteraturgeschichte* 4 (1891), p. 234.

12 To Nicolai, 4 April 1772: P. Leemann-van Elck, 'S. Gessners Briefe an F. Nicolai', *Zürcher Taschenbuch* (1934), pp. 150f.

13 To Ramler, 18 April 1772: Schüddekopf, pp. 108f.

14 V, p. 184 (*Brief über die Landschaftsmahlerey*).

15 V, p. 185.

16 V, p. 186.

17 6 June 1788: *S. Gessners Briefwechsel mit seinem Sohne*, pp. 210f.

18 See Johann Heinrich Füssli, 'Brief des Conte di Sant' Alessandro', *Geist und Schönheit im Zürich des 18. Jahrhunderts* (Zurich, 1968), pp. 9–13.

19 12 Feb. 1775: Schüddekopf, pp. 112f.

20 Leeman-van Elck, 'S. Gessners Briefe an F. Nicolai', p. 152: letters of 12 Feb. 1775 and 8 Aug. 1777.

21 F. X. Bronners Leben, von ihm selbst geschrieben, Vol. 2 (Zurich, 1797), p. 168.

6. THE GESSNER CULT

1 *Journal Étranger* (Dec. 1761), pp. 87f.

2 See T. Süpfle, *Geschichte des deutschen Kultureinflusses auf Frankreich*, Vol. 1 (Gotha, 1886), pp. 183, 187, 191.

3 Cited F. Jost, *La Suisse dans les lettres françaises au cours des âges* (Fribourg, 1956), p. 212.

4 See Baldensperger, 'Gessner en France', p. 437.

5 N. G. Léonard, *Oeuvres*, Vol. 1 (Paris, 1798), p. 142.

6 Léonard, *Oeuvres*, Vol. 2 (Paris, 1798), p. 161.

7 Grimm, *Correspondence Littéraire*, Vol. 7, p. 182.
8 A. Berquin, *Recueil complet des idylles* (London, 1776), p. iii.
9 Berquin, p. 72.
10 Blin de Sainmore, *Joachim, suivi d'un choix de Poésies fugitives* (Amsterdam, 1775), p. 156.
11 J. B. Leclerc, *Mes promenades champêtres ou poésies pastorales* (Paris, 1786).
12 Mlle Levesque, *Idylles ou contes champêtres* (Paris, 1786), p. 45.
13 J. J. Rousseau, *Oeuvres complètes*, Vol. 1 (Paris, 1959), p. 586.
14 J. P. Florian, *Oeuvres*, Vol. 9 (Paris, 1793), p. 8.
15 See P. van Tieghem, *Le préromantisme*, Vol. 2 (Paris, 1930), p. 282.
16 See B. Reed, *The influence of Solomon [sic] Gessner upon English Literature* (Philadelphia, 1905), p. 52.
17 Hugh Blair, *Lectures on Rhetoric and Belles Lettres* [1783] (Philadelphia, 1857), pp. 439f.
18 John Aikin, *General Biography*, Vol. 4 (London, 1803), p. 394.
19 See E. C. Mason, *The Mind of Henry Fuseli* (London, 1951), pp. 110f.
20 See C. P. Moritz, *Journeys of a German in England in 1782* (London, 1965), p. 44.
21 See F. W. Stokoe, *German Influence in the English Romantic Period 1788–1818* (Cambridge, 1926), p. 39.
22 See *Quarterly Review* (1814), p. 78.
23 *Thoughts on some late pieces, particularly The Death of Abel and The Messiah* (London, 1766), p. 5.
24 *The Eclectic Review* (1810), pp. 946f.
25 W. H. Hall, *The Death of Cain in five books. After the manner and as a sequel to The Death of Abel* (London, 1804).
26 John Macgowan, *The Death of Abel. The Death of Cain* (Plymouth, 1821).
27 Reed, passim; see van Tieghem, p. 211.
28 See S. T. Coleridge, *Collected Letters*, ed. E. L. Griggs, Vol. 2 (Oxford, 1956), pp. 809f.
29 Coleridge, *Collected Letters*, Vol. 2, pp. 813f.
30 Coleridge, *Collected Letters*, Vol. 3, p. 313.
31 *The Works of Mrs. Hemans*, Vol. 2 (Edinburgh and London, 1843), p. 254.
32 See Reed, pp. 18f.
33 See Reed, pp. 20f.

7. GERMAN REACTIONS

1 K. W. Ramler, *Einleitung in die schönen Wissenschaften nach dem Französischen des Herrn Batteux, mit Zusätzen vermehrt*, second edition, Vol. 2 (Leipzig, 1762), pp. 395f.
2 J. G. Sulzer, *Allgemeine Theorie der schönen Künste, Zweiter Theil* (Leipzig, 1786), p. 458.
3 J. J. Eschenburg, *Entwurf einer Theorie und Literatur der schönen Wissenschaften* (Berlin and Stettin, 1783), pp. 68f.
4 Eschenburg, *Beispielsammlung zur Theorie und Literatur der schönen Wissenschaften*, Vol. 1 (Berlin and Stettin, 1788), p. 431.

5 J. J. Schlegel, *Anfangsgründe einer Theorie der Dichtungsarten*, second edition (Berlin and Stettin, 1804), pp. 87f.

6 *Briefe, die neueste Literatur betreffend.* 5. *Theil* (Berlin, 1762), 85th letter.

7 Friedrich II von Preussen, *Über die deutsche Literatur, die Mängel, die man ihr vorwerfen kann, die Ursachen derselben und die Mittel, sie zu verbessern* (Vienna, 1781), pp. 8f.

8 Joseph Freiherr von Penkler, *Abhandlung vom Schäfergedichte* (Ausburg, 1767), p. 165.

9 Cited by P. Leemann-van Elck, 'S. Gessners Beziehungen zu Zeitgenossen', *Zürcher Taschenbuch* (1930), p. 157.

10 See Leemann-van Elck, 'S. Gessners Beziehungen...', pp. 175f.; also J. H. Merck, *Briefe*, ed. H. Kraft (Frankfurt a.M., 1968), p. 73.

11 Unpublished letter dated 14 Jan. 1780, Zentralbibliothek Zürich.

12 Unpublished letter dated 30 March 1774, Zentralbibliothek Zürich.

13 J. G. Herder, *Sämmtliche Werke*, ed. B. Suphan, Vol. 1 (Berlin, 1877), pp. 337f.

14 Herder, *Sämmtliche Werke*, Vol. 18 (Berlin, 1883), p. 120.

15 J. W. von Goethe, *Werke* (Sophienausgabe), Vol. 37 (Weimar, 1896), pp. 284f.

16 A. W. Schlegel, *Kritische Schriften* (Zurich, 1962), pp. 117f.

17 *Dichtung und Wahrheit*, Book 18: *Werke*, Vol. 29, p. 83.

18 Karl Christian Reckert, *Vermischte Schriften*, Vol. 2 (Münster and Hamm, 1772).

19 F. X. Bronner, *Fischergedichte und Erzählungen* (Zurich, 1787), pp. 123f.

20 Maler Müller, *Idyllen*, ed. O. Heuer, Vol. 3 (Leipzig, 1914), p. 10.

21 See B. Seuffert, *Maler Müller* (Berlin, 1877), p. 124.

22 Müller, *Idyllen*, Vol. 1 (Leipzig, 1914). pp. 177f.

23 Müller, *Idyllen*, Vol. 1, pp. 147f.

24 Müller, *Idyllen*, Vol. 1, p. 158.

25 Müller, *Idyllen*, Vol. 1, pp. 118f.

26 Müller, *Idyllen*, Vol. 3, p. 6.

27 See W. E. Delp, 'Goethe and Gessner', *Modern Language Review* 20 (1925).

28 See K. L. Schneider, *Klopstock und die Erneuerung der deutschen Dichtersprache im 18. Jahrhundert*, second edition (Heidelberg, 1965), pp. 92f.

29 See U. Eisenbeiss, *Das Idyllische in der Novelle der Biedermeierzeit* (Stuttgart, 1973), pp. 22, 26f.; F. Sengle, *Biedermeierzeit*, Vol. 2 (Stuttgart, 1972) pp. 743f.

CONCLUSION

1 L. Tieck, *Schriften*, Vol. 4 (Berlin, 1828), pp. 417f.

2 Jean Paul, 'Vorschule der Aesthetik', *Sämtliche Werke*, Vol. 11 (Weimar, 1935), p. 240.

BIBLIOGRAPHY

PRIMARY SOURCES

GESSNER, S.: 'Werke', ed. A. Frey, *Deutsche National Litteratur* Vol. 41(i) (Berlin and Stuttgart, no date).

Sämtliche Schriften ,[reprint of 1762 *Schriften*] ed. M. Birchner, Vols. 1, 2 (Zürich, 1972), Vol. 3 [reprint of 1772 *Schriften*] (Zürich, 1974).

Idyllen, Kristische Ausgabe, ed. E. T. Voss (Stuttgart, 1973).

Die Nacht (Zürich, 1753).

Idyllen vom Verfasser des Daphnis (Zürich, 1756).

Inkel und Yariko, Zweyter Theil (Zürich, 1756).

Gedichte (Zürich, 1762).

Schriften (Zürich, 1770, 1777, 1782, 1817).

Salomon Gessners Briefwechsel mit seinem Sohne 1784–85, 1787–88 (Bern and Zürich, 1801).

'Fragment eines Briefes von 1751 von S. Gessner'. *Neue Schweizer Rundschau* 23 (1930).

'Briefe von S. Gessner an J. G. Zimmermann', *Zürcher Taschenbuch* (1862).

'Gessner an Michele de Sorgo in Ragusa', *Neue Zürcher Zeitung* (7 Dec. 1924).

'Gessner Nachlass' in the 'Zentralbibliothek Zürich'.

For other published correspondence, see under Körte, Loomann-van Elck, Schüddekopf, Usteri, Wölfflin and V. pp. 307ff.

A bibliography of editions of Gessner's works, in German and in translation, is given in Leemann-van Elck, *S. Gessner* (see below); that volume also includes a catalogue of Gessner's engravings and paintings.

ANONYMOUS: *Cain's Lamentations over Abel, in six books* (Portsea, no date).

Neue Idyllen eines Schweizers (Zürich, 1780).

Thoughts upon some late pieces, particularly The Death of Abel and The Messiah (London, 1766).

PERIODICALS: *Das Angenehme mit dem Nüzlichen* (1755, 1756).

Année Littéraire (1760).

Annual Register (1761).

British Critic 20 (1802).

The Critical Review 10 (1762), 89 (1803).

Crito: Eine Monat-Schrift (1751).

The Eclectic Review 6 (1810).

Freymüthige Nachrichten (1757, 1762).

The Gentleman's Magazine 46 (1776).

Helvetischer Kalendar (1780).

Journal Étranger (1761).

Le Journal des Sçavans (1760, 1762).

The Literary Magazine and British Review (1789).

The Quarterly Review 11 (1814).

Der Übersetzer. Eine moralische Wochenschrift (1753, 1754).

AIKEN, J.: *General biography or lives critical and historical of the most eminent persons*, Vol. 4 (London, 1803).

BÄCHTOLD, J.: 'Briefe von J. G. Schulthess an Bodmer', *Zürcher Taschenbuch* (1894).

BADEN, T.: *Briefe über die Kunst von und an C. L. von Hagedorn* (Leipzig, 1797).

BERQUIN, A.: *Recueil complet des idylles* (London, 1776).

BERTOLA, GIORGI D': *Lobrede auf Gessner* (Zürich, 1789).

BLAIR, HUGH: *Lectures on rhetoric and belles-lettres [1783]* (Philadelphia, 1857).

BODMER, J. J.: *Johann Miltons Episches Gedichte von dem Verlohrenen Paradiese [1742]* (Stuttgart, 1965).

    Die Discourse der Mahlern (Zurich, 1721–3).

    Neue Critische Briefe (Zurich, 1749).

    Pygmalion und Elise (Zurich, 1749).

    Jacob und Joseph (Zurich, 1751).

    Jacob und Rachel (Zurich, 1752).

    Der Noah (Zurich, 1752).

    Joseph und Zulika (Zurich, 1753).

    Der gepryfte Abraham (Zurich, 1753).

    Der Syndflut (Zurich, 1753).

    Inkel und Yariko (Zurich, 1756).

BONSTETTEN, K. V. VON: 'Briefe über ein schweitzerisches Hirtenland', *Der teutsche Merkur* (1781).

BREITINGER, J. J.: *Critische Dichtkunst* [1740] (Stuttgart, 1966).

BROCKES, B. H.: *Aus dem Englischen übersetzte Jahreszeiten des Herrn Thomson* (Hamburg, 1745).

    Irdisches Vergnügen in Gott [1721–48] ed. A. Elschenbroich (Stuttgart, 1963).

BRONNER, F. X.: *Fischergedichte und Erzählungen* (Zurich, 1787).

    Leben, von ihm selbst (Zurich, 1795).

BRÜCKNER, E. T. J.: *Gedichte* (Neubrandenburg, 1803).

    Selection in *Deutsche National-Litteratur*, Vol. 125 (i) (Stuttgart, no date).

COLERIDGE, S. T.: *The poetical works*, ed. E. H. Coleridge (London, 1912).

    Collected letters, ed. E. L. Griggs, Vols. 2 and 3 (Oxford, 1956, 1959).

COXE, WILLIAM: *Travels in Switzerland*, 3rd ed. (London, 1794).

CUNNINGHAM, JOHN: 'Poems', *The works of the English poets*, ed. S. Johnson, Vol. 14 (London, 1810).

DROLLINGER, C. F.: *Gedichte* (Frankfurt a.M., 1745).

EBERT, J. A. *Übersetzungen einiger poetischen und prosaischen Werke der besten englischen Schriftsteller, Vol. 1: Edward Youngs Klagen oder Nachtgedichten* (Braunschweig and Hildesheim, 1751).

ENGEL, J. J.: *Anfangsgründe einer Theorie der Dichtungsarten* (Berlin and Stettin, 1804).

    Review of Gessner, *Neue Bibliothek der schönen Wissenschaften und der freien Künste* 14 (1773).

ESCHENBURG, J. J.: *Entwurf einer Theorie und Literatur der schönen Wissenschaften* (Berlin and Stettin, 1783; another edition 1805).

    Beispielsammlung zur Theorie und Literatur der schönen Wissenschaften, Vol. 1 (Berlin and Stettin, 1788).

FÉNÉLON (F. de Salignac de la Motte Fénélon) *Les aventures de Télémaque* [1700] (Paris, 1821).

FLORIAN, J. P.: *Oeuvres*, Vol. 9 (Paris, 1793).

FONTENELLE, B. DE: 'Discours sur la nature de l'églogue', *Oeuvres complètes*, Vol. 3 (Geneva, 1968).

FRIEDRICH II VON PREUSSEN: *Über die deutsche Literatur* (Vienna, 1781).

GENLIS, MME S. F. BRULART DE: *Les souvenirs de Félicie L...* (Paris, 1804).

GLEIM, J. W. L.: *Sämtliche Werke*, ed. W. Körte (Leipzig, 1811–13).

GOETHE, J. W. V.: *Werke* (Sophienausgabe), Vols. 19, 24, 25, 29, 37 (Weimar, 1891ff.).

GOTTSCHED, J. C.: *Versuch einer kritischen Dichtkunst* (Leipzig, 1730).

GRIMM, F. M.: *Correspondence littéraire, philosophique et critique*, Vols. 2, 7 (Paris, 1812).

GÜNDERRODE, H. W. V. [GÜNDERODE]: *Versuch in Idyllen* (Karlsruhe, 1771).

HAGEDORN, F. V.: *Gedichte*, ed. A. Anger (Stuttgart, 1968).

HALL, W. H.: *The Death of Cain* (London, 1804).

HALLER, A. V.: *Tagebuch seiner Beobachtungen über Schriftsteller und über sich selbst* (Bern, 1787).
   Die Alpen und andere Gedichte, ed. A. Elschenbroich (Stuttgart, 1965).

HEGEL, G. W. F.: *Sämtliche Werke* (Jubiläumsausgabe), Vols. 12, 14 (Stuttgart, 1927, 1928).

HEMANS, F.: *The works of Mrs. Hemans* (Edinburgh and London, 1839–40).

HERDER, J. G.: *Sämtliche Werke*, ed. B. Suphan, Vol. 1 (Berlin, 1877). Vol. 18 (Berlin, 1883).

HIRZEL, J. C.: *Die Wirtschaft eines philosophischen Bauers* (Zürich, 1761).

HÖLTY, L. C. H.: *Sämtliche Werke* (Weimar, 1914–19).

HOOD, T.: *The complete poetical works*, ed. W. Jerrold (London, 1906).

HOTTINGER, J. J.: *Salomon Gessner* (Zurich, 1796).

JEAN PAUL: 'Vorschule der Aesthetik', *Sämtliche Werke*, Vol. 11 (Weimar, 1935).

KELLER, G.: *Sämtliche Werke*, Vol. 9 (Zurich, 1944).

KELLETAT, A.: *Der Göttinger Hain*, ed. A. Kelletat (Stuttgart, 1967).

KLEIST, E. V.: *Werke*, ed. A. Sauer (Berlin, 1881–2).

KLEIST, H. V.: *Sämtliche Werke* (Berlin and Darmstadt, 1960).

KLOPSTOCK, F. G.: *Der Tod Adams* (Berlin, 1787).
   'Werke', ed. R. Hemel, *Deutsche National-Litteratur* Vols. 46, 47 (Berlin and Stuttgart, no date).

[A Lady]: *The Death of Cain, by a Lady* (London, 1789).

LANGE, S. G.: *Horazische Oden* (Halle, 1747).

LA ROCHE, SOPHIE: *Rosaliens Briefe* (Frankfurt and Leipzig, 1781).

LECLERC, J. B.: *Mes promenades champêtres ou poésies pastorales* (Paris, 1786).

LEEMANN-VAN ELCK, P.: 'Ein Brief von S. Gessner an Christian von Mechel', *Zürcher Taschenbuch* (1929).
   'S. Gessners Beziehungen zu Zeitgenossen. Mit 28 ungedruckten Briefen', *Zürcher Taschenbuch* (1931).
   'S. Gessners Briefe an F. Nicolai', *Zürcher Taschenbuch* (1934).
   'Ungedruckte Briefe von Wieland an Gessner und Orell, Gessner und Cie', *Zürcher Monats-Chronik* (1934).

BIBLIOGRAPHY

'S. Gessners Freundschaft zu E.v. Kleist' [with 3 letters], *Zürcher Monats-Chronik* (1937).

'S. Gessners Freundschaft mit A. Graff' [with letters], *Zürcher Taschenbuch* (1938).

LÉONARD, N. G.: *Oeuvres* (Paris, 1798).

LESSING, G. E.: *Sämtliche Schriften*, ed. K. Lachmann, 3rd ed., Vol. 8 (Stuttgart, 1892).

LEVESQUE, MLLE [M. L. R.]: *Idylles ou contes champêtres* (Paris, 1786).

LONGUS: *Daphnis and Chloe*, translated P. Turner (Harmondsworth, 1956).

MACGOWAN, J.: *The Death of Abel. The Death of Cain* (Plymouth, 1821).

MARMONTEL, J. F.: *Oeuvres complètes*, Vol. 7 (Paris, 1787).

MATTHISON, F.: *Briefe* (Zurich, 1795).

MENDELSSOHN, MOSES: *Briefe die neueste Literatur betreffend* (Berlin, 1760).

MERCK, J. H.: *Briefe*, ed. H. Kraft (Frankfurt a.M., 1968).

MORITZ, C. P.: *Journeys of a German in England in 1782*, transl. and ed. R. Nettel (London, 1965).

MÜLLER, F. [MALER MÜLLER]: *Dichtungen*, ed. H. Hettner [1868] (Bern, 1968). *Idyllen*, ed. O. Heuer (Leipzig, 1914).

MURALT, B. L. DE: *Lettres sur les anglois et les françois et sur les voyages* [1728], ed. C. Gould (Paris, 1933).

PENKLER, FREIHERR J. V.: *Abhandlung vom Schäfergedichte* (Augsburg, 1767).

POPE, A.: 'A discourse on pastoral', *Poems* (Twickenham edition), Vol. 1 (London, 1961).

PYRA, J. I./LANGE, S. G.: 'Thirsis und Damons freundschaftliche Lieder', *Deutsche Litteraturdenkmale des 18. und 19. Jahrhunderts*, Vol. 22 (Heilbronn, 1885).

RAMLER, K. W.: *Einleitung in die schönen Wissenschaften nach dem Französischen des Herrn Batteux, mit Zusätzen vermehrt*, 2nd ed. (Leipzig, 1762–3). *Salomon Gessners auserlesene Idyllen in Verse gebracht* (Berlin, 1787).

RECKERT, K. C.: *Vermischte Schriften*, Vol. 2 (Münster and Hamm, 1771).

RICHARDSON, W.: *Poems, chiefly rural* (Glasgow, 1774).

ROST, J. C.: *Schäferzählungen* (Berlin, 1742).

ROUSSEAU, J.-J.: *Oeuvres complètes*, Vol. 1 (Paris, 1959).

SAINMORE, BLIN DE: *Joachim, suivi d'un choix de poésies fugitives* (Amsterdam, 1775).

SCHEUCHZER, J. J.: *Beschreibung der Natur-Geschichten des Schweizerlandes* (Zurich, 1706).

SCHLEGEL, AUGUST WILHELM: *Kritische Schriften und Briefe*, Vol. 3, 4 (Stuttgart, 1964, 1965).

SCHLEGEL, JOHANN JACOB: *Anfangsgründe einer Theorie der Dichtungsarten*, 2nd ed. (Berlin and Stettin, 1804).

SCHMIDT, KLAMER E. K.: *Idyllen der Deutschen* (Frankfurt and Leipzig, 1774).

SCHÜDDEKOPF, C.: 'Aus dem Briefwechsel zwischen Gessner und Ramler', *Zeitschrift für vergleichende Litteraturgeschichte* New Series 5 (1892).

SCOTT, JOHN: 'Poems (1782)', *The works of the English poets*. ed. S. Johnson, vol. 17 (London, 1810).

SOUTHEY, R.: *The poetical works collected by himself* (London, no date).

BIBLIOGRAPHY

STEPHENS, G.: *The Death of Cain, intended as a companion to The Death of Abel* (Portsea, 1810).

STOLBERG, F. L. GRAFZU: *Die Insel [1788]* (Heidelberg, 1966).

SULZER, J. G.: *Allgemeine Theorie der schönen Künste* (Leipzig, 1771); another edition (Leipzig, 1786).

TAYLOR, WILLIAM: *Historic survey of German poetry*, Vol. 1 (London, 1828).

THEOCRITUS: *Theocritus*, ed. A. S. F. Gow (Cambridge, 1950).

THOMSON, J.: *The Seasons*, [1730] (London, 1825).

TURGOT, A. R. J.: *Oeuvres*, ed. G. Schelle, Vol. 1 (Paris, 1913).

USTERI, P.: 'Briefwechsel Salomon Gessners mit Heinrich Meister 1770–1779', *Archiv für das Studium der neueren Sprachen und Literaturen* 120 (1908).

'Lettres inédites de Melchior Grimm à Gessner', *Revue d'histoire littéraire de la France* 15 (1908).

VIRGIL: *The Pastoral Poems*, translated by E. V. Rieu (Harmondsworth, 1954).

VOSS, J. H.: *Idyllen* [1801] (Heidelberg, 1968).

WERDMÜLLER, J. R.: *Die vier stufen des menschlichen Alters* (Zurich, 1753).

WIELAND, C. M.: *Ausgewählte Briefe an verschiedene Freunde 1751–1810* (Zurich, 1815).

WILHELM, F.: 'Briefe von und an K. W. Ramler', *Vierteljahrschrift für vergleichende Litteraturgeschichte* 4 (1891).

ZERNITZ, C. F.: *Versuch in moralischen und Schäfer-Gedichten* (Hamburg and Leipzig, 1748).

SECONDARY LITERATURE

ANONYMOUS: 'Gessner und Rousseau', *Neue Zürcher Zeitung* (14–15 Dec. 1916)
'S. Gessner der Sihlherr', *Neue Zürcher Zeitung* (11 May 1924).

ANDREEN, G. A.: *Studies in the idyl in German literature* (Rock Island, Illinois, 1902).

ANGER, A.: 'Landschaftsstil des Rokoko', *Euphorion*, 51 (1927).
Literarisches Rokoko (Stuttgart, 1962).
Deutsche Rokoko-Dichtung. Ein Forschungsbericht (Stuttgart, 1963).
Dichtung des Rokoko nach Motiven geordnet (Tübingen, 1958).

BÄCHTOLD, J.: *Die deutsche Literatur in der Schweiz* (Frauenfeld, 1892).

BALDENSPERGER, F.: 'Gessner en France', *Revue d'histoire littéraire de la France*, 10, (1903).

'L'épisode de Gessner dans la littérature européenne', *Salomon Gessner 1730–1930, Gedenkbuch zum 200. Geburtstag* (published by Leserzirkel Hottingen, Zurich, 1930).

BENNING, L.: *J. H. Voss und seine Idyllen* (Diss., Marburg, 1926).

BERGEMANN, F.: *Salomon Gessner. Eine literarisch-biographische Einleitung* (Munich, 1913).

BERIGER, L.: 'Poesie und Prosa. Eine grundsätzliche Betrachtung', *Deutsche Vierteljahrsschrift für Literaturwissenschaft und Geistesgeschichte*, 21 (1943).

BERNARD, S.: *Le poème en prose de Baudelaire jusqu'à nos jours* (Paris, 1959).

BERNOULLI, R.: 'Der Kupferstecher und Buchkünstler Salomon Gessner', *Salomon Gessner 1730–1930* (Leserzirkel Hottingen, Zurich, 1930).

BETZ, L.: 'J. J. Bodmer und die französische Literatur', *Johann Jacob Bodmer*,

Denkschrift zum CC. Geburtstag (Stiftung Schnyder von Wartensee, Zurich, 1900).

BIANCHI, L.: *Untersuchungen zum Prosa-Rhythmus J. P. Hebels, H. v. Kleists und der Brüder Grimm* (Heidelberg, 1922).

BLACKALL, E.: *The emergence of German as a literary language 1700–1775* (Cambridge, 1959).

BODEMANN, E.: *Johann Georg Zimmermann* (Hannover, 1878).

BOGDAN-DUICĂ, G.: 'Salomon Gessner în literatura romînă', *Convorbiri literare* 35 (1901).

BORELIUS, H.: 'Gessners inflytande på svenska litteraturen', *Samlaren* 22 (1901).

BÖSCHENSTEIN-SCHÄFER, R.: *Idylle* (Stuttgart, 1967).

BRAUER, W.: *Geschichte des Prosabegriffes von Gottsched bis zum Jungen Deutschland* (Frankfurt, a.M., 1938).

BRÜGGEMANN, F.: *Utopie und Robinsonade. Untersuchungen zu Schnabels Insel Felsenburg* (Weimar, 1914).

BRUNNER, H.: 'Kinderbuch und Idylle. Rousseau und die Rezeption des Robinson Crusoe im 18. Jahrhundert', *Jahrbuch der Jean-Paul Gesellschaft* 2 (1967). *Die poetische Insel. Inseln und Inselvorstellungen in der deutschen Literatur* (Stuttgart, 1967).

CANO, J. L.: 'Gessner en España', *Revue de littérature comparée* 35 (1961).

CARRARA, E.: *La poesie pastorale* (Milan, no date).

CLAYTON, V.: *The prose poem in French literature of the 18th century* (New York, 1936)

CLOSS, A.: *Die freien Rhythmen in der deutschen Lyrik* (Bern, 1947).

CORRODI, P.: 'Besuch bei Salomon Gessner im Sihlwald', *Die Schweiz* 23 (1919).

CURTIUS, E. R.: *Europäische Literatur und lateinisches Mittelalter* (Bern, 1946).

DAVIS, G. N.: *German Thought and Culture in England 1700–1770* (Chapel Hill, N. Carolina, 1969).

DELP, W. E.: 'Goethe and Gessner', *Modern Language Review* 20 (1925).

DENK, F.: *Friedrich Müller* (Speyer, 1930).

DEDNER, B.: *Topos, Ideal und Realitätspostulat. Studien zur Darstellung des Landlebens in Roman des 18. Jahrhunderts* (Tübingen, 1969).

EISENBEISS, U.: *Das Idyllische in der Novelle der Biedermeierzeit* (Stuttgart, 1973).

EPTING, K.: *Der Stil in den lyrischen und didaktischen Gedichten Friedrich von Hagedorns* (Stuttgart, 1929).

ERMATINGER, E.: 'Salomon Gessner, der Mensch und der Dichter', *Salomon Gessner 1730–1930* (Zurich, 1930). *Dichtung und Geistesleben der deutschen Schweiz* (Munich, 1933).

ERNST, F.: 'Turgot und Gessner', *Neue Schweizer Rundschau* 23 (1930). 'Kleinjogg der Musterbauer', *Essais*, Vol. 1 (Zurich, 1946).

ESTÈVE, E.: 'Gessner et Alfred de Vigny', *Revue d'histoire littéraire de la France* 17 (1910).

FABRE, J.: *A. Chénier* (Paris, 1963).

FAESI, R.: 'Die Dienstags-Compagnie, eine unbekannte literarische Gesellschaft aus Bodmers Kreis', *Zürcher Taschenbuch* (1918). *Heimat und Genius* (Frauenfeld and Leipzig, 1933).

FEUERLICHT, I.: 'Analyse des Idyllischen', *Psychoanalytische Bewegung* 5 (1933).

'Vom Wesen der deutschen Idylle', *The Germanic Review* 22 (1947).

FINCH, R.: *The sixth sense. Individualism in French poetry 1686–1780* (Toronto, 1966).

FINSLER, G. *Zürich in der zweiten Hälfte des 18. Jahrhunderts* (Zurich, 1884).

FREI, K.: 'Salomon Gessner und die Porzellanmanufaktur in Schooren', *Salomon Gessner 1730–1930* (Zurich, 1930).

FREY, A.: 'Salomon Gessner', *Deutsche Rundschau* 54 (1888).

FÜLLEBORN, U.: *Das deutsche Prosagedicht* (Munich, 1970).

GEISSLER, R.: 'Versuch über die Idylle', *Wirkendes Wort* 11 (1961).

GUITTON, E.: 'Folklore ou pédantisme: les vicissitudes de la pastorale française au XVIIIᵉ siècle', *Actes du 6. congrès national, société française de littérature comparée* (1965).

GUTHKE, K. S.: 'Zur Frühgeschichte des Rousseauismus in Deutschland', *Zeitschrift für deutsche Philologie* 77 (1958).

HAFEN, H.: *Studien zur Geschichte der deutschen Prosa im 18. Jahrhundert* (Diss., Zurich, 1952).

HENKEL, H.: 'Über rhythmische Prosa in der deutschen Dichtung des vorigen Jahrhunderts', *Zeitschrift für den deutschen Unterricht* 12 (1898).

HESSE, H.: *S. Gessner, Dichtungen, ausgewählt und eingeleitet von H. Hesse* (Leipzig, 1922).

HIBBERD, J. L.: 'Salomon Gessner's Idylls as Prose Poems', *Modern Language Review* 68 (1973).

'Gessner in England', *Revue de littérature comparée* 47 (1973).

HILTBRAND, R.: *Hirtenkultur in Europa. Programm der Sonderausstellung 1966–67, Schweizerisches Museum für Volkskunde Basel*, ed. R. Hiltbrand (Bâle, 1966).

JOST, F.: *La Suisse dans les lettres françaises au cours des âges* (Fribourg, 1956).

KLUCKHOHN, P.: *Die Auffassung der Liebe in der Literatur des 18. Jahrhunderts und in der deutschen Romantik* 3rd. ed. (Tübingen, 1966).

KORMANN, H.: *Johann Christoph Rost* (Diss, Erlangen, 1966).

KYRRE-ÖLSEN, O.: *Salomon Gessners skrifter i Denmark og Norge* (Bergen, 1903).

LAMM, M.: *Upplysningstidens Romantik. Den mystiskt sentimentalen strömningen i svensk litteratur* (Stockholm, 1918).

LANGEN, A.: 'Verbale Dynamik in der dichterischen Landschaftsschilderung des 18. Jahrhunderts', *Zeitschrift für deutsche Philologie* 70 (1948–9).

Der Wortschatz des deutschen Pietismus (Tübingen, 1954).

Anschauungsformen in der deutschen Dichtung des 18. Jahrhunderts (Darmstadt, 1965).

Dialogisches Spiel. Formen und Wandlungen des Wechselgesangs in der deutschen Dichtung 1600–1900 (Heidelberg, 1966).

LEEMANN-VAN ELCK, P.: *Salomon Gessner. Sein Lebensbild mit beschreibenden Verzeichnissen seiner literarischen und künstlerischen Werke* (Zurich and Leipzig, 1930).

MASON, E. C.: *The mind of Henry Fuseli* (London, 1951).

MENNE, K.: *Der Einfluss der deutschen Litteratur auf die niederländische um die Wende des 18. und 19. Jahrhunderts* (Weimar, 1898).

MERKER, E.: 'Zu den ersten Idyllen von J. H. Voss', *Germanisch-Romanische Monatsschrift* 8 (1920).

MEYER, HERMANN: 'Hütte und Palast in der Dichtung des 18. Jahrhunderts', *Formenwandel, Festschrift P. Böckmann* (Hamburg, 1964).

MÖLLENBRUCK, K.: 'Die Idyllen des Maler Müller', *Dichtung und Volkstum* 40 (1939).

MÖRIKOFER, J. C.: *Die schweizerische Literatur des 18. Jahrhunderts* (Leipzig, 1861).

MORNET, D.: *Le sentiment de la nature en France de J. J. Rousseau à B. de St-Pierre* (Paris, 1907).

MÜLLER, A.: *Landschaftserlebnis und Landschaftsbild. Studien zur deutschen Dichtung des 18. Jahrhunderts und der Romantik* (Stuttgart, 1955).

MÜLLER, N.: *Die deutschen Theorien der Idylle von Gottsched bis Gessner und ihre Quellen* (Diss., Strasbourg, 1911).

NADLER, J.: *Literaturgeschichte der deutschen Schweiz* (Leipzig and Zurich, 1932).

NAGEL, W.: *Die deutsche Idylle im 18. Jahrhundert* (Diss., Zurich, 1888).

NETOLICZKA, O.: 'Schäferdichtung und Poetik im 18. Jahrhundert', *Vierteljahrschrift für Litteraturgeschichte* 2 (1889).

OEFTERING, H.-G.: *Naturgefühl und Naturgestaltung bei den alemannischen Dichtern von Beat L. Muralt bis Jeremias Gotthelf* (Berlin, 1940).

PANOFSKY, E.: 'Et in Arcadia ego. On the conception of transience in Poussin and Watteau', *Philosophy and History, Essays presented to Ernst Cassirer*, ed. R. Klibansky and H. J. Paton (Oxford, 1936).

PESTALOZZI, O.: 'Ein Besuch bei Salomon Gessner in Sihlwald im September 1787', *Zürcher Taschenbuch* (1924).

POMEZNY, F.: *Grazie und Grazien in der deutschen Literatur des 18. Jahrhunderts* (Hamburg and Leipzig, 1900).

PRICE, L. M.: *Inkle and Jariko Album* (Berkeley, Cal., 1937).

PRUTZ, R. E.: *Der Göttinger Dichterbund* (Leipzig, 1841).

RASCH, W.: *Freundschaftskult und Freundschaftsdichtung im deutschen Schrifttum des 18. Jahrhunderts vom Ausgang des Barock bis zu Klopstock* (Halle, 1936).

REED, B.: *The influence of Solomon Gessner upon English literature* (Philadelphia, 1905).

REHM, W.: *Der Todesgedanke in der deutschen Dichtung vom Mittelalter bis zur Romantik* (Halle, 1928).

Griechentum und Goethezeit. Geschichte eines Glaubens (Bern, 1936).

REYNOLD, G. DE: *Histoire littéraire de la Suisse au XVIIIᵉ siècle, Vol. 2: Bodmer et l'école suisse* (Lausanne, 1912).

RITTER, O.: 'Gessner und Thomson', *Archiv für das Studium der neueren Sprachen und Literaturen* III (1903).

RYCHNER, M.: 'Salomon Gessner als Verleger', *Salomon Gessner 1730–1930* (Zurich, 1930).

RÖTTEKEN, H.: 'Weltflucht und Idylle in Deutschland von 1720 bis zur Insel Felsenburg', *Zeitschrift für vergleichende Litteraturgeschichte* New Series 9 (1896).

RUPRECHT, W. K.: 'Felicia Hemans und die englischen Beziehungen zur deutschen Literatur im ersten Drittel des 19. Jahrhunderts', *Anglia* 48 (1924).

SCHIRMER, W. F.: *Der Einfluss der deutschen Literatur auf die englische im 19. Jahrhundert* (Halle, 1947).

SCHMIDT, ERICH: 'Salomon Gessners rhythmische Prosa', *Zeitschrift für deutsches Alterthum und deutsche Literatur* 21 (1877).

SCHMITZ, R. M.: *Hugh Blair* (New York, 1948).

SCHNEIDER, F. J.: *Die deutsche Dichtung der Aufklärungszeit* (Stuttgart, 1948).

SCHNEIDER, K. L.: *Klopstock und die Erneuerung der deutschen Dichtersprache im 18. Jahrhundert*, 2nd ed. (Heidelberg, 1965).

SCHÖFFLER, H.: *Das literarische Zürich 1700–1750* (Frauenfeld and Leipzig, 1925).

SCHULTZ, F.: 'Die Göttin Freude', *Jahrbuch des Freien Deutschen Hochstifts* (1926).

SECKEL, D.: *Hölderlins Sprachrhythmus* (Leipzig, 1937).

SENGLE, F.: *C. M. Wieland* (Stuttgart, 1949).

'Wunschbild Land und Schreckbild Stadt', *Studium Generale* 16 (1963).

'Formen des idyllischen Menschenbildes', *Arbeiten zur deutschen Literatur 1750–1850* (Stuttgart, 1965).

Biedermeierzeit, Vol. 2 (Stuttgart, 1973).

SEUFFERT, B.: *Maler Müller* (Berlin, 1877).

SNELL, B.: 'Arkadien. Die Entdeckung einer geistigen Landschaft', *Die Entdeckung des Geistes*, 3rd ed. (Hamburg, 1955).

SØRENSEN, B. A.: 'Das deutsche Rokoko und die Verserzählung im 18. Jahrhundert', *Euphorion* 48 (1954).

STEFFAN, T. G.: *Lord Byron's Cain* (Austin, Texas, and London, 1968).

STETTBACHER, H.: 'Salomon Gessner und Pestalozzi', *Atlantis* 2 (1930).

STOCKLEY, V.: *German literature as known in England 1750–1830* (London, 1929).

STOKOE, F. W.: 'The appreciation of German literature in England before 1820', *Publications of the English Goethe Society* New Series 3 (1926).

German influence in the English Romantic period 1788–1818 (Cambridge, 1926).

STRASSER, R.: *Stilprobleme in Gessners Kunst und Dichtung* (Diss., Heidelberg, 1936).

SÜPFLE, T.: *Geschichte des deutschen Kultureinflusses auf Frankreich*, Vol. 1 (Gotha, 1886).

TIEGHEM, P. VAN: *Le préromantisme*, Vol. 2 (Paris, 1930).

VEREKER, C.: *Eighteenth-century optimism* (Liverpool, 1967).

VETTER, T.: *Zürich als Vermittlerin englischer Literatur im 18. Jahrhundert* (Zurich, 1891).

'Bodmer und die englische Literatur', *J. J. Bodmer, Denkschrift zum CC. Geburtstag*, published by Stiftung von Schnyder von Wartensee (Zurich, 1900).

WANIEK, G.: *Gottsched und die deutsche Literatur seiner Zeit* (Leipzig, 1897).

WARTMANN, W.: 'Der Maler und Zeichner S. Gessner', *Salomon Gessner 1730–1930* (Zurich, 1930).

WEISS, L.: 'Der Rats- und Sihlherr S. Gessner, *Salomon Gessner 1730–1930* (Zurich, 1930).

WENDLAND, U.: *Die Theoretiker und Theorien der sogenannten galanten Stilepoche und die deutsche Sprache* (Leipzig, 1930).

WÖLFFLIN, H.: *Salomon Gessner. Mit ungedruckten Briefen* (Frauenfeld, 1889).

'Zur allgemeinen Charakteristik von Gessners Kunst', *Salomon Gessner 1730–1930* (Zurich, 1930).

ZOEPFL, F.: *Der Maler-Dichter Salomon Gessner und der Wechinger Pfarrer Johann*

BIBLIOGRAPHY

Wilhelm Schlegel. Sonderdruck aus dem 16. Jahrbuch des Historischen Vereins für Nördlingen und Umgebung (Nördlingen, no date).

ZÜRCHER, R.: 'Salomon Gessner 1730–1788', *Geist und Schönheit im Zürich des 18. Jahrhunderts, Jubiläums-Publikation der Art. Institut Orell Füssli AG* (Zurich, 1968).

INDEX